THE PEABODY INFLUENCE

THE
PEABODY
INFLUENCE

HOW A GREAT NEW ENGLAND FAMILY

HELPED TO BUILD AMERICA

BY

EDWIN P. HOYT

ILLUSTRATED

DODD, MEAD & COMPANY

NEW YORK

Library of Congress Catalog Card Number: 68-57197
Printed in the United States of America
by The Cornwall Press, Inc., Cornwall, N. Y.

*For all the librarians everywhere who have
helped me with this and so many other books*

INTRODUCTION

OVER THE PAST decade I have made a series of studies of the lives of prominent American families such as the Vanderbilts, the Morgans, and the Guggenheims. In their stories, I came across important clues to the pattern of monetary success in a capitalistic society. First, there was luck—great good luck repeated, not once, but several times. Second, there was an ability by some strong character to take a road quite different from that of all his contemporaries. Some might call it vision. Third, in every instance, there were hard work and growing technical skill in the application of a special knowledge. For example, the luck of the old Commodore Vanderbilt was phenomenal. Vanderbilt was fortunate enough to have a father who would let him work for himself, using the family boat—which let him into the ferrying trade and gave him a nest egg. Most poor Staten Island farmers in those days (circa 1800) demanded the full labor of their sons until they reached their majorities, but not Cornelius' father. At the end of the War of 1812 he built an oyster schooner, and he sailed her to the Virginia banks and back, filled to the gunwhales with oysters. The immense good luck here was that he and his equally greedy partner did not founder in their ship. Later, Vanderbilt was lucky enough to be taken as a junior partner by Thomas Gibbons, the first steamboat man truly to oppose the Fulton-Livingston monopoly. Vanderbilt might have had a job as a captain with the Fulton crowd, but then he would never have advanced further. As it turned out, he was able to buy several steamboats from the Gibbons firm later. Gibbons led him to a larger nest egg by giving him and inn to operate. The wealthy Gibbons family, in other words, did a number of favors for Cornelius Vanderbilt, and made it possible for him to move along the path to success.

There were others of Vanderbilt's kin who were as hard-working as he, but not so lucky. His brother Jake had a steamboat before he was of age, yet he never did more than work for his brother. Vanderbilt's brother-in-law, John De Forest, his partner in the oystering venture, never amounted to very much, because he stayed in the oystering trade, handling the Vanderbilt–De Forest sailing ship business, while Corneel went on to the opportunity offered by steamboats.

Might not one say, then, that Vanderbilt exhibited superior capability and understanding of his environment and its opportunities? Quite so—but not at this stage of his life. The Commodore did exhibit unusual characteristics when he got into Wall Street twenty-five years later. But as for his canny reading of the signs of the future in 1818 (when Vanderbilt went work for Gibbons), Corneel at that moment had absolutely no faith in steamboats, although he signed on to captain one. He had made a trip across New York harbor in a steamer, had inspected its strange machinery, and had phophesied that in ten years the fad would be done. As a captain he received a mere sixty dollars a month. He went to work for Gibbons only because he saw where he might make money in the keeping of the inn at New Brunswick, called Bellona Hall, that Gibbons gave him free of rent and that Vanderbilt's wife Sophia ran for him.

No, one must truly say that Commodore Vanderbilt was a very lucky man. He went into steamboating at just the right time and was carried along by the tide from one venture to another. There luck ended, of course. He manipulated his growing empire, ex-

panding, cheating the customers, endangering their lives, but giving them what the public demanded, which was fast, ever faster
service. This aspect of the Vanderbilt career was not dictated by
luck or vision, but by hard work. His judgment came into play
when Vanderbilt sensed just the right time to move out of steamboating and into railroads and made his first raid on Wall Street
to acquire control of the New York and Harlem Railroad.

At the same time, fortune played less happy a role in the careers
of some of his contemporaries such as E. K. Collins, who started
a transatlantic steamship line in competition with Vanderbilt and
the Cunard Line of Britain. Collins was doing well until his two
prize steamships, the *Arctic* and the *Pacific*, were sunk with tremendous loss of life. The *Arctic* collided in fog with a small French
steamer; the *Pacific* simply disappeared, probably the victim of an
iceberg. And were it not enough to lose wealth and his good name
in the sinking of the *Arctic*, his wife and two of their children
were drowned in the disaster.

As for luck, the story of the Morgan bankers can also be said
to have begun with a good share of it. The Morgans were Massachusetts men. The first Morgans came to America in 1636 to escape
the persecutions of the Papist-oriented Bishop Laud against the
overwhelming majority of Englishmen, the Puritans. The Morgan
banking business began with Joseph Morgan, who had inherited
enough wherewithal to begin lending some of it out to his less
fortunate neighbors around 1812. Then this Morgan took a big
step; he left the farm and went to Hartford to become an innkeeper. He worked hard and made a certain amount of money,
but never enough to place him in the pages of history, other than
as innkeeper Morgan, or as an organizer of one of America's insurance companies. Of such material fame is not made. No, the
luck of the Morgans truly began when Joseph's grandson was
chosen by the American Banker George Peabody to become his
assistant in the Peabody banking firm in London. Peabody was already a millionaire; his offer to young Morgan was tantamount to
handing him a million dollars. If Junius Spencer Morgan chose to

go to England, and comported himself properly, his fortune was assured.

In studying the path of fortune of the Morgan family, the differences in attitude toward riches between the Morgans and George Peabody became apparent. Why would Peabody behave in one way and the Morgans in another? And as this problem bedeviled me, I began studying the fortunes of the Morgans and the fortunes of the Peabodys with a more interested eye.

Peabody turned his wealth over to the man he chose, but the man was not a member of his own family, large as that family had grown. In this fact came the glimmering of something else—another factor which determines the course of family wealth in the United States. It is a matter of ego. George Peabody was deficient of ego, unlike the Commodore or Junius Morgan or old Meyer Guggenheim. What Peabody had built in his British-American banking enterprise was incalculable in terms of money alone. Yet he walked away from it and left the field to Junius S. Morgan. Furthermore, George Peabody is one of the few millionaires to have left his money to the people of the United States and Britain, in charities, for good works—and one must say ruefully that this is part of the reason he is virtually unknown a hundred years after his death (1869) when he died one of the richest of all Americans. We recognize the name, in Peabody Institutes, Peabody Museums, Peabody Funds; but aside from the few who are benefited by or operate these charities and institutions, Americans know little of the man who founded them, and most Englishmen know very little about his benefactions to their country, although he refused high honor from Queen Victoria herself, and the British gratefully erected a statue of him in that inner sanctum of London known as The City, where Peabody operated for so long as a banker.

As for Meyer Guggenheim, how lucky that man was! He was persuaded by his father Simon to come to America when he did not much want to go. Simon was driven by a combination of personal consideration, regard for his good name, and a search for freedom. The Guggenheims were Jews in Lengnau, Switzerland,

and Simon, a widower, wanted to marry a widow Myer, but was restrained by the authorities because he was not rich enough. So Simon Guggenheim decided to seek the land of the free in the middle of the nineteenth century, and he came to Philadelphia with his family, including the reluctant son Meyer, who was making a very good living as a traveling salesman, working in Germany along the Rhine. But that was hardly the end of it: Meyer's real stroke of luck came when he invested $5,000 in a mine that most of the wise money men of Leadville, Colorado, would not touch, and the mine came up a bonanza. Thereafter, the Guggenheim fortune became a compendium of smart operation and egocentric empire building. Meyer determined that each of his seven sons would have a million dollars, and he saw that the smelting business was a much better way to earn it for them than to trust to the luck of the miner. But the luck of the miner had started it all.

Yet luck is never enough; it is only one essential. For every Vanderbilt there is an E. K. Collins; for every Guggenheim there is an H. A. W. Tabor (who virtually owned Leadville when Meyer Guggenheim arrived there, but who all too quickly went stone-broke). For every Morgan there is a failed bank. For every story of every American fortune there are a dozen stories of failure of men who did not have luck, ability, or timing. Fortunately in America those are the important attributes. So fortunes are made, and sometimes lost.

Then there is another aspect of the baronial American families, which I was taught to cherish by no less an expert than Stewart Holbrook, an apt student of Americana. Holbrook's *The Age of the Moguls* is a classic study of fortune hunting in America. With joy and gusto the author chronicled the making and the spending of the fortunes of the very rich Americans. One point of interest to me was the rapidity with which the fortunes ran downhill once they got into the hands of the spenders. Money attracts money, if let alone. How many men can spend a million dollars a year on pleasure? Well, some did (maybe some still do); the stories of the Vanderbilts are evidence enough. Commodore Vanderbilt was the richest man in the United States and perhaps the world when he died in 1877, and a hundred years later his family's fortune is hardly worth counting among those of the really rich.

Starting with my book on the Morgans came the nagging idea of studying an American family that was not terribly rich, and whose place in American life did not depend either largely or entirely on the luck of one great ten-strike, compounded by being caught up in the grand trends of the nation's history. For example, once Collis P. Huntington, Leland Stanford, Mark Hopkins, and Charles Crocker secured the western part of the Transcontinental Railroad their fortunes were made, one might say, not by a ten-strike of luck so much as the juggernaut of "Manifest Destiny," the expansion of the nation, which sent millions of men west to line the pockets of these four. All these make likely studies, and some of them have been made, more or less respectably; but what about an "ordinary" family, one unblessed by the ten-strike, a family that came to America early and remained?

Many thousands of such families exist. Some twenty thousand Englishmen came to New England between 1620 and 1640, and then there were the Dutch and the French and Spanish, to say nothing of the later migrating groups: Swedes, Germans, and the rest. The problem, however, is to find a family about whom a body of information exists, spanning a long period of time. Most of us, even if we are descended from the Pilgrim fathers or the early Puritans, come from families which have largely lived below the level of "historical scrutiny."

Remembering old George Peabody's story and then examining the genealogy of the Peabodys, I was struck by the pattern of Peabody life. Rich men arose in this family, but wealth has never been an overriding factor among them. Accomplishment has been a matter of concern—and in this aspect of life they are probably a good deal more typical of the men and women who came to America than the handful of lucky ones whose success stories we usually read.

The vast majority of Peabodys who have raised their heads

above the crowd have done so in fields other than the acquisition of material goods. One might say—and I propose to show in these pages how—Peabodys contributed directly to the establishment of American freedom, to the wars against American enemies, to the unleashing of the American spirit, to the broadening of American religious practice, to the edification of mankind through the printed word, to the establishment and furthering of the American educational processes; and over all, militarily, religiously, and in a score of other ways, they bettered America and helped make it grow and prosper.

The Peabodys were an uncommon family, but not unique, and they were and are contributing notably to the peculiar ambience of the United States that gives this nation its individuality. After some thirty-five generations the mark of the Peabodys has touched all of us a little bit, and those who peruse these pages, noting how the Peabody influence moved north and south, east and west, will see how a gentility and a spirit that can be traced to one family and a way of life have become part of the American mystique.

EDWIN P. HOYT

Bomoseen, Vermont

CONTENTS

PART III

Man of Affairs

PART IV

The Literati

PART V

Men of Affairs

ILLUSTRATIONS

PART I

The Forgers of the Tools

———

Each is given a bag of tools,
A shapeless mass,
A book of rules;
And each must make,
Ere life is flown,
A stumbling-block
Or a stepping stone.
—R. L. Sharpe

CHAPTER 1

THE COMING OF THE PEABODYS

THE NAME PEABODY is an old one in Anglo-Saxon history, going back to the days of the Caesars, when the wild tribes of the British Isles were becoming civilized enough to need such names. Even after the conquest of Britain by the Romans the kings and queens of the isles retained a certain amount of independence. The wise King Prasutagus of the Iceni was an astute student of Roman politics. He learned with horror of the intrigues of the court of the Caesars, but his awe was mixed with a certain understanding of the wheels that made the Roman world turn, and to grease those wheels for his own people the shrewd Prasutagus, long before his death, willed half his estate to the reigning Emperor Nero and let it so be known, in the hope that the independence of his people would be respected by Rome. Prasutagus lived out his days, and on his death his queen, Boadicea, looked forward to a continuation of her role without disruption or dissent. But it was not to be.

The Emperor Claudius had married his niece, Agrippina, who was determined that her child by her first marriage, the lad Nero, should become Emperor of Rome. Thus, in the fifties of the years of our Lord the Roman court crackled with intrigue, and in 54, Anno Domini, Agrippina caused Claudius to be poisoned at his dinner by a wretched woman named Locusta. The instrument of poison was a dish of mushrooms, which the gourmand Emperor was expected to find irresistible. So he did; Claudius gobbled the poison hungrily and all seemed to be up with him. He collapsed on his couch, moaning and sweating, but instead of dying as he ought, the Emperor heaved and panted for a time, then gave signs of revival. The startled Agrippina felt a surge of horror and fear. What if, after all, her lord should regain consciousness? Undoubtedly he would learn of her treachery, and neither her life nor that of her beloved son would be worth a lead-filled Greek drachma, a coin of no account at all in the empire then.

Agrippina was a Caesar by birth as well as by marriage. She, the last surviving daughter of Germanicus, was as steadfast of purpose as the first of the line who cast the die of fate when he crossed the Rubicon. The court physician Xenophon was summoned to attend his Emperor, but this physician was another whom faithless Agrippina had cajoled within her power, and the physician came, not to help his Emperor, but to do away with him. As there were guards (and who knew what other eyes about) the snuffing out of life must take the form of saving it. For poisoning, the standard Roman treatment involved forced regurgitation, induced by a long feather to tickle the palate. Xenophon knelt by his Emperor's side and tickled the royal palate, but with a feather dipped in poison.

So Claudius the mighty died a wretch's death, and the young Nero became Emperor of Rome. Immediately Nero indulged himself in every extravagance: he never wore the same piece of clothing twice; it was said that he would wager 400,000 sesterces on a throw of the dice; twice as much, or $40,000 a day, was spent on the entertainment of the visiting eastern king Tiridates, who was nine months in Rome as guest of the state; and this Caesar Nero traveled his realms incessantly, never with fewer than a thousand baggage carts in his train.

For the first four years of Nero's reign, he seemed to be a benevolent if wasteful monarch, but soon he fell into the most vile of excesses. Murder of family and peers became commonplace. Following the first years of the Neroic period, when it was said that Rome had not been so well governed since the days of the first Caesar, Nero then murdered his mother, Agrippina, and his wife Octavia; he began an assault on all Octavia's friends and adherents, and persecuted the Christians. No promise made by any predecessor was sacred; no promise made by the young Nero could be remembered; no obligation was carried on save the obligation of royal self-indulgence.

Seven years after the murder of Claudius the young Emperor was in his twenty-fifth year when King Prasutagus died in Britain. Half the royal estates, as promised, were dedicated to the Emperor of Rome, and it was devoutly believed in Britain that even Nero would be satisfied, for these were the most lush properties in all the British isles. Yet Prasutagus and his court were sadly deceived; no sooner had the royal funeral been carried out than Nero's tax collectors arrived to announce insolently that they were seizing *all* the king's possessions, including Queen Boadicea, in the name of the Roman Emperor.

Queen Boadicea was a woman of rank and spirit. She resisted the tax collectors, who sent emissaries to Rome to discover the will of Nero. These messengers traveled back to Britain bearing the Emperor's offhand judgment. He had scarcely paused in the royal round of intemperance to announce the judicial verdict; it was cast over his shoulder as a phrase caught on a trailing toga: the property was to be seized for the Emperor and the unworthy Boadicea was to be whipped publicly in front of her court.

The word reached Britain and traveled to Boadicea's court even more quickly than the couriers. The Queen's anger rose in her breast, and she called on her own people for support. They came rallying against the hated Romans.

At the head of Boadicea's kinsmen was the patriarch Boadie. Before he could rush to the court in Norfolk the sentence had been carried out: Boadicea was publicly scourged in her own capital, and to show the Roman contempt for these petty Celtic kings, her two daughters were raped by the Romans, and those chiefs who came within the view of the Roman legions on hand were murdered or robbed of all their holdings.

So Boadie, the bearded, brown-haired warrior, came down from the hills to the Queen's lands in what is modern Norfolk, and there he consulted with Boadicea for many nights. Messengers were sent speeding to all the other kingly courts of East Anglia, and it was learned that Caesar's governors had tapped them all with a single wand. Every princeling was weary and ready for rebellion.

At this time, Governor General Suetonius Paulinus was traveling in North Wales and Anglesey, putting down rebellions and enforcing the rule of the Caesars wherever he went. In the absence of Roman power the rebellion had a chance.

Boadie and Boadicea began by burning the Roman chartered town of Colchester and putting its Romanophiles to the sword. Suetonius soon had the news, and so outraged was he, so sure of Roman power, that he set off to quell this rebellion without his troops, who were busily occupied in bringing peace with the sword to Wales. It was not until Suetonius reached central England that he learned he was dealing with a trend, not with a single outraged queen. The Romans had become too greedy, the moneylender Annaeus Seneca had called loans from a dozen British princes, the demands of Nero's Rome were endless, and the Britons were ripe for battle.

The outraged Britons were not interested in the peaceful overtures of the Governor General without his army, and they marched next on the marketplace of the region, London, which they burned. They set fire to the tribal capital of Verulam and bore down on the posts of the Roman legions. From Lincoln, Governor Suetonius called the IX Legion to his rescue, but the Britons caught the legion on the road and nearly annihilated it. In the weeks that followed, Boadie and his men, exhorted by Boadicea, burned and pillaged, killing some seventy thousand Romans and Britons who had shown themselves to be friends of Romans.

Then the Roman legions returned in force, ten thousand strong, and began to restore the Pax Romana to the countryside. Governor General Suetonius Paulinus himself led his troops into action in a decisive battle fought at what is now Towcester, between London and Chester. The superior weapons and training of the legions carried the day, the Britons were defeated and dispersed, and the Romans set about hunting them down and killing the warriors. Boadicea took poison, and the people of the Icentri tribe were crushed, never to rise again as a serious threat against Rome.

The bearded, hulking Boadie fought fiercely that day near Chester. Men fell all around him, but armed with battleax and stout shield he smote Romans to the ground time and again and held the little knoll on which he had chosen to make his stand. But the battle was so obviously lost, and the vengeance of the Romans so near and so apparent, that eventually he and a handful of followers turned and escaped through the fens. Lucky they were, for during the next ten years not for a moment were the people of Norfolk allowed to forget the rebellion. Indeed, through all the rest of Roman rule Norfolk was a veritable wasteland, whose nobles were degraded if allowed to live, whose common men were chosen endlessly for every form of labor needed by their conquerors.

Boadie's escape from the Roman legions was possible because his stout defense had brought confusion to the ranks of the enemies around him. He had sought out the Roman officer Galbuta, had killed him in combat and seized his helmet and armor, making his flight from the field before the confused enemy could regain their wits.

Up into the mountains of Wales Boadie fled with his handful of followers and what little they managed to save from the disaster. They became crag dwellers, poor mountain men ennobled in their own minds by their refusal to surrender to their enemies and by their choice of freedom in poverty as against wealth in slavery. Outlaws they were and they lived as outlaws, spurning the ways of farmers and taking their living by preying on Romans and the servants of Romans in the valleys below their mountains.

Boadie's last Roman victim, the centurion Galbuta, had been a loyal soldier of his Emperor and had been granted, for some previous act of bravery, the right to wear a special crest on his helmet: two Roman suns and a likeness of the Empress Poppaea, successor to Octavia as Empress. This trophy was preserved and handed down by the descendants of Boadie, all of whom kept that name as their badge of rank and honor. And after many generations, in the language they spoke in those mountains, *boadie* came to mean "body" or "person," and *pea* came to mean "mountains." So the leader was named *Peabodie*, or the mountain man, and his followers all accepted that designation as their tribal name. As ruler of his mountain, Peabodie was entitled to a crest or coat of arms, which consisted of a Roman eagle above a Roman casque, this adorning the top of a shield, the upper half on red with two Roman suns, the lower half on blue cut off by a crenellated line, sporting a golden sheaf of grain, and beneath all the motto: *Murus Aereus Conscientia Sana.*

These were the arms of the Peabodys.

CHAPTER 2

THE FAMILY CHARACTER

BEFORE A.D. 100 the forebears of the Peabody clan in England had risen to wealth and power in the fen country, had been subdued by war, and had fled to the mountains in retreat. There they lived for a thousand years. Some Peabodies became tillers of the rich soil to be found in the mountain valleys—but not many of them. Some changed their names and followed other leaders of peripheral relation to the mountain tribe, and so came the names of *Mann*, and *Hill*, and *Pea*, and *Mont*, and *Mountain*—all deriving from the ragged fleeing mob that made its way from the plains near London into the safety of the mountains. The Peabodies, staying in the mountains, were the most rugged individualists of all these. And they so distinguished themselves, time and again. In the sixth century, when King Arthur attempted to unify England, Peabodie was one of his trusted chieftains, and the Peabodie arms were made official, it is said, in the court of the Round Table.

The Peabodys, then, represented an ancient and honorable line in England, but not one that was notable for its acquisition of great wealth or great power under the Danes or the Saxons or the Normans of William the Conqueror. The Peabodys, one might say, were notable from the day of old Boadie for a certain stubbornness and firmness of belief that precluded the compromises usually necessary in acquisition of wealth, except by the sword.

By the beginning of the seventeenth century, however, the Peabodys of England—or some of them—were back in the old stamping grounds around London, specifically in Hertfordshire, where they were small landholders, minor officials, and among the lesser of the landed gentry. If the Peabodys profited, it was to a modest degree, and by the time of the Reformation they were scribes and soldiers for the most part. They were also Protestants, a matter that was to assume vague and then vital importance to their future in the years that followed the death of Queen Elizabeth I.

On the death of Elizabeth, James I became King of England, and thus the first of the Stuarts brought a Catholic tradition back to an unwilling England. James was not only Roman-inclined, he was deluded into believing that he could bring back the days of absolute monarchy, and he so declared early in his rule. There began then after 1604 a long and evil-tempered struggle between monarch and the nobility and merchant classes, a struggle fought in the halls of Parliament, which was out of session and out of power more than in, usually by royal decree of dissolution.

Parliament listened coldly as James outlined a program of reconciliation with Spain. Before the end of his reign even this Stuart's ministers were turned against him, with the exception of the powerful Duke of Buckingham and a handful of lesser lights. The heir apparent, Charles, was packed off to Spain to marry the Infanta. The Spanish were unwise enough to pass by their opportunity, and quite by accident England was saved from an alliance the majority of Englishmen considered to be most unholy.

On the death of James, Charles I came to the throne. It was 1625, and at that time, the thirty-five-year-old John Peabody was living at St. Albans in Hertfordshire, with his wife, three sons, and one daughter. One of his sons, Francis Peabody, was at that time eleven years old. He would grow up to become a sergeant of infantry in the army of the king, and he would be promoted to lieutenant in his regiment by the time he was twenty-one years old.

No matter what service this and other Peabodys were embarked upon in those years, they were Protestants, Puritans by nature and upbringing, in a region that seemed bent on once again becoming Roman Catholic. Like their other Protestant brethren, the Peabodys did not like the look of affairs in the homeland.

One group of Puritans had left England's shores for the Low Countries, but found the economic climate inhospitable, returned to England, and made their way to the New World in 1620. The word of their exploit spread quickly through England and the other territories of Britain; everywhere Puritans began to talk about this experiment which offered them their first real alternative to unhappiness, dissent, and even treason against the Crown.

No greater revolution ever came to any country than the Reformation which came to England, and in the assessment of the Peabody clan on the eve of departure for the New World, it is useful to examine the motivating force that caused them to depart along with thousands of their brethren, to sacrifice hearth, relative comfort, and, above all, the known for the unknown. The breach with the church of Rome took time and toll. For this story of the Peabodys, suffice it to say that by the middle of Elizabeth's reign the Bible had been translated into English and had become the cornerstone of a new literature. For the common people, the Bible was *the* literature—all they had. The commoners could not read Greek or Latin or even French, and these were the languages of literature in England. But the common folk could hear the Bible read to them in their own tongue, and the more ambitious among them could acquire cheap Geneva Bibles and learn to trace the passages. Many thousands of Englishmen learned the rudiments of reading thus. When Bishop Edmund Bonner of London set up the first six Bibles in St. Paul's, members of the congregation used to come into the church and arrange for someone with a clear, loud voice to read to them. A few had recourse to Chaucer, a few others had bits of poetry to read, but for the mass there was the Bible and no other book. Thus it must be realized that to an ambitious, intellectually inclined Englishman of the common people in the sixteenth century the Bible represented joy and opportunity, stimulation and intellectual exercise, and not simply cold duty or hot faith. Their constant quotation from the Bible in common speech was a sign of neither affectation nor excessive religious zeal; the Bible was as much a part of ordinary daily life as eating and drinking.

In *A Short History of the English People*, which contains a long study of the Puritans, John Richard Green noted that great as the effect of the Bible on literature and social usage might have been, its far greater effect was exerted on the character of the English. "The whole moral effect which is produced nowadays [late nineteenth century] by the religious newspaper, the tract, the essay, the lecture, the missionary report, the sermon, was then produced by the Bible alone; and its effect in this way, however dispassionately we examine it, was simply amazing." Or, to bring the comparison into twentieth-century terms: the Bible in the sixteenth century was capable of arousing Englishmen as Billy Graham was capable of arousing Americans four centuries later, except that because it was all new and unjaded and the English people were hungry for intellectual challenge and moral guidance, the Bible alone affected a far greater slice of the English population than Billy Graham or any Evangelist could hope to arouse in the America of the later period.

To attest the strength of religion, note that from Holland came Grotius at the end of the century, and this learned Dutch jurist looked around him and went home. "Theology rules England," he said, meaning that law did not. And the French intellectual Casaubon followed Grotius in visit and in comment: "There is a great abundance of theologians in England. All point their studies in that direction."

Now among these theologians were the Roman Catholics, brought back to power and to prominence by James and encouraged by the later Charles I. But more virile, more striking, and far more popular were the rising theologians of the native reformed English church. It suffices to remark that the Puritan faith burgeoned in the face of open opposition from the Crown. These were

days when Parliament could be—and was—dismissed by the wave of
a lacy royal wrist, when dukes could be—and were—imprisoned
unto death in the Tower of London, when the common people
could be drawn and quartered on no more than the say-so of anyone who wore silver buckles.

The new religious sense brought with it to England a renewed
morality. Falstaff was out, Colonel Hutchinson was in. That meant
that among the gentility, coarse jests, open sexuality, overindul-
gence in food and drink were no longer favored, but a man was
measured by his quiet dress, self-control, and love of family life.
Coming within a hundred years as the change did, it was earth-
shaking. The puce and pink of the Renaissance disappeared in favor
of gray and white, although, of course, the influence was most
apparent among the Puritans and least apparent at the court of
James I.

In John Milton we can see something of the earliest of the American Puritans like the Peabodys, for Milton, born in 1608, was very
nearly of an age with Francis Peabody, born six years later. Milton
was the highest type of Puritan, a member of the privileged class
who could choose to say in England and fight the battle of his
beliefs, for he had the power to make his will felt. The early Puritan home was not a prison, far from it: Milton's youth was gay and
marked with the sound of music in the house. His father, a scriv-
ener, was a Puritan but not a prude. Young Milton studied Greek,
Latin, Hebrew, Italian, and French—but he also studied the drama
and Ben Johnson and Spenser.

Even as Milton and Francis Peabody were growing to manhood,
however, the excesses of the court of James seemed to push the
Puritans toward an evermore straitened way of life.

Milton went from St. Paul's school in London to Cambridge and
came out a gentleman, but one more inclined to strong views on
the matter of morality than the gay youth who entered Cambridge's
Christ's College. The Puritans were herding out from the Romans,
and even the Presbyterians, who had their center north in Scotland.

Puritan began to turn to other Puritan, rather than professing love for all mankind.

The Puritan felt apart, by this time, and his bonds were with others of the belief. The Puritan leaders hardened their hearts against the excesses of the worldly followers of King James, and all their goodnesses were turned in toward their own kind and their own God.

By 1600 the Puritans were totally devoted to the Supreme Will; by the time of Francis Peabody's coming of age the Puritans had quite lost their sense of humor, and zeal took the place of laughter as the spice of life. Oliver Cromwell and John Bunyan grew up in households saddled with constant vision of hellfire and brimstone. Bunyan related that when he was but nine or ten years old, a child in an artisan family (his father was a tinker in Bedfordshire), his dreams were troubled with visions of Heaven and Hell, and he feared mightily that he was going hellbound because he could not rid himself of his "sins." The terrible sins he admitted? A love of hockey and dancing on the village green.

Early in the seventeenth century, Catholicism began to gain ground in central Europe (where it had lost much in the early days of the Reformation). Consequently, the Catholics of England took heart and pressed their luck with James I. Their dream—a heartfelt longing for a universal church of England—came to an abrupt end, and the borders of English Catholicism began to shrink while those of Protestantism began to expand beneath the anguished, ever sterner eyes of the Puritan fathers. Of the eight thousand clergymen in the realm, ten percent were stern Puritan by belief; the others were more lenient, ranging from what we would now know as high to low Church of England, or Episcopal in America.

James I broke with the Catholics and reinstituted punitive laws against them, but he also broke with the growing body of the Puritans at about the same time.

Late in the sixteenth century the most formidable and stern of the Puritans became so disgusted with the "Romanish" forms of worship that persisted in the English church that they began to withdraw from public worship, and to go to church only among themselves to worship in their own way. Such Separatism soon frayed the nerves of all concerned—the lesser Puritans, the bishops of his Majesty, the Presbyterians. The stern "Separatist Puritans" soon had every man's hand against them, and led by Robert Brown, their founder, they immigrated gladly to Holland when opportunity came. Others might not call it opportunity: Parliament, even though Puritan, passed a statute against he Separatists, and Brown fled the country. Others followed him, others were driven into exile.

The neighbors of the Separatists quite gave up on them: these crazy folk flatly rejected the authority of the bishops and the old religious ceremonies as idolatry. After many misadventures a large colony of these people settled at Amsterdam and another at Leyden. These latter were the Pilgrims.

Life in the Low Countries was hard for the Puritans. The language difficulties precluded steady employment, and few men saw how they could amass property, provide for their children, and maintain the Englishness of their group for long. So with the opening of the New World across the Atlantic, Robert Brown and his followers decided to go there, and did so, securing the *Mayflower*, which made the voyage (and another small vessel which failed), landing at the spot they named for their last landfall in England. They secured a patent of the land they occupied. They underwent the most serious of privations, and at the end of ten years their colony still numbered only three hundred persons.

By 1630 that was the state of affairs. In England, as the conflict between King Charles I and the nobles and independent churchmen grew more virulent, the eyes of the Puritans turned ever more to the New World. Here was a place of escape, and one need not be a harsh Puritan to feel put upon and trammeled by the actions of a lawless king. After a long and vigorous quarrel, in 1629 Charles I dissolved Parliament, but at almost that same moment he granted a charter establishing the Massachusetts colony. When that word was out, thousands of Puritans began making their plans to leave

the strictures of the Old World for the unknown dangers of the
New.

Within five years thousands of Puritans would flee the strife and
growing repressions of an unfriendly England. Among them would
be John Peabody and his sons William and Francis.

CHAPTER 3

THE NEW WORLD

THE GRANTING of the Massachusetts charter in 1629 set off a wave of emigration from England by those who sought to avoid repression of their freedom and were willing to undergo present hardship in the promise of future well-being to secure their ends. Within a year of Charles' dissolution of Parliament, nearly two thousand Puritans had migrated. These were not necessarily poor men, or men who either had failed or believed it unlikely they would succeed in their native land. They were professional men— lawyers, doctors, and representatives of the landed gentry. They left because they did not believe in the future of an England ruled by a despot. Things were going all the wrong way; rather than increasing, their portion of freedom as citizens was being decreased, and they felt it would become far worse before changing, if indeed they might expect any betterment in their lifetimes.

The bulk of the emigrants were God-fearing men from the Eastern Counties, and as the repressions on the nine tenths of the English people who were Puritans increased, so did the emigration. Five years after the suspension of Parliament, the Peabodys were on their way out of England.

The length of time they waited indicates that the Peabodys were not among the more militant of the Puritan families, and this, too, was the way it seemed in the New World. The father, John Peabody, settled in Plymouth colony at first, along with his son William. What happened to Thomas Peabody, the firstborn son, no one knows. Daughter Annis went to the New World with her father and brother William, and there she married John Rouse.

John and William Peabody were close and remained so. They pass from this narrative, however, almost immediately because they were not to perpetuate the Peabody line. On arrival in the New World, John and William became known as Paybody, and in later years their family would be called the Rhode Island branch.

John Paybody had no particular skill aside from farming. He took up land at Bluefish in Plymouth, and two years after arrival was admitted as a freeman. William stayed with his father, as he ought to have done, being only fifteen years old at the time of the emigration. Nine years later he married Elizabeth Alden, child of John Alden and Priscilla Mullins, whose courtship became so famous in history through the imagination of Henry Wadsworth Longfellow. But they were all Paybodys, no longer Peabodys, and of no more concern to the line than the Manns and Peas who had remained behind in the Welsh mountains for a thousand years.

So brisk was the passage of Puritans and other malcontents between England and New England in 1635 that Lieutenant Francis Peabody was not accorded a berth on the same ship as his father, brother, and sister. He came at a time when some ten thousand Englishmen had already crossed the Atlantic, in a hundred ships. He found passage aboard the *Planter*, on which Captain Nicholas Trarice was making a career of the transatlantic trade. Before he could leave England it was necessary that Francis Peabody clear all his debts (for a man could be thrown into debtor's prison, after all) and pay his taxes and be quits with all authority, religious and temporal. He secured a certificate of clearance from the minister of Great St. Albans, and cleared his debts and crimes with the Justices of the Peace. His clearances were duly registered in the Augmentation Office of the Rolls Court at Westminster, and his name was placed on the manifest of the *Planter*. He was free to go.

Francis Peabody came to the New World, looked about him, and settled at first in Ipswich, where he lived for three years. Then he moved with a group of New Englanders to found the village of Hampton in the north. A dozen families established Hampton, and among them Francis Peabody was a respectable and honored citizen, serving on the grand jury and on the juries that were called together from time to time to try men accused of crimes against their fellows. In 1649 he was chosen as one of three men to hold administrative-judicial posts which were designed to "ende small causes" without resorting to trials at law. It was a responsible post and apparently he fulfilled it competently.

In 1650 it was discovered that Hampton was located inside the colony of New Hampshire. Suddenly Francis Peabody was taken with a desire to live closer to the big city of Boston, and he sold his house and fifty-five acres of land to Robert Drake of Exeter and moved to Topsfield, where he bought a small farm.

Over the years Peabody prospered there. He married Mary Foster, about whom nothing else is known. He acquired more lands. He planted an orchard and it grew and increased. He built a mill for grain, powered by the river that ran through his property. He bought more lands adjoining his own, and soon owned a pretty farm of meadows, brooks, and upland.

As the old man aged and his children grew (fourteen were born to him), he acquired more lands, both adjoining his holdings and elsewhere. He bought large farms in Boxford, and several hundred acres nearby, as well as other houses, where he settled his sons and sons-in-law. He built up his own house until it was nearly a manor, with several cellars where provisions were stored over the cold winter and ice cut from the ponds was kept in sawdust during the hot summer. He grew corn, malt, rye, and wheat, and raised pigs, sheep, and cattle for beef and milking. He kept a good stable and several carts. He had nothing so fine as a carriage, nor did his country neighbors; only in the cities were such luxuries available or useful on the roads. In the country both men and women rode astride and sidesaddle.

Old Francis lived a long time; he was eighty-four years old when he died, and he outlived four of his fourteen children. He was perhaps the most prominent man in Topsfield at the hour of his death, and his holdings made him nearly as important in Boxford and Rowley. He was not an intellectual, or at least he gave no outward signs of being so, but these were days of discovery and settlement, and by far the most of his waking moments were spent in husbanding the land and protecting it from enemies. What Francis did, if nothing else, was to leave an estate large enough to give a good start to his ten surviving children and provide amply for the needs of his widow.

When he died in 1698 the eastern half of Massachusetts was becoming well civilized, although the west was still to be won entirely, and the Peabody children—all grown to maturity—took their places as responsible and respectable members of the community. John, born in 1642, served in the colonial forces and became a captain of colonial militia. He also went as representative to the Massachusetts assembly from 1689 to 1691; which meant, of course, that he was more than usually respected by his peers. Joseph, the second son, two years younger, took up lands left him by his father in Boxford, improved and increased them, and lived the life of farmer and ardent churchman until his death in 1721. William, the third son, also lived in Boxford until his untimely death in 1699; Isaac, the fourth, born in 1648, lived in Topsfield in the family house. He kept his mother there with them until she died in 1705, and then lived on until 1726, leaving a dozen children of his own, but still enough substance to keep them all from want.

Finally, among the males of the line, there was Jacob, born in 1664, who also lived in Topsfield until his death in 1689. Oddly enough, the children after the first four were not long-lived, and the last of them, Nathaniel, born in 1669, lived only until 1716 and died without heirs. Of the fourteen, six were girls who passed from the direct line to marry young, or die early—as did Damaris, Samuel, Jacob, and Nathaniel. Nevertheless, John, Joseph, William, Isaac, and Jacob left forty descendants, and taking account of the females and the early deaths of some males, there were fourteen Peabodys of the male line in the third generation of American Peabodys who married and begat, to further the line. It was the line that counted, the material possessions were simply something to be used up or sold off—from the beginning the Peabodys were a scattered lot, in no sense a dynasty. Francis had established the pattern by sharing his worldly goods as equally as possible among sons and sons-in-law, where he might have kept the lion's share for Captain John. There was, it seemed, little sense of acquisitiveness or retention among the clan, certainly no sense of destiny to lead Francis to bring to America the English tendency toward primogeniture.

Other families, the Morgan bankers for example, would pass down major holdings in a fashion more inclined to keep the fortune together. And it was a fortune that Francis Peabody left. It means nothing to speak in terms of pounds, shillings, and pence but is only meaningful if one considers the way of life of the Peabodys and their ladies. By the second generation, freemen though they called themselves, they were of the privileged group; they were leaders among Massachusetts men, and the name was well known in eastern Massachusetts, for how many other penniless immigrants to the colonies acquired far more than a thousand acres of good farmland in a few years?

CHAPTER 4

THE REVOLUTIONARY

A LARGE NUMBER of the Peabody tribe served with some distinction, along with thousands of their fellow Americans, in the War of the Revolution against the tyranny of an unthinking England, but of all the distinguished sons of the Revolution who were Peabodys, the name of Nathaniel Peabody leads the rolls.

Nathaniel was the son of Dr. Jacob Peabody, of Topsfield, and Susanna Rogers, daughter of the minister at Boxford who claimed a line that led back to John Rogers, the Smithfield martyr, who was burned at the stake for his beliefs in England ten generations earlier.

Dr. Jacob Peabody must have found the area around Topsfield restricting to a medical man, not an unusual situation where a doctor learned his calling by going on rounds with an established man. He could hardly set up in practice to rob his teacher, so he usually moved on to a less settled place where the demand for a physician was always great. So it was that Jacob finally went in 1745 from Topsfield to Leominster in Worcester County, Massachusetts, and lived there for the rest of his life.

Nathaniel was a bright and slender young man who decided very early to follow his father's calling. He was fortunate in having so educated a father who could teach him to read and write, to do mathematics, to translate Latin, and to practice medicine. As a consequence, all of Nathaniel's scholarly education was at the hands of his father, and he never attended a formal school. As for his other education, it came at the hands of boys with horses and other men. Early in life he suffered a broken nose which gave him an unusual appearance, for in healing the nose developed a pronounced hook.

When Nathaniel was eighteen years old his father died, but luckily the young man had acquired as much medical knowledge as was deemed necessary, and he soon set up practice in Plaistow, New Hampshire—a village that almost as soon became a part of Atkinson (where the Reverend Stephen, his cousin, would become the pastor). In Plaistow, Nathaniel married Abigail Little and settled into a comfortable life as doctor and squire, trusted by the colonial authorities so that he was made a justice of the peace by Governor John Wentworth. Dr. Peabody also held the more exalted post of justice of the quorum, which was a sort of combination coroner's jury and district court with considerable power over the lives of the colonists. He was liked and trusted by authority.

Yet all the while, Dr. Peabody's sympathies were with the growing tide of revolution. He hated the imposition of taxes, the disregard of the rights and complaints of the colonies, the sneers and unpleasantnesses of the king's men. Yet it did not show—he kept his own counsel—and he was still considered a loyal subject of King George. So loyal was he thought to be that in the fall of 1774 the doctor was appointed lieutenant colonel of the Seventh Regiment of New Hampshire Militia. He was still doctor, but he was also judge and lieutenant colonel.

Such was his status in April, 1775, when the British and the Minutemen met at Lexington. The sound of the shots was heard quickly enough in Plaistow, and the first American to so declare himself in New Hampshire was Lieutenant Colonel Peabody—who resigned his royal commission because he no longer believed in the British policies and took his stand with the Revolution.

The resignation, of course, made Nathaniel a marked man in New Hampshire, and he was forced to flee and to hide from the authorities on several occasions. In December, he participated in an act of violence against the Crown: he, Major Sullivan, Captain John Langdon, Josiah Bartlett, and several other men marched against Fort William and Mary at Newcastle, seized and bound the captain and his men in the fort, and then marched off with a hundred barrels of powder in wagons to deliver to revolutionaries.

On November 26, 1776, Colonel Peabody, as he was still known, met with some forty other men, each delegated by his own town, to consider the serious situation of New Hampshire. They all met at the house of Major Joseph Varnum in Dracut, elected officers for the meeting, and got down to business. Captain John Bodwell was the chairman, and Nathaniel Peabody, as the best-educated man, was clerk. The purpose of the gathering was to try to organize, to bring some reason into the affairs of the rebelling colony, to stop the spiraling of prices. The committee of town representatives considered the problem, and then sent Nathaniel and Oliver Barron to Boston to make the case before the General Court of the State of Massachusetts Bay.

So Nathaniel went to the warring colonial legislature that December, and again in 1777. He served well on various committees and in the deliberations of the whole body of the representatives to the General Court. His most important post was on the Committee of Safety, which considered the secret measures that must be taken to rid the area of spies and protect the warring colonists. Only men of the most hard-tried patriotism were considered for such tasks, for the committee was given powers similar to those attributed to the old Roman dictators by the Senate in times of war. Nathaniel Peabody served on this committee six or seven different times in 1777, 1778, and 1779.

But that was hardly all he did in these early days of war. Colonel Peabody went down to Springfield in the summer of 1778 to meet with committees from the states of Massachusetts Bay, Rhode Island, Connecticut, and New York to try to control the inflation and come to some understandings about the use of the Continental currency which was fluctuating wildly in value.

Then came the involvement he had been seeking. On July 19, 1778, Nathaniel Peabody was appointed Adjutant General of Militia of New Hampshire, with the rank of colonel. A few months later he went to Rhode Island with his troops, to serve under General Whipple.

Colonel Peabody was a good officer. The officers of higher command liked him because he could train the men in a hurry, and the men liked him because he was compassionate although a stickler for discipline and close-order drill. As an officer, Peabody had another attribute that made him invaluable to the military: his medical experience. After several months in Rhode Island this knowledge was called into play, when he was sent with Josiah Bartlett to Bennington to care for and supervise the sick and dispirited troops who had fought at Ticonderoga and at Bennington.

The duties piled up on him. He was a delegate to a colonial congress in New Haven, called by the Continental Congress in an attempt to control prices and services. He was chosen to perform the duties of Attorney General during the crisis, along with General Blanchard of New Hampshire. He rubbed shoulders with Roger Sherman of Connecticut, Robert Treat Pain of Massachusetts, and many other celebrated revolutionary leaders, such as Thomas Cushing; and then in the spring of 1779 he was elected delegate to the Continental Congress from New Hampshire.

Spring was no time to be traveling to Philadelphia, with the roads turned into quagmires and the mosquitoes on the Jersey flats as thick as flakes in a snowstorm. It was June 22 before the Colonel managed to make his way by coach and horse down to the City of Brotherly Love, put up at a tavern, and take his place in the little hall. Soon he was elected chairman of the Medical Committee of Congress, and put in charge of the Hospital Department of the Continental Army. Congress did not believe in delegating authority and letting its executives alone. The committee supervised the actual work in the hospitals, and Doctor-Colonel-Delegate Peabody was forever snooping around the bedsides. His committee issued directives on everything from antisepsis to hospital labor management.

Again in 1780 he met with other delegates to discover what might be done to alleviate the ever worsening economic situation of the various, colonies in the drawn-out war. The budding nation was on the brink of ruin. The treasury was empty. The paper currency was "not worth a Continental"—that is how the people designated anything totally worthless. The public in every state had lost faith in the promises of the state governments as well as the Congress. The army was falling away and could not be successfully replenished; men would not enlist to starve and go in rags, to go unpaid; and some units were talking of mutiny and returning home. There was speculation in the banking districts, and speculation in public office. Those who held gold were charging usurious rates of interest and seizing properties of the unfortunate who had invested in the Continental currency. The Revolution, in other words, was very nearly lost at the time that it was very nearly won, because the resources of the American farm economy were giving out in the blockade and the absence of the men from the farms.

In this parlous state of affairs, Congress appointed a committee with orders to go to the headquarters of the Commander-in-Chief, General Washington, there to settle on a revised military plan. The committee had tremendous power. It was to establish a commissary and quartermaster system anew, if necessary, after talking with General Washington, his Commissary General, and his Quartermaster General. The committee could consolidate regiments, abolish posts, discharge unnecessary officers, retrench or expand, or do anything that was necessary to win the war. On April 13, 1780, Congress met in Philadelphia and chose the committee. Its members were Philip Schuyler (later general) of New York, John Matthews (later governor) of South Carolina, and Nathaniel Peabody of New Hampshire.

Off the men went, posthaste, on the road to Morristown, to visit

General Washington and do the bidding of Congress. The muddy season was nearly over, but not quite, and their coach lurched through ruts and slime until it reached the big house where the General had his headquarters.

The committeemen arrived just in time, for Washington was about to lose control. On May 9, the committee reported back to Philadelphia:

> . . . we observed that if the spirit of discontent which then prevailed among the soldiery should fully establish itself it would be productive of the most serious consequences.

On May 23 the committee reported:

> . . . The causes which contributed to the first rise of dissatisfaction continuing, have increased and ripened into mutiny. Two entire regiments of the Connecticut line, paraded on Thursday evening with their arms, accoutrements, and packs, intending to march off and return to the state. They complained of inability any longer to endure the torture of famine and the variety of distress they experienced. On this serious occasion the officers displayed a wisdom and prudence which does them honor; their exertions reduced the disorder to bounds of moderation, and the soldiery were prevailed upon to desist from intentions so injurious to their country, so derogatory to their honor: they retired to their huts with passions cooled down indeed, but with evident signs of discontent and chagrin, and left their officers with a painful reflection that a repetition of similar distress was only wanting to complete a scene which they cannot contemplate without horror. The brave, patriotic and virtuous band of officers of every line have already given up their rations to the soldiery, submitted literally to bread and water as their only sustenance. By this scanty fare, they continue to set an example to and keep the soldiery in tolerable temper; but with tears in their eyes, such as men who feel for the distresses of their country may shed without pusillanimity, stated their apprehensions, that the dissolution of the army was at hand, unless constant supplies of provisions at least were kept up . . . .

Over coffee on the bare tables of the mess in General Washington's headquarters the committeemen met with the General and his staff, their black coats in sharp contrast to he blue and buff and red and white of the Continental uniforms, but all dimly seen by the light of the guttering candles that fluttered in the drafty room. The commander outlined the problem; the committee members listened and asked him to reduce to writing his needs.

Unless he had specific requisitions from the states for men, provisions, forage and the means of transportation, he must give up, General Washington said. The promises of Congress were no longer "worth a Continental" either. The men were ready to rebel unless their bellies were filled and their bodies were clothed.

The committeemen sympathized, and drafted a strong letter to Congress, in which the meaning was plain: ". . . something more is necessary than mere recommendation," they wrote back to Philadelphia. "Times and exigencies render it sometimes necessary for the governing power to deviate from the strait line of conduct which regular constitutions prescribe." Such conditions now prevailed in their opinion, delegates Schuyler, Matthews, and Peabody said. If their comrades were shocked, then their comrades must see for themselves the situation which had become so desperate that this committee would recommend strong, even dictatorial action to states, which guarded their powers so diligently that Congress was often left without any power at all.

So they recommended dangerously, these three, knowing they were letting themselves in for criticism from their fellow congressmen, that they might be recalled by their states, but also knowing that the gallant Washington could not go on, his army could not live on unfilled promises, and the horses could not substitute encouragement for hay.

Congress assembled in Philadelphia and was not pleased, but could not refrain from discussing the recommendations of its own committee of hitherto responsible men who suddenly seemed to have gone wild. The word of the serious condition of the Continental Army got out in a few days and was the subject of talk in every state capital and in every large city controlled by the Americans.

On July 18, Schuyler and Peabody wrote to Congress again, better pleased this time:

> It was reasonable to conclude, that every State, so fully advised of the alarming situation of public affairs, would not have left any measure, to which it was equal, unassayed, to preserve the empire from the impending ruin with which it was threatened, support its honor, and maintain its character amongst the powers of the earth; and especially to establish the great object, to accomplish which they had already expended such a deluge of blood. We have learnt, with the most sensible satisfaction, that the people in most of the States are aroused from the torpor which had generally prevailed; that a due sense of duty to their country has, with all ranks of men, been productive of a patriotic activity, evincing that they mean effectually to support the common cause; that some of the States, from whom aid has been required, have explicitly advised us of their intentions; whilst others have been partial, and some altogether silent on the subject.

So in part, at least, the mission could be marked "accomplished." The committee, just in time, had aroused the country to see the danger that General Washington's pleas had not succeeded in showing, so ingrained is the politician's distrust of the military claim. In Congress what General Nathanael Greene called a "wicked cabal" sought to dishonor the committeemen and disregard their recommendations, but they persisted until the crisis was past. Indeed, all through they had understated, rather than overstated, the case. In the disturbance of the Connecticut regiments in May, the committeemen did *not* report all the facts: that loyal Pennsylvania troops had to be rushed to the scene to quiet the Connecticut men and get them back to bivouac.

But the cabal persisted in its attempts to dishonor Schuyler, Matthews, and Peabody, so much so that General Greene wrote Colonel Peabody that autumn expressing sympathy: "Congress seems to have got more out of temper with the committee than with me," and he gave the committeemen high compliment: "The committee stand fair with the army, and I believe with the public at large; and, bad as our condition is, I believe we are altogether indebted to the committee for the tolerable state we are in."

The struggle went on. Colonel Peabody was ill during the summer and fall of 1780, and he wanted to resign his seat. He had letters of encouragement from Richard Henry Lee of Virginia and his fellow committeeman John Matthews, but his health continued to be poor, and he found that his personal fortunes in New Hampshire were suffering seriously from inattention. In January Peabody asked New Hampshire's General Court to relieve him and bring another man to Philadelphia, but his plea went unheeded. He asked again in February, and then in March the General Court adjourned, still not letting him go, which meant he had another year to serve.

That autumn Peabody was in frequent touch with General Greene and General Washington, and in October gave Washington some intelligence about the military situation in the south that evoked a grateful reply from the Commander-in-Chief and a wish that Peabody would come to Morristown for a visit when he was able.

But in November, Peabody was at last relieved of his post as Delegate, and rushed home to New Hampshire to do what he could to straighten out his affairs. In 1781 he was again serving in the House of Representatives of New Hampshire, but in the next three years he served only as a legislator and turned down an appointment as a justice of the court of common pleas.

In 1785, while serving in the New Hampshire State Senate, Nathaniel Peabody was elected Delegate to Congress again but he did not serve. Instead, he was appointed brigadier general and given a corps of light horse: two regiments of six companies and several independent companies for disposal as he saw fit. The war was then ended and the army disbanded, but each state found it necessary to provide for its own defense, all the more so since the common cause seemed gone.

For the next five years Nathaniel Peabody was active in the legislature, mostly as a member of the House of Representatives, where he performed such tasks as codification of the state laws. He was also at this time one of the founding members of the New Hampshire Medical Society. In 1791, as a member of the State Senate, Peabody was chairman of a committee that promoted a constitutional convention, and when called he was vice chairman of the convention. That same year he was given an honorary degree of Master of Arts by Dartmouth College.

In 1793 Nathaniel Peabody was elected Speaker of the State House of Representatives, and that same year he was appointed major general of the militia.

So it went until 1798 when Nathaniel was fifty-seven years old, and he resigned all his offices except that of justice of the peace, and devoted himself to his medical practice and the life of a country squire. The reason for this retirement was that about 1794 the doctor's finances became burdensome. Until that time his debts did not exceed twenty percent of the money owed him by creditors, but he spent so much time on public affairs that he was forced to put his lands and collections into the hands of agents. The agents cheated him, ran him into debt—and he was slapped into debtor's prison at Exeter, where he extricated himself from time to time by making some arrangement with the creditor who had him confined, only to be recommitted by demand from another. It must be said that the good doctor was partly responsible for his own troubles, for he was a vain and arrogant man, who insisted on riding the best of horses, wearing the best of clothes, being served on silver, and drinking the finest of wines. These habits, combined with his zeal in public service, diminished his fortunes and made his creditors loath to forgive his debts—creditors were seldom concerned with the greater public interest, and the doctor's were no exception.

By 1805, many of the doctor's troubles were over. (He was sixty-four years old and some of his failings had been corrected by time.) He took an ever greater interest in natural history and studied the stars, particularly. Such study brought him a new misfortune, one which is surprising for a man of medicine: he injured his left eye seriously by gazing openly at the sun in the total eclipse of 1806.

His last years were spent in more squabbling with his creditors, and people in New Hampshire tended to forget him. Yet at one time it is said that he was so powerful a member of the legislature that he and three or four other men actually ruled the state. On his eightieth birthday, going blind, Dr. Peabody summed up his life and found it good in spite of his troubles. "Though laboring under many bodily infirmities," he said, "such as would make many stout hearts shrink from business and the world, yet through the unceasing mercies of an indulgent Parent and Benefactor, I still retain sufficient energy of body and mind to earn means of support for myself, partner, her attendants, and to afford a little aid to others in distress."

The doctor spent his birthday in practice of medicine, dining with his wife, and staying up until eleven o'clock to write in his diary that he was engaged in much thought of the future and contemplation of his past. He was not entirely happy with what he found:

> . . . the main object of my pursuit, by honest industry, fair undisguised upright dealing, [has been] to earn and obtain a decent living and support for myself, family and immediate dependents so as not to be burdensome to my friends nor the community; and with the means and opportunities in my power to exert every honest effort in promoting the cause of truth and justice; to support the feeble, relieve the oppressed, secure the rights, preserve the morals, meliorate the condition and increase the happiness of man; nor am I conscious of having intentionally injured any of my fellow mortals—yet my whole life has been interspersed with scenes of imbecility, errror and disappointment, and I am with deep regret compelled to look back and reflect that, for want of prescience and calculation, many of my well-meant pursuits have in their results proved injurious both to myself and others; well aware that, although the mind of man may be free from inherent

turpitude, yet the wisdom and knowledge of those that are ranked among the great and wise are limited. . . .

He was a sad philosopher, this eighty-year-old man who looked forward to continued daily work in his consulting room, that he might provide for his wife and family support. There were no children of the marriage, there was no one to help him, and he continued to work at medicine until his death three years later.

Yet sadness over the human condition and his own past foibles did not make Dr. Peabody an embittered man. He never lost his sense of humor, and a few months before his death, when called upon to treat a young girl, he showed both that humor and his skill as physician. The girl came with glandular swelling on her neck, worried sick about herself. She had visited all Dr. Peabody's younger colleagues and not one of them had been able to help her. She and her mother feared that she had scrofula, which they called "the King's evil," and they came into the consulting room with the words on their lips.

"The King's evil," scoffed Dr. Peabody. "I know of none who have the King's evil but Tories."

And assured that she did not have the King's evil, the young lady followed Dr. Peabody's advice and proceeded to get well.

He worked and joked, and lived on in a fair state of happiness during the last months of his life. Although theoretically he was still confined to debtor's prison, the authorities actually left him alone, for he was too well respected a man for them to touch without arousing the people of New Hampshire. He died on June 27, 1823, and was mourned by the officials of the state as well as his many friends.

The man named Nathaniel Peabody was Jeffersonian in stature; he was a medical doctor, a man learned in law, languages, literature, and political science. He was a soldier who led military forces in the field, but then found that his political accomplishments were more in demand in the service of the Revolution. Had he wished, he might have continued on as a representative of New Hampshire in the federal government, and who knows how high he could have

risen then? Perhaps to Speaker of the House, perhaps even to aspire
to the Presidency, for this Peabody was a man of such ability and
was liked that well by his fellows.

Where was his influence? Where was it not in the formation of
the character of New Hampshire? He was colonial legislator, law-
giver; he helped devise the new government of the rebellion and
helped to carry it out as a member of Congress. He advised with
General Washington in the weaker moments of Congress and was
very much responsible for awakening the fighting states to their
near-defeat through lassitude and for the salvation of the ragged
army camped in New Jersey. He was constitutional reformer and
legislator in his chosen state, and only by his own choice did he
fail to go to Philadelphia and New York and then to Washington
to participate in the federal government.

Few Americans have heard of Nathaniel Peabody, but obviously
in one way or another his activity has touched our lives.

CHAPTER 5

THE MINISTER

THERE WAS ANOTHER aspect of public affairs in which the Peabody family was to distinguish itself. In the formative years, when the vast majority of Americans were God-fearing and church-going, dozens, even scores of Peabodys joined the ministry. It was one of the areas in which the family as such seemed to shine best. It would be impossible to chronicle the activities of all the churchly Peabodys, for when Selim Hobart Peabody compiled a genealogy of Peabodys in the year 1909 there were already more than 1,200 listed descendants of old Francis of Topsfield, and in the ensuing half century the number increased by the hundreds.

But the influence went a long way back. One of the most effective of Peabody ministers of the Gospel was the Reverend Stephen Peabody of Atkinson, New Hampshire, a direct descendant of Francis. Here was a man who would be the first minister to settle in Atkinson. Outside New England he would not be known at all, so one might be tempted to ask why bother with his story? But to understand Americans and American growth is to understand the influences of many periods, and the influence of Stephen Peabody of Atkinson was definite, strong, and pervasive in its own mild way.

Most of this Peabody's life was wrapped up in one small northern New England town. He was born in Andover, Massachusetts, in 1741, and grew up in a poor Peabody family, so poor that although he was sent to Harvard College his family could not help him much. Poor is a relative term, and certainly this definition was relative in the middle of the eighteenth century. The father, John Peabody, was the son of William, who was the third son of old Francis, the founder of the line. William had received several hundred acres of land from his father, Francis; more than some of the others because he was severely handicapped: he had lost an arm. But William had four sons, and John, the father of Stephen, was the fourth of them, so when he grew to manhood and married, there was not much chance for him to secure a large share of the family holdings. The trouble—part of it at least—was that John was born just four years before his father's death, and it was apparent that the estate would not go so very far. Stephen (uncle of future Reverend Stephen) was the firstborn, in 1685, which meant he was fourteen years old when his father died, and it was necessary for Stephen to grow up almost overnight and become the man of the farm. John remained in Boxford all his early years, married there when he was twenty-seven, and when it became apparent that his share of the estate would never support him, he disposed of it and went to Andover, where he settled down as farmer and raised a family of ten children.

Ten children, that was the trouble. The estate was valued at 806 pounds when John died, but divided among ten children that was little enough, and much of it was in the land and the house, which would remain the widow's for her use. All during Stephen Peabody's boyhood there was the land, and that meant a living for those who worked it; but there was little to divide and less cash, which was needed for college and seminary education.

So it was a long time before Stephen Peabody got that education or was able to respond to the call of the Gospel. He went off to Cambridge when he was twenty-five years old, and graduated when he was twenty-eight. He managed to acquire his degree then only through such economies as waiting on tables for money and doing his own laundry.

Next, Stephen studied theology in the manner of the poor boy—he became in essence an apprentice to a minister, lived with the family, pumped the organ, worked on the minister's farm (for even the clergy farmed for a living), and taught school during the winter season.

In 1767 a group of inhabitants of the town of Plaistow decided to break away and form their own town government. The reason was that they were too far away from the meetinghouse, and it was a hardship for them to go to church on Sundays. Furthermore the meetinghouse at Plaistow was so small that only half the towns-people could get inside at one time. So they petitioned the legisla-ture for the right to withdraw, and since this was for the most logical and law-abiding of reasons, the petition was granted.

Having established their freedom, as the town of Atkinson, these citizens then built their own meetinghouse and set about the search for an ordained minister, which was more easily said than done, for few settled clergymen wanted to come to the frontier.

The situation, however, suited Stephen Peabody. On November 25, 1772, he was ordained, and very shortly afterward he made his compact with the people of Atkinson. He would go there and live and be their pastor. They would pay him 160 pounds as a settlement, to get him started in the community, and then pay 66 pounds per year plus 13 shillings and 4 pence, that first year, then adding 40 shillings per year until the salary mounted to 80 pounds. It would be roughly seven years, then, before Stephen Peabody would receive his full salary, and that was not a particularly princely one. If he were to survive, he would have to settle land and farm, just like the others.

Stephen Peabody was ready, however. He was thirty-one years old, a big burly fellow, with a square face and the family's black eyes, heavy beetling brows, and already a high forehead with wispy hair that darted all over. He wore the simple black vestments of a Puritan minister with the two-tailed white stock that hung down the front of his chest. He settled gladly for the small salary, which was augmented only by the gift of ten cords of wood a year. (It was not always easy to get the wood before the cold weather set in, because the farmers thought of their problems first and the minister's welfare a poor second.)

It was the custom in these early days for the minister to settle down for life with his parishioners. Only much later with a change in the times would there come the practice of ministerial itineracy. Stephen Peabody came to Atkinson to stay, and he did remain for the next forty-seven years.

In the year after his ordination, Stephen was married and took his wife, who was born Polly Hasseltine, to live in the rough house he was able to build for her with the help of his neighbors. Almost immediately Polly was pregnant, and their first child was born late in the autumn. They were late in starting the family, as far as Stephen's age was concerned, and there was only one more child, Mary, born the beginning of 1775.

By that time the fever of revolution was heavy in the air, and Stephen, although the minister, was as much a revolutionary as any man in Atkinson. When the trouble began in Boston harbor and elsewhere along the coast, and the Continental Congress met, the Congress sent out to the various towns of the many colonies a circular declaration, so the leaders would know how they stood before matters went too far. To Atkinson came this declaration, with the request that it be signed by as many of the men of the town as agreed:

> We, the subscribers, do hereby solemnly engage and promise that we will do the utmost of our power, at the risk of our lives and fortunes, with arms, oppose the hostile proceedings of the British fleets and armies against the United American Colonies.

A serious matter that, and it required the most serious deliberations. A meeting was called, and the various members of the town, the freeholders, spoke their minds on the subject of British taxes and freedom. The Reverend Stephen Peabody arose and spoke, and his thoughts were more revolutionary than religious. The colonists had put up with much in the Stamp Act and the various exorbitant levies on imports, to say nothing of the supercilious treatment accorded the colonies by their brethren so far away across the Atlantic. It was as if the brethren were not brethren at all—a fact that the Reverend Stephen Peabody was quite willing to accept, for he was of the fourth generation of American Peabodys. His father was born an American. His grandfather was born an American. Only his great-grandfather, Francis, had ever seen the green shores of England; and Francis, it must be remembered, had died a very old man forty-six years before Stephen was born. Like the others of the community, and of the colonies for that matter, Stephen was an American, and the land meant much to him, almost as much as his freedom, while loyalty to the British Crown meant nearly nothing at all.

So these Americans, sons of Americans, and grandsons of Americans were not long in making up their minds when it came to such a vital matter as their freedom and the common good. Solemnly, every male citizen of Atkinson, ninety-seven of them in all, signed the pledge and vowed to risk their lives, to give up their property, to save American colonies from brutalization.

It was not long before most of them were called to redeem that pledge, and among them was Stephen Peabody. He joined Colonel Poor's regiment as Chaplain, and he spent long months in the field.

Stephen's service was arduous, uncomfortable, and dangerous, but it was not much unlike that of most of the able-bodied men of Atkinson or the other colonies. Within this one family, the Peabodys, there is enough variety of Revolutionary War military experience to give some picture of the American scene, as it was in 1776.

Look at the stories of Stephen's cousins: First there was Nathaniel, also of Atkinson, whose story has been told as one of the most prominent of the Revolutionary Peabodys, and who, probably, was responsible for Stephen's coming to Atkinson in the first place.

Then there was Ebenezer Peabody of the fifth generation. Eb-

enezer was a descendant of Francis's eldest son, John, and a third
cousin (or so) of Stephen's. Ebenezer had stayed in Boxford and
married one of the Pearl girls in 1764. He was bright and had some
education together with a great deal of courage. Soon he was a
lieutenant, and he was in command of his troops at the Battle of
Bunker Hill, where he distinguished himself by yielding only inch
by inch and refusing to turn his back on the enemy. As it turned
out that day—not a particularly honored one for Americans—he
was one of the last to leave the field and he left with honor. Later
Lieutenant Ebenezer Peabody served with Colonel Alden in the
burning of Cherry Valley (when the Indians attacked); he was
with Colonel Brooks at the taking of Burgoyne; he traveled
through the Indian country on a wild and dangerous mission with
General Sullivan. Lest there be any doubt about his services, after
his death at the age of eighty-seven, long after the war ended, his
widow was granted a pension of $400 a year in honor of Ebenezer's
valiant services for his country.

Also, there was Henry, descended from Joseph, the second son
of old Francis, who stayed on in Boxford. He was killed in the
Revolutionary army, at the age of twenty-seven. A second cousin
of Reverend Stephen's with the same name was also a colonel, and
his eldest son Thomas served. Still another Stephen served as a
private beginning in 1776 when he was seventeen years old, but
that feat was surpassed by his brother John who went to war at
thirteen. Joseph, who would be the shipping king of Salem, served
as a private, and one of his cousins, Dr. Thomas Peabody, a descendant of Francis's fifth son, Jacob, was in at the surrender of Burgoyne. He had served as regimental surgeon to Colonel Evans's
New Hampshire regiment all through the war. He died as result
of his exposures and war experiences in 1777, and thus extinguished
the branch of Jacob, for he was the only surviving son—his brother,
Jacob, having been killed with Wolfe on the Plains of Abraham
at the battle of Quebec. And finally there was Richard, of the line
of William, who had remained in Boxford. Richard became a captain in the Revolutionary army, commanded a company at Ticon-

deroga, and served along Lake George in the decisive days of that campaign.

One of Richard's brothers, Francis Peabody, had moved his wife and children from Boxford to St. John River, Nova Scotia, and later settled in New Brunswick. So the Peabodys had men on both sides of the lines with very different sympathies during this war of revolution. They were fairly unusual among old American families, in this regard, but far from unique, although usually the transference was the other way around—the families who went to what is now Canada decided to opt for the warmer climate south and sent some of their representatives to the colonies that would rebel.

Rebels and loyalists—it can be seen that the Peabodys were in the thick of the Revolutionary War and that they were not without influence in its outcome.

When that war was over, and not really until then, the Reverend Stephen Peabody returned to his flock at Atkinson and began to settle down to a peacetime career. He kept a diary that first year of peace when he returned to the unfamiliar routine, and that journal tells much about his life and about life in Atkinson in 1783. Congress began furloughing the soldiers in the spring, and by October nearly all the soldiers were discharged and Chaplain Peabody was at home on the farm.

Oct 3. Catechised the children at John Dustin's.

The entry was laconic, but it told much. The children were forced to learn the Westminster catechism. Each Sunday during services the minister informed the congregation that he would travel among various families during the week "to catechise the children," questioning them on the points of religious doctrine in this book of guidance. So on the appointed day he would call at the house, and there would be the children in the parlor, dressed in their Sunday clothes, faces washed and shoes brushed.

"What is the chief end of man . . . ?" he would begin. And by rote, the children would answer what they had been taught from the book.

April 13. Write John Little's will.

As town scholar, with no lawyer yet settled in Atkinson, it was the task of the minister to see to the normal legal papers of the families in his charge. He wrote the wills, not an unhandy device for keeping track of sources of potential trouble and for exerting his influence for the betterment of the community.

July 16. Went to Commencement.

The Reverend Stephen Peabody went back to Harvard College for the ceremonies that year. It was not a totally nostalgic trip, but a renewal. For Harvard College then was a borning place for ministers and scholars, and in going back Stephen Peabody secured information and sources of inspiration for the months to come.

Nov. 6. At Mr. Dow's mill raising.

He was there, along with everyone else in the town. The mill could not be raised—the big timbers could not be managed, with less than a dozen men to haul on them. Beforehand the affair was opened by the Reverend Peabody, who offered a prayer. Then came the work, lubricated by a little rum, and when it was finished the women came forth with a feast.

Dec. 26. Got my wood.

The wood was late coming this year, but that was to be expected because nearly all the men had been away. On the appointed day, set by the town selectmen, everyone would come and contribute his share of the minister's wood for the season.

Then there were other entries, referring to his sermons, for he preached two on Sundays—morning and evening—and they were different at each meeting. These were long sermons, as most of the congregation wanted them long, because there were no movies, no lectures, no amusements of any kind except those of children; such new ideas as the adults received they got through these sermons and the movement through the town of the tinkers and peddlers.

There were few enough other travelers, few enough new ideas, and the townspeople were content that the Reverend Stephen Peabody exhort them to goodness.

Also, there were frequent reports of weddings and christenings and funerals—all the tasks of the minister who is father to his flock, who lived and felt more than any other member of the congregation the ebbs and flows of life.

For Stephen Peabody it was a busy life, because he plowed his own fields as well as those of the Lord. He got in his corn, having sowed it in the spring, and he husked it, and he raised his own cow for milk and his hog for meat and when the cow went dry he killed her for meat. He was strong and healthy and the farm work increased his burliness until he was known as one of the most muscular men of the town, and perhaps its best wrestler. Sometimes, when someone in the town had given him cause to anger, the Reverend Stephen Peabody was known to take it out in a friendly little wrestling match, and he had a reputation throughout New Hampshire for his "muscular Christianity."

He was a generous man. After the prayers at a house raising or a barn raising, he would pitch in and help put up the building. At home, he kept his doors open for visitors, day and night, and his cupboards and his pots full for them. There were no railroads, and the farmers of New Hampshire took their produce to town in their carts during the winter season, before the snow became too thick, so in late fall and early winter his house was always filled with arriving and departing guests, but he never complained, nor did Polly, his wife.

He worked the fields in rude farmer's homespun, but when visitors came to call, and Polly came after him or sent one of the children, he would rush into the house and put on his black suit, his white cravat, his silk stockings, and his shoes with the silver buckles that marked him as a gentleman.

Four years after Stephen Peabody's return from the Revolutionary War, he established Atkinson Academy, to give the youngsters of the town a better education. The stumbling block was money, so he set out to raise funds, and in 1791 petitioned the legislature to allow a lottery, which petition was granted. Since Atkinson was close to the Massachusetts border, he also petitioned the Massachusetts legislature for the same privilege, but was refused, because the Bay State's lawmakers did not want any New Hampshireman selling lottery tickets in their territory.

The lottery scheme was hardly successful, with so few people in New Hampshire, but Stephen Peabody did not despair, rather he went into debt personally to see his dream come true, and the academy was founded.

The Atkinson Academy was one of the first to take girls, and its most famous female student was Grace Fletcher, who would marry Daniel Webster. Among the boys were Levi Woodbury, Governor Kent, and Jonathan Cilley, who would all become more or less well known in New England.

The academy was simply the Peabody house built onto, and soon it was full. The Reverend Peabody found it hard to refuse those who requested his help, and he took many charitable or scholarship students whose families could pay only part or none of their expenses.

So the Peabody influence was exerted very early in the matter of education—and not content with founding a school that ran him into debt, the Reverend Stephen Peabody would start a subscription library, gathering together the leading citizens of Atkinson and bludgeoning them, most of whom did not care a fig, into putting up money for the purchase of books.

The books tended toward *Pilgrim's Progress*, religious tracts, a *History of England*, treatises on mathematics, and similar useful material. There was certainly no "popular fiction," for popular fiction was not yet in being; it would be a product of an easier time. The Reverend Peabody would never have permitted it in his library in any event, for he was a stern Puritan preacher. In the church at the close of the services the congregation rose and remained standing while Peabody and his wife went out. And when the members of the parish met him on the street they called him

"Sir" and "Parson Peabody." There was never any familiarity with the parson in Atkinson, for he was a taskmaster in the house of the Lord and out of it. Any disturbances, particularly by boys, were quelled immediately during church services, and the wardens sometimes took offenders by the ear and escorted them out of the building. Then, the poor boys had to face further punishment from the fathers in expiation of the disgrace they had brought on the family. The Reverend Peabody was not loath, either, to stop his sermon or the services, fix the offender with a stern and cold eye, and speak up about the offense.

The time in which Stephen held the pulpit in the town church at Atkinson was a most difficult one for a preacher of the old faith, for all around him was growing the new Unitarianism and other offshoots of the hard line of Puritanism. Yet while he was the town's minister there was no break—no one dared stare him down or start another church, and when an old Bostonian who had strayed into Unitarianism settled in Atkinson to spend his declining days, he very carefully concealed his estrangement from the mother church lest he get into serious difficulties by showing himself an unbeliever. Just as everybody else, the old Bostonian attended the services, twice on Sundays, and contributed to the support of the parish.

Had he not been a preacher, Stephen Peabody might have been a joyful and contented man. He had a fine voice, and he liked to sing—but he sang hymns. He played the violin, and played it well—but he played only religious music. Some said that in his youth, before he took his vows, he had even *danced!*

In 1793, when the Reverend Stephen was fifty-two years old, his wife died, and it was a measure of his vigor that his parishioners thought nothing of it when he began to seek another partner almost immediately. As was befitting a widower, the Reverend Stephen looked for a widow to become his second wife. In such matters a man needs a friend, and he turned to the Reverend and Mrs. John Shaw of Haverhill, Massachusetts.

The Reverend Stephen had known the Shaws for many years. Their parishes were only six miles apart, although separated by the state line, and there had been much visiting back and forth. The preachers of the region held frequent meetings, sometimes for as long as two or three days, in which the men discussed theological matters and the women talked about housewifely problems. Some, like Elizabeth Shaw, led excursions into more esoteric matters, for Mrs. Shaw was that rarity, an educated woman, and a person in her own right. She brought a certain eclat to the whole region, in fact, because her sister Abigail was married to John Adams, who was to be second President of the United States.

So when he was bereaved, and the sorrow of loss gave way before the senses of frustration and panic that overcome a man who has been deprived of a woman's help in running a house filled with children, the Reverend Stephen Peabody turned to the Shaws.

"What kind of a woman do you want?" Elizabeth asked when the three of them had discussed his problem and agreed that he must remarry.

"One just like yourself," was Stephen's gallant reply.

So Elizabeth Shaw counseled with her friends and searched her memory for the names of all the widows in the countryside twenty or thirty miles around. Finally she recommended one particular widow who seemed most suitable for the parson. He was on his way to visit this candidate one day, when he learned of the untimely death of John Shaw in Haverhill. Suddenly, he turned his horse and went home, abandoning his mission.

Some weeks went by, during which the widow Shaw adjusted herself to her new status in life, but not very many weeks at that, because the Puritans of New England were realists, and one of their realizations was that in the long cold winters of New England, man and woman were not made to sleep alone.

It did not appear unseemly, then, when the Reverend Stephen Peabody came calling on the widow Shaw less than three months after her bereavement. Indeed, he was not the first, but the second suitor to come and sit in the widow Shaw's parlor. The first was the Reverend Isaac Smith, a tall, slender figure of a man, who had courted Elizabeth Smith twenty years before. He was her cousin and had always hoped to marry her until she was swept away by John Shaw before his very eyes. Now, in his forties, given a second chance, Isaac was determined that Elizabeth would be his wife. He held an excellent post, as praeceptor of the Byfield Academy, the oldest school in Massachusetts, and thus the most prestigious. His luck seemed to be running, so every week he rode the fifteen miles from the academy to Haverhill.

When Stephen learned of this courtship, he examined his situation. The Reverend Smith knew Elizabeth better than he; the Reverend Smith had the advantage of kinship—definitely an advantage rather than a disadvantage as might be thought in the twentieth century—and the Reverend Smith had a higher post in life. All the considerations seemed to favor his rival—for Stephen was in debt, he ran a poor school that seemed more millstone than asset, and his prospects were largely writ: he would be the pastor of Atkinson for all the rest of his life, and Atkinson was not and never would be much more than a village.

But this accounting did not reckon with two advantages which Stephen possessed. One was an ardent temperament. His outdoor farming life had kept him in a fine state of bodily preservation— he was a handsome figure of a man, only slightly graying in his fifty-third year. And he had the advantage of propinquity—he was only six miles from Haverhill. Stephen did all he could with those advantages. He visited the widow Shaw oftener and stayed later than the Reverend Smith.

Both ministers persisted in their suits, and both declared themselves the same week. The widow Shaw was undecided, and she prayed for time, which, of course, must be granted to her. Both suitors were sent away with instructions not to return—she would call the one she wanted.

But a few days later, before the day on which she had promised to make her decision known, a terrible storm struck the area. The rain camed down in sheets. The farmers gathered their cattle in the barns and the sheep were pushed in, too, underfoot, lest they bog down in the mud and suffocate or drown in ditches that suddenly became roaring rivers. The trees bowed down under the weight of rain and wind, and even the wolves sought shelter in the depth of the forest.

The Reverend Smith sat in his lonely pastorate before his fire and was suddenly struck by inspiration. He would go and make his plea. Seeing him come so far, so wet and bedraggled, so willing to brave lightning and the cold and wet for her sake, the fair widow would judge that he loved her more than his rival, and would accept him. So Isaac mounted his horse and rode the miserable fifteen miles, through morass and torrent, to reach the side of his ladylove.

Luckily for him he had still another advantage in this courtship —the support of the widow Shaw's maid, Lydia. She had been with Elizabeth for many years and had looked with favor on Isaac Smith's courtship of her mistress in the first place. Now she was in league with him to persuade the widow.

But unluckily for Isaac, when he arrived at Mrs. Shaw's house, the maid had to tell him bad news.

"You are altogether too late, sir," Lydia said to the determined suitor as she took his dripping coat and hung it near the fire. "Parson Peabody has long since dried his coat by the kitchen fire and has been sitting with Mrs. Shaw a whole hour in the parlor."

A look at her face told the Reverend Smith all he needed to know. His instinct had been right, his timing wrong. Yielding the field to his rival, he picked up his wet coat, put it on, turned and went out of the house into the storm with Lydia looking mournfully after him. Isaac Smith was too proud to let Mrs. Shaw know he had come so fruitlessly, and he would not disturb Stephen Peabody's belief that he had triumphed through thoughtfulness rather than the difference of nine miles.

So that is how Parson Stephen Peabody got his second wife and his great happiness, and how Atkinson Academy secured a new mistress who added immeasurably to the cultural blessing of the place. She was much more cultivated and refined than the rude folk of Atkinson. Her roots were in Boston and Quincy, and she returned there frequently, coming back to Atkinson with infusions of ideas and styles that quite bedazzled the townspeople. There could be no criticism of her, because she was the wife of the preacher, and she never comported herself in such a way as to arouse the slightest whisper of gossip.

She could quote readily from Shakespeare, Pope, and Addison, and she committed to memory much of Hannah Moore's new *Tracts* when they came out. She was aware of all that was published and all that was going on in the infant republic to which she kept the school alert. But with all that she was a housewife about whom no criticism could be raised. She mended stockings and sewed up torn breeches, she cleaned along with Lydia. Always she was dressed as a lady with the most elaborate headdress (which was her hallmark), but she did not avoid the barnyard if there was reason for her to go there.

Through Elizabeth, Stephen Peabody became an intimate of the John Adams family, and an influence on young John Quincy Adams, because of his rectitude and courage, just as Elizabeth brought playfulness, a good humor, and love of beauty to the Adams household whenever they visited there. Elizabeth's son, who grew up in the household at Atkinson and later attended Harvard College, became private secretary to his cousin when John Quincy was President, studied law, and became clerk of the United States District Court in Boston. This man, William Smith Shaw, was one of the principal founders of the Boston Athenaeum. Of course, he was not a Peabody, but a stepson of a Peabody—and how does one measure the influence of pure environment on the future of a man or a nation?

In the spring of 1815, Elizabeth Peabody died, ending a real romance—as real as that of John and Abigail Adams—which had lasted for twenty-two years. The Smith girls had a penchant for romance, it seemed, to turn such men as John Adams and Stephen Peabody into romantics; and their influence, from White House to Atkinson parish house, was for culture, gentleness, honesty, and honor always. These two women brought much grace to the nation in their own ways, within their own spheres, and Elizabeth's influence was far wider than one might expect because of the respect and love for her borne by her sister Abigail. "I scarcely ever received a letter from her," Abigail wrote on Elizabeth's death, "which did not draw involuntary tears from my eyes. Her imagination was brilliant, her affections pure and ardent, her wit and playfulness full of good humor, unalloyed with acrimony. To know her was to love and respect her. How many owe to her the good seed which she planted in their infant minds, and which, I doubt not, will be her crown of rejoicing!"

How very intertwined the influences were.

Stephen Peabody survived Elizabeth by only four years, and that was due to his splendid constitution, for on her death his will to live was gone and he lost strength visibly month after month. He did not joke with his parishioners any longer, he did not sing or play the violin. He rarely wrote a new sermon, but relied upon ones given before. All that remained of the old Stephen was his charity and his upright character.

He died on May 23, 1819, and was buried in the burying ground in the center of the village, by the side of Elizabeth, as he wished, in a plot overlooking the Monadnock Mountains to the west and north, and the spires of the villages that sprawl their way along the south and eastern plain toward the sea.

CHAPTER 6

THE PRIVATEER

NATHANIEL PEABODY was certainly the most celebrated member of the clan during his lifetime, and as for the rest of the Peabodys, a family growing large as all "original" American families seemed to do in the healthy atmosphere of the new continent, they were, as L. H. Butterfield put it in relation to the Adamses before John, "a family of farmers, maltsters, and holders of town office who lived their lives below the level of historical scrutiny." They were, in other words, like the vast majority of us. For four generations most of these Peabodys stayed close to Essex County, with a hand-ful wandering off romantically to such far reaches as Nova Scotia and the Deep South.

Isaac, fourth son of Francis, the founder of the American Pea-body line, was one of the most unfortunate of men. Early in life he lost one of his legs. In consideration of this disability he received the manor house and mill when Francis died. Isaac's eldest son, also named Francis, moved to Middleton where he took up farming in the family tradition. He served as a cornet (junior officer) in the militia and retained that title until his death from a stroke in 1769. His son, who had a definite bent toward the church, although he, too, was a farmer, became known in Middleton as Deacon Peabody, although he, too, was a Francis.

It is Deacon Francis's ninth child, Joseph, who was the next Peabody to come into the ken of historians. His fame parallels a significant development in the American story: the rise and decline of the great American shipping merchants, of whom this Joseph Peabody was perhaps to be paramount.

There was no particular indication of this boy's future in his early years. As a stripling of eight he was sent from the over-crowded family hearth to life on the Boxford farm of his eldest sister, Ruth, who had married farmer John Curtis. For ten years, Joseph Peabody had his keep from his sister and her husband, in exchange for doing farm work. He received no wages, but he was allowed to keep hens and sell eggs. This servitude, which began in 1763 and lasted until just before the American Revolution, was typical of the American farm system, for the boy's wages and labor belonged to his elders. He did not resent the system, nor would any youths of his day have done so; they accepted it and would expect to receive the same service from their own progeny.

Following the practice of four generations in America, and two generations before that in England, this Joseph's education came largely from learning to read the Bible. He went to school only during one season (some say for only two weeks), and his sister taught him to read, using the same good book from which she had learned herself.

Joseph was an ambitious lad. He became the family shoemaker and perfected his cobbling so that he could do far more than make rough boots or repair farm shoes. Soon he became the neighbor-hood cobbler, in demand by the farm families around. He liked the work because it took him away from the pigpens and sheep enclosures for a time. In 1775, just after the battle of Lexington, Joseph took up a musket and joined the local militia with his sister's blessing. They marched through Wilmington to attack the British, but came too late. Finding the British gone, they scattered and went home in a most unmilitary fashion, as was the way of these independent Minutemen. Joseph Peabody, having no British to shoot, spent his bullets on the countryside, and managed to bag a wild goose, which brought him some glory at home as a provider, if not as a rebel against the King that day.

That excursion was not typical. Instead, while his brother-in-law went off to fight the war, Joseph ran the farm by himself for the year 1776. When John Curtis came trudging home after his year of service, it was agreed that Joseph, having served out his time and paid for his keep, might do what he wished with his life. He returned home for a visit, to decide what to do. At Middleton, however, he discovered there was really no place for him. He was a virtual stranger, and his brother Stephen, three years younger, was taking care of the farm and seemed likely to inherit it. Joseph therefore decided that he would make his fortune as a sailor, and he marched off to Salem to discover the wide, wide world.

At Salem, the world did indeed beckon. Around the docks were advertisements from the Congress and from private shipowners, asking for men to sign on as seamen. It was a dangerous time to be shipping out, for the war was raging, and any American ship was subject to sinking or seizure by the British. But where there was danger there was also opportunity for gain. Joseph Peabody joined the American privateer *Bunker Hill* as an apprentice seaman and sailed to war with a promise of a share in the proceeds if they were successful. But the *Bunker Hill* accomplished little on this voyage in 1777. She moved into southern climes where fever predominated, and there Joseph Peabody contracted malaria. When he came home to Massachusetts at the end of the voyage he was ill for several weeks. He recovered and shipped out again in 1778 aboard the *Pilgrim*, owned by a Cabot of Beverly, to seek fortune and damn the eyes of the British under the command of an Irishman, Captain Hugh Hill.

The cruiser headed toward the coast of Ireland, waters the captain knew like the back of his hand, where he might expect to find unarmed merchantmen rather than British frigates or ships of the line. On May 14, 1779, the *Pilgrim* closed up on a sail, and discovered that she had overhauled a British privateer, the ship *Success*.

On coming alongside and ordering her "to strike her flag," the English captain exclaimed lustily, "I must fight you."

"Very well," said Captain Hill, "just say when you are ready."

After waiting for a considerable time, which was improved to the utmost by the Englishman in clearing for action, loading and pointing his guns, Captain Hill, beginning to grow impatient, cried out "Are you ready?"

"Yes, damn you," said the Englishman.

"Then, my boys," said Hill, "let him have it." In a few moments the ship was a prize and the unfortunate Englishman paid the debt due to his folly, being the first man that fell on board his ship.*

Joseph Peabody was one of the men assigned to board the *Success* and take her to America as a prize. They sailed to Thomaston, Maine, and he went home again, to await the return of his ship to American waters. When the *Pilgrim* arrived, having taken eleven prizes in all, Joseph Peabody shipped out aboard her once again. But this third voyage was an unsuccessful as his first, for soon out of port the *Pilgrim* was dismasted in a storm and had to put back for repairs.

Young Joseph was a lanky, thoughtful youth, with large head and mouth, characteristic of the family line. After three sea voyages he found that he liked the life, but he also recognized his own deficiencies. He could scarcely read and write, and he observed that the officers of the ships he served were educated men. He had no desire to spend his life before the mast; from the day that he left his sister's farm, he had been determined to make his fortune, and at the conclusion of the *Pilgrim* voyage he decided the time had come to prepare himself for a more valuable career at sea.

Joseph returned to his family home at Middleton, where he could be assured of bed and board in exchange for helping around the farm. He had earned some money in his second privateering voyage, and this was put by for the future. He arranged his affairs so that he could take time off from the farm chores in order to

* Notes of George Peabody on the early life of his father in the Peabody Museum of Salem.

study with the local parson, the Reverend Elias Smith, a graduate of the class of 1753 at Harvard College.

There was a year of study at Middleton, where it appeared that Joseph got on better with the parson and his wife than he ever did with his own family, who did not hold much with learning for its own sake. Joseph, alone among them, had been out in the world and knew the values of education, not only for such essentials as celestial navigation but also for traffic among men.

Joseph went back to Salem in 1781, to undertake a fourth voyage. As the *Pilgrim* was not available to him, he shipped out on the privateer *Rambler*, and so distinguished himself with his deportment and his new education that on a fifth voyage in that same year he was appointed prize master of the privateer *Fish Hawk*.

The *Fish Hawk* sailed in the summer of 1781 out into the Atlantic to look for prizes, and moved north, hoping to find them in the waters off Newfoundland. Unfortunately, on September 21 they ran afoul of a British ship-of-war, and the *Fish Hawk*'s predatory career came to an untimely end. Joseph Peabody was sent with the other captives to a British prison ship off St. John's, Newfoundland. With his usual energy he contrived to make the experience useful: he persuaded an educated man named Cowan to conduct classes in arithmetic, and he perfected his understanding of that subject.

After a few months Joseph was exchanged by the British in a general turnover of prisoners between Canada and the United Colonies; and he went back to preying on British commerce, this time as second mate on the privateer brig *Ranger*. The *Ranger* carried cargo between the Colonies and Havana, including two hundred barrels of flour from George Washington's plantation at Mount Vernon. The ship was anchored one night downriver from what is now Washington near Georges Island, a notorious hangout for pirates, when the watch passed the word that boats were seen coming from the shore. The *Ranger* carried a crew of only twenty, and they were being attacked by two barges, each of which held about fifty men. Obviously the situation was desperate. The captain, named Simmons, was aroused, and he began issuing orders.

"Mr. Peabody, let no boats come alongside; no one has any business here," he said as he encountered his second mate in the companionway on their way to the upper deck. Just as they stepped on deck a discharge of muskets blazed in their faces, and the captain fell back, wounded in the leg.

The fight went on from there. Mate Peabody was still in his nightshirt. He had not even had time to dress when the alarm was sounded. He rushed forward, yelling at the crew to seize their pikes and repel boarders. He grasped a boarding pike himself and leaped to the bow, followed by a man named Kent. They arrived just as the pirates were clambering over the gunwhales and were able to drive the invaders back down into their boat.

Scarcely losing a moment, Mate Peabody and Seaman Kent dashed back amidships, where the other boat was alongside. Peabody led the men in the rush, standing out in his white linen shirt, making a fine target for a musket ball. But he was unhurt, and after the charge, he stood in control of the deck. For some reason the first mate of the vessel was down in the magazine, not on deck, where he should have been, so Second Mate Peabody led the defense. The cannon of the *Ranger* were not shotted, and could scarcely have been of much use at such close quarters, but on deck lay pyramids of shot for the guns, and they gave Peabody an idea. In a moment of respite, before the next attack which they knew would be mounted, the men seized up the cold round shot, rushed to the starboard rail, and rained the heavy ammunition down on the pirates in the craft alongside. It was an excellent ploy. The shot crashed through the bottom of the frail barge, and she began to sink. The pirates yelled and suddenly became far more interested in swimming for shore than in attacking the brig.

Seeing their advantage, Mate Peabody urged the men forward to the port side with shout and gesture, picking up another shot himself to illustrate how he wanted the same treatment given those rogues below.

"We have sunk one, my boys, now sink the other," he cried.

Hearing this shout, the pirates on the barge to port pushed away from the brig, which was all the while drifting slowly downstream, having cast loose her anchors at the first sign of trouble. The barge began dropping back, and the men on the deck of the *Ranger* could only heave their shot, hoping to land it among the enemy. Soon the barges were out of sight, and calm descended on the river.

Mate Peabody then called the men together, to check his casualties. One crewman was found dead and three men were wounded, plus the captain. Only when the action was ended did Joseph Peabody notice that his own left wrist felt stiff, and he found that he had been hit by a pistol ball. Further, his right elbow had been laid bare to the bone by a cutlass slice, and his left shoulder had been clipped by a ball from a gun. Not until later did he discover that his pigtail had been shot off the back of his head. It was found next morning, lying on the deck, severed as cleanly as if by a barber's shears.

After the action, First Mate Thomas Perkins appeared on deck to take command because the captain could not stand on his leg. Joseph Peabody then became acting first mate of the ship.

The *Ranger* sailed back up to Alexandria next morning to report on the encounter. There the first mate discovered that the pirates were actually refugee loyalists, who had taken possession of these islands in the river rather than be imprisoned or shipped north to Canada. When the ship came sailing in with her news, the town erupted in excitement, and the merchants sent out spies to discover how badly the Tories had been hurt. They found, to their great pleasure and comfort, that the enemy had lost fifteen men killed and thirty-eight wounded in the encounter with the brig. So pleased were the merchants with this defense that they got up a purse for the ship. One reason they were so delighted was that a few days earlier the Tories had captured and destroyed a vessel in a similar encounter. Captain Simmons, the wounded master, was honored by presentation of a silver-mounted boarding pike, which

he accepted gratefully. Afterward, he had the grace to will the
pike to Joseph Peabody, who had really won it.

From Alexandria, Captain Simmons returned to Salem to nurse
his wounds, and the new Captain Perkins and First Mate Peabody
took the ship on her voyage to Havana, then went back to Salem.
By the time of their return, Captain Simmons was ready for sea
again, and Captain Perkins went to a new command. Joseph Peabody's rank of first mate of the *Ranger* was confirmed, and he
sailed again on an eighth privateering voyage, which was to be an
exciting one. One day out of Curaçao the *Ranger* was chased by a
British man-of-war, but Mate Peabody laced on every stitch of
canvas she would hold, and after thirty-six terrifying hours, the
Ranger made her escape in a squall and came home safe to Salem
a few months later.

By this time it was 1783, and peace came to the New World, at
least outside the waters of the pirates in the south. Joseph Peabody
had served aboard enough ships and knew enough now to have
his master's ticket, and he was given command of a series of packets
owned by the Gardner family of Salem. He spent several adventurous years at sea in the employment of the Gardners, making
most of his voyages in the Americas. He caught smallpox on one
trip and nearly died. He had fever and other ailments. But he
survived and bought a share of the ship *Three Friends*, which he
then took voyaging to Europe and other waters.

For several years Captain Peabody was almost constantly afloat,
but he had other matters on his mind. He was still determined to
seek his fortune, and he knew that vast wealth was not acquired
by sea captains, save perhaps in the dangerous, lucrative opium
trade. He was not the kind of man to join other Salem captains in
this dope traffic, however, and he kept to more normal pursuits,
nursing his ambitions. When he had accumulated enough capital,
he turned over his command to another and went ashore.

Captain Peabody was then in his thirty-fourth year. One has a
hint of the kind of man he was, a strong, stouthearted fellow of
absolute conviction in his own abilities and in very little else in

this world. Who would have known, in all those years of seafaring, that the sea was but the means through which he would gain his end: fortune? Who would have suspected that he could quit the sea? Certainly few of his acquaintances in Salem town would have guessed, for Captain Peabody was a taciturn officer, who kept his business to himself and his owners.

On August 28, 1791, Joseph Peabody married Katherine Smith, daughter of the Reverend Elias Smith, his mentor in Middleton. Like all else in Joseph Peabody's life, this marriage was carefully planned months in advance. Almost a year earlier he had bought a house on Essex Street in Salem. It was a handsome old place. Chimneys rose three stories above the nearly flat roof with its railing and middle skylight. The house was boxlike, shuttered, with Greek porticoes at the entrance and latticework for climbing vines. The property was surrounded by an iron fence, as was the neighboring house; it was a solid businessman's residence in a busy town, substantial and comfortable.

Poor Katherine. She was nearly thirty years old when wed, and most unwell. Her health had been delicate for some time, and it was believed that she was on the verge of consumption. Enough reason, then, that her husband should forsake the sea to help nurse her back to health. John Endicott (mark the name) had been put in charge of the *Three Friends* for two voyages, about the time of Joseph's marriage. In the spring of 1792, however, Peabody took his old ship out again himself, leaving on April 30 from Salem port for the West Indies and returning on August 13.

When he arrived back home, he discovered that Katherine's health had worsened considerably. What promise did he make to her then, in the joy of homecoming and the anxiety of examining a beloved face and finding it ravaged by disease in only a matter of months? Perhaps he promised her he would never go to sea again or leave her side. At any rate, that is what happened. Captain John Endicott and others sailed the *Three Friends* across the brimming sea, and Captain Joseph Peabody stayed in Salem, tending the garden of his love. After but a year all this attention proved useless, for Katherine Smith Peabody died, leaving the young widower distraught.

What now? Back to sea, to live the life of adventure that had brought him health, fame, and profit? No, that was not to be the course. It may be that Joseph was permanently scarred by the death of this gentle, long-suffering creature, that he considered his promise binding, if indeed he had truly made one. But more likely is the ruder alternative—adventure and romance had been thrust upon Joseph Peabody by the circumstances of war. His earlier training and his whole background until the date he set out to sea were dull by comparison. How many youths, taking up a musket to hunt Redcoats, would be satisfied to spend their ammunition on so crass a target as a gray goose? How many youths, studying with the village pastor, would listen attentively and make a record of the homilies or maxims, then use those throughout the rest of their lives as guides to their own conduct and quote them to their descendants as guides for theirs?

"You need not tell all the truth, unless to those who have a right to know it all. But let all you tell be truth." There was a maxim for a New England merchant prince. Truth and honor were fine in their place, and it simply behooved a man to be sure he knew their place. In a sense, this maxim became the guide of Captain Joseph's adult life: the truth, but not all the truth. . . .

There were other maxims to be followed; he had copied down far more than a hundred of them and in copying them he learned them as perfectly as a Harvard boy might learn his Latin lessons.

Captain Joseph settled down to the good solid American practice of making money. To his interest in the *Three Friends* he added other ventures with Jonathan Gardner, and as they profited he reinvested. Soon he owned a full half of the *Three Friends*. He did not confine himself to partnership with Gardner, either. His old first mate, Thomas Perkins, put together a little capital, and Joseph joined Perkins in another operation, with Perkins taking the ship out to trade, and Joseph handling the work of provisioning, bringing the cargo to Salem, and collecting the bills. In 1793

Joseph and Perkins went to the shipbuilder Enos Briggs in Salem and had him build for them the schooner *Cynthia*, which became their joint venture. Her first trip was so successful that the same year they bought a brigantine named the *Three Brothers* and put her out to trade under another captain.

Next year, the *Cynthia* went out under Captain Hezekiah Flint. There is a hint of the uneasy situation of post-Revolutionary America in her fate during the autumn of 1794. She was out in Bermuda waters when suddenly she was stopped and boarded by a British privateer. On the pretext that the *Cynthia* was carrying contraband destined for the French, with whom Britain was at war, she was seized as a prize, her crew was taken off and impressed into the British service, and six British sailors were put aboard her to sail her to a friendly port. Only Captain Flint, one able-bodied seaman, and one boy were left of the Americans, to prove that the *Cynthia* was not the victim of an act of pure piracy.

But six men is a small crew, and not one to dismay two men and a boy who had their wits about them and knew the boards on which they walked so well they could traverse the ship in the dark without once stumbling. Night came, and the captain and his supporters overwhelmed the watch, shut the British securely in the cabin, and sailed the *Cynthia* back to the safety of Martha's Vineyard.

The salvation of the *Cynthia* was due entirely to the toughmindedness of Captain Flint, but he does not seem to have been overgenerously rewarded, for we see him appear later in the life of Joseph Peabody only as a casual master of his ships, not a firm friend or a trusted employee, certainly not a partner. It was Peabody and Gardner, and Peabody and Perkins, not Peabody and Flint.

In 1795, affairs had so prospered for the youthful merchant that he and Perkins went further afield and bought a 113-ton schooner, the *Nabby*. Peabody also joined Gardner and others in a venture into the lucrative but dangerous Far Eastern spice trade, buying a share of the 181-ton brigantine *Sally* which was bound for

Batavia. Captain Joseph was by then successful, with a counting-house in his Essex Street residence and plans for the future. He would have a separate countinghouse and his own wharf, and he would become the foremost merchant of the town.

At thirty-eight Joseph Peabody was a good catch for any girl. He could now be called rich: a single voyage might bring him a gross return of $50,000 or more, and in the spice trade there would be even higher profit. But the maidens of Salem were doomed to disappointment, for the Captain was a creature of habit. When his wife's father had died, mother Smith had moved to Salem to be near her ailing daughter, and after Katherine's death, her mother had stayed on. In November, 1795, Joseph Peabody married his dead wife's sister, Elizabeth Smith.

Elizabeth possessed sterling qualities, but physical beauty was not one of them. Her nose was long and not quite straight, with a tendency to hook which seemed to grow more pronounced in her old age. Her forehead was high, but she appeared to have nearly no eyebrows and such scanty lashes that her eyes stuck out of her face like pumpkin seeds. Her mouth was straight and slightly grim-set. As she aged, long lines extended down from the corners of her nose past the edges of her lips, giving her a positively mournful appearance. Her neck was long, and her hair was dark and tended to be oily. Though wealthy, Captain Joseph was physically not so great a prize himself, and his attention was given totally to his account books.

Joseph Peabody never fully recovered from the loss of his first wife. Just once, he spoke to one of his and Elizabeth's children about Katherine, briefly but with much feeling. She was "a very different woman from your mother," he said. Elizabeth was younger by ten years, but she did not look it. She had seven chil-dren and childbearing aged and tired her. The family lived in an atmosphere of wealth but never of luxury.

Joseph had bought the house on Essex Street for Katherine, and he brought Elizabeth there to live. She did not like inhabiting an-other woman's house, and finally as the children began coming along she had her own way, and her husband moved them across to 134 Essex Street. This was a house built in the year of Katherine's death for Nathan Read, who later moved to a farm in Danvers to live. William Prescott, the historian of Mexico, lived there for a time with his parents, but the property was put up for sale a few years after Captain Joseph's marriage to Elizabeth and she persuaded him to buy it.

The house was handsomely done, inside and out, with delicate carved woodwork wrought by expert artisans. To furnish the inside, Captain Joseph was persuaded to ask his Leghorn correspondent for assistance, and several Italian carved marble pieces came to Salem in Peabody ships. One day there was much excitement when a drayman's cart arrived from Peabody wharf, and workmen unloaded a heavy, padded crate to take inside. When it was undone before the admiring eyes of mistress, maids, and children, there was revealed a mantel with Medusa heads atop it, a present from the merchants of Leghorn to the admired merchant Peabody. Other carts were constantly pulling up to the house in those early years, delivering chairs, glassware, china, and silver from the Peabody ships that ranged across the globe.

The house was entered through a double mahogany door with silver hardware, and the rooms were furnished sumptuously in silks and satins and heavy brocades. But after the furnishing, which represented "investment," as Joseph Peabody would have put it, expenditure for living was another matter. Captain Joseph believed in investing his money in the business, not in wasting it on high living. For years the expense of running the household was kept at $3000 a year, although his earnings might be twenty times as much.

There was no hint of scandal about Joseph Peabody in Salem. Any merchant in town would have scoffed if Captain Peabody had been accused of any crime, save usury. For Captain Peabody was a stern man who kept his own counsel and cared only for his business.

"Make your company a rarity, and people will value it," was one of his maxims. "Men despise what they can easily have."

So he was solitary. Actually, for several years his one confidant, if you could call him that intimate, was Judge William Prescott, father of the historian. Few other men knew Captain Joseph Peabody well or favorably.

The Captain was close with his money, but he was not stingy to his family. When the children came along, they received as good educations as anyone in the country. Two of the boys died in infancy. Eight-year-old Charles fell from the yard of one of his father's ships while playing during a deserted noon hour, and struck the ground so forcefully that his head was jammed into the mud. No one was near to rescue him, and the poor boy suffocated, adding a few more grim lines to his father's visage.

The first child, Joseph, born in 1796, was sent to private school in Salem, and then to Harvard College, after which he was given the "grand tour." With a letter of credit and notes of introduction the boy went abroad to learn the ways of he world. He stayed in England and on the Continent for a year and a half. When he came home, he went into business with his father, the most pleasant occasion that Captain Joseph had enjoyed for many a year. He believed strongly that business ought to be kept in the hands of the oldest son. He had caught the rich man's fever, the yen for power and immortality, and primogeniture was a way of realizing these goals.

With the first son his heir apparent, the second son killed in a grisly accident, and the third son dead as a baby, the fourth son, Francis, was allowed to do much as he would. He went to Dummer Academy as a boy. His health proved frail, and he was sent on a Peabody ship to Russia to recover in the healthful climes of the frigid north. While there he visited Cronstadt and went overland to Moscow; then he came home, a young man celebrated for his travels.

Francis might have gone to Harvard, but he was of a more scientific than literary turn of mind. Rather than go to college, he chose to stay at home where he dirtied the air with his chemical experiments and filled the house with mechanical devices. Finally,

Francis went into business in Salem, pulled into the world of trade by his chemical interests. His first venture was in white lead, and then he became a producer of lead products such as lead sheet and lead pipe. He manufactured fine book paper, and went into the refining of whale oil and the making of candles. Yet he was not all businessman like his father; he was elected to the American Academy of Arts and Sciences and later became President of the Essex Institute of Salem. He would play a role, too, in the establishment of the Peabody Museum of Salem, and would interest his distant relation George Peabody in the philanthropic support of public institutions.

The fifth son of Joseph Peabody, also named George, went to Jacob Knapp's school in Salem and then to Harvard. He was a member of the rebellious class of 1823, most of whose degrees were held up. George did not receive his bachelor's degree from the college until twenty years after his senior year, and then probably only because of his accomplishments in nonacademic matters. He learned the violin, and went to Paris on his grand tour. He came back to settle down in the banking business, the railroad business, and shipping ventures on his own. He was an alderman and three times a state legislator. He married Clarissa Endicott, a relative of Samuel Endicott's and of John Endicott's who had been one of Captain Joseph's master mariners. Older brother Francis married Clarissa's sister—Martha.

The two Peabody girls married successfully, as was to be expected, because their father was an important man in Salem by the time they were grown. Martha and Elizabeth married brothers, Richard Denison Rogers and Jacob Crowninshield Rogers—but both were childless and so became relatively unimportant to the tale of the Peabodys.

Overseeing the growth of his children, educating his sons, and marrying off his daughters occupied some of Captain Joseph's waking moments, but relatively few compared to those devoted to his business life. Very early in his own marriage he built his wharf and countinghouse, on Derby Street, a little east of the Charter

Street Cemetery. Ten years after he quit the sea, he was worth $286,000, a very large fortune in that day. But he regarded this wealth as only a beginning and spent long hours in his counting-house to increase it, growing red-eyed, lined, and stooped in the process of making money.

There were dozens of ships and they went everywhere in the world. The *Three Friends* carried lumber, butter, casks, and cod-fish to ports in the south in the beginning, but by 1796 she was sailing to Surinam for coffee, cocoa, and spices. The *Three Brothers* traveled to the West Indies carrying rum, brown sugar, and pimentos home. The *Cynthia* was in the rum trade, and then in 1796 moved into the more lucrative spice islands voyaging. Soon most of the Peabody ships were in the spice trade, for where else could a man legally, and without fear of reprisals, earn as much *700 percent* on his investment in a single voyage?

Each year the fortune increased, and the figures were jotted down in neat numbers in Captain Joseph's ledger, under such headings as:

Profits	Property, Dec. 31	Household Expenses	Bills Payable, Dec. 31

That is how the ledger was kept year after year, and up, up, up went the profits and net worth, because the Peabodys spent only $3000 a year, and the ships continued to increase apace. There came the *Neptune*, the *Cincinnatus*, the *Franklin*, the *Catherine*, the *Mount Vernon*, the *Janus*, the *Augustus*. Eventually there were eighty-six of them. All were small, tight vessels managed by small crews (the largest, the *Franklin*, was 296 tons). There lay the profit. Small crews, small cargo representing high value, traded for cargo of even higher value, brought home and sold at as much as seven times its cost.

All went well for Captain Joseph in his countinghouse during these early days of the Republic. When the revered President Washington retired and John Adams became Chief Executive of the nation, Captain Joseph was content. Adams was a correct sort of man, a Federalist as was the Captain, a conservative, God-fearing Massachusetts man of Puritan background and sensible upbringing. But four years later, in 1800, Thomas Jefferson was elected President, bringing to the nation the hated libertine philosophy of the detestable French. Captain Joseph was at war with France, even though his country was not. He had sent his vessels out in 1799 as privateers to prey on French shipping. The *Neptune, Sally, Three Friends,* and *Cincinnatus* all went to war, and all were successful in their piratical trade, save the *Neptune,* which was captured in June by French privateers, much to the annoyance of Joseph Peabody.

By 1800, when he expanded his activity to become an incorporator of the Salem Marine Insurance Company, Captain Joseph was recognized as one of the two most prominent merchants in Salem— the other was his partner, Thomas Perkins. Two years later Peabody had committed much of his shipping to the Sumatra pepper trade, which proved to be a bonanza that would last for the next forty years. Captain Joseph's ships would win the honors of being first and foremost in the trade, and one of them, the *Francis,* actually held the record of most voyages to Sumatra—seventeen between 1809 and 1836.

Joseph Peabody and his Federalist friends hated the Jeffersonian policies. The Captain was a thoroughgoing supporter of Timothy Pickering and the Essex Junto, that wild-eyed group of anti-French extremists. Peabody at least had a good solid reason for his enmity: money. The French with their undeclared war threatened his well-being, and he was glad to reciprocate by sinking them on the high seas with his privateers and trying to sink them in Congress with his influence. He opposed Jefferson all the way, and when in 1806 the President began laying down restrictions on trade, Captain Joseph was nearly beside himself. With the declaration of the Embargo, threatened to keep the Peabody ships at home, the Captain became livid. He even bestirred himself to journey to Topsfield for a political meeting, and there concluded with other Federalists that Jefferson's policies were leading the country directly to an unnecessary and unwanted war with Great Britain.

As for the Embargo, it affected Joseph Peabody very little because he simply ignored it—broke the law of the land— and sent his ships off trading although Jefferson said they were to be tied up in Salem port.

Captain Joseph reached and passed his fiftieth birthday, and the years rolled on. His hair grew gray and then white, and moved back from his temples. His mouth was thinner and sharper. His eyes grew steely, and his voice became shrill when he contemplated the sins of the Republican administrations. In 1811 he had this to say about the Madison administration:

> The conduct of our national government the past year has been marked by complete acquiescence in the views of the French government, a dishonorable defiance and resistance towards that of England; and by the most arbitrary and oppressive laws against the commercial interests of ourselves.*

He went so far, in his virtuous anger, as to suggest that he would prefer a limited monarchy to the Republican government that countenanced such frightful activity in the name of good management.

Captain Joseph was hardly alone. All the Salem merchants agreed with him, though not all of them showed such high profits as he from blockade running. During 1808, the first year of the Embargo, his profits leaped to $72,000, and in 1810 they jumped again to $126,000. In 1811, as the authorities cracked down on Salem, his profits fell to $36,000, a loss designed to make any merchant furious.

In 1812 Captain Joseph and the far more celebrated Nathaniel Bowditch were deputized by their fellow citizens of Salem to draw up a memorial to Congress opposing the War of 1812. But the war came anyhow, and it brought Joseph Peabody even more profit. In 1813 his earnings came to nearly $200,000, which must have represented either the highest prices in trade (dangerous trade certainly with the British blockade outside his door) or some income from privateering. The blockade was far more effective in

* Peabody Papers, Salem Museum.

the next three years, and the Peabody income dropped down to the $20,000 and $30,000 level, which meant small trade indeed, and very dangerous at that.

The war worried Captain Joseph in many ways, not the least of them concerning the safety of his family. He bought a farm in Danver Centre and shipped the family there along with much of his wordly fortune, to have a sanctuary from the threat of British seizure. The war ended, but he kept the farm, by only that much increasing the luxury of hs living.

Business, trade, and the family, these were Captain Joseph's preoccupations. His countinghouse would have endeared him to that other master businessman, the old Scrooge, before the Ghost of Christmas past took him in hand: it was a huge loft of a room, with an inner sanctum in which the Captain sat before the only fire, while in the outer offices his clerks shivered at their high desks, poring over his bills of lading and making out his charges against those who bought from him.

In 1817, Joseph Peabody was honored among his neighbors for what he had become, the most important man in Salem. More than that, he was the wealthiest merchant in the United States, and when President Monroe came to Essex County on his goodwill tour of the nation, and to Salem during the Era of Good Feeling, Monroe was advised to call on Joseph Peabody, the powerful Federalist merchant—and he did so. "This day the President waited upon Joseph Peabody, Esq., merchant of Salem and the wealthiest man now living in it, "went a contemporary account of the meeting.

And thus the years passed, each one seeming shorter and more like the year before. Captain Joseph was a strange man, a narrow man, a man who kept his own affairs to himself. He lived up to his maxims: "As you are going to a party of mirth, think of the hazard you run of misbehaving." Captain Joseph never went to "parties of mirth." "Never offer advice, but what there is some possibility of its being followed." Save in the anxiety of his concern during the War of 1812, and in the bosom of the family, Captain Joseph never offered advice.

And yet, his children thought well of him and his son George wrote long after the old man's death that outside the family the world was unaware of the strength of his father's intellect and the "true refinement and delicacy of his sentiments." The son gave the father credit for "lofty moral tone" and "dignity of character." Captain Joseph was a much misunderstood man, said his son—courteous and yielding to friends and family, gentle and friendly and kind. He was hasty of temper, but he was always right, said George, and he never had cause to regret anything he said in anger.

Others had different views. Those who worked in the Captain's countinghouse did not agree with George Peabody, except perhaps to comment on the Captain's uncommon agility and attentiveness to the affairs of this world.

On January 4, 1844, the old man, who was eighty-seven, arose and walked to the countinghouse as was his habit, and there he snooped about suspiciously, watching his clerks at their drab work to be sure they kept their noses in his ledgers. He was busy settling bills, paying his debts and collecting his profits, for that year his profits were $44,000 and his net worth was over $2,000,000, which represented one of the largest fortunes in the country. At the end of the day at five o'clock he put on his stovepipe hat, donned his greatcoat, picked up his stick, and walked home again. Tucker Daland, one of his clerks for thirty-three years, walked with him, granted the privilege by long service. They reached the iron gates of the big white house at 134 Essex Street and the old man turned round and looked to the west with a sailor's eye, thinking of those ships in the spice trade. The sky was bright that night, and he looked long and hard.

"We shall soon have longer days," he said, and went inside the iron gate.

Next day the old man was dead, and the legend of Salem was no more.

The fortune was divided up among the living sons and daughters. There was no Peabody to continue the business, because Joseph, Jr., had died, victim of a fever he caught while checking the lading of one of his father's ships inbound from the treacherous tropics. The other brothers had gone their own ways and were too old to change.

So the Peabody firm passed out of existence with the old man, and the fortune was cut up into chunks, sizable enough to provide a handsome living for all the Captain's descendants, but not sizable enough to rock the nation, or to give these others the measure of economic control of affairs in the region that Joseph Peabody had exerted. The will was short but complicated, for its purpose was to assure that the grandchildren each had a share of the fortune to start off life. Captain Joseph's major preoccupation was with their education and upbringing, and in this he showed the unusual side of his character mentioned by George. But to the wide world in general, there was no such recognition of the piety and love of the old man as he might in his last hours have wished there could be. Quite the contrary, for a man who contributed an estimated $200,000 a year in taxes to the common good, who gave constant employment to hundreds of his townsmen, and created so brisk an atmosphere in Salem, his fellows thought very harshly of old Captain Joseph.

There is a tale that when Augustus Peabody Gardner, one of his many descendants, was running for Congress just after the turn of the twentieth century, the young candidate toured Essex County looking for votes, and at one village the oldest inhabitant was brought forward to take a look at the whippersnapper and vouchsafe an opinion.

"Be you Augustus Peabody Gardner?" he asked.

"Yes, sir."

"Be you the grandson of Joseph Peabody of Salem?"

"No, sir. I am his great-grandson."

"Be you as mean as he was?"

Sic transit gloria mundi.

PART II

Growing with the Nation

It may be said that it is the vehemence of their desires that makes the Americans so methodical; it perturbs their minds, but it disciplines their lives.

Alexis de Tocqueville,
Democracy in America, Chapter 17

CHAPTER 7

THE JUDGE

GOING BACK to retrace the ancient Peabody line, one comes to William Peabody, son of old Lieutenant Francis, the original American Massachusetts Peabody, William grew up in Topsfield, married Hannah Hale of Newbury in 1684, and when he died in 1699 left eight children. Among these was an Oliver Peabody, eighth of the line of William, and Oliver grew up to be the most prominent of this group in the early days of the eighteenth century. One of the first Peabodys to become a minister, he was well known in Massachusetts in the very early years of America; and when he died in 1752 at Natick, his name was chiseled into a gravestone, and the townspeople went to the trouble to give him a Latin inscription in honor of his rectitude and learning. Tranlated, it said:

> Here are deposited the remains of the Reverend Oliver Peabody, a man venerable for the faculties of his mind and for all needful learning. He delighted much in theological investigations. He discharged the pastoral office with great renown for thirty years—ministering to the people of Natick, especially to the aborigines, in the cause of sacred learning. He was a model in social life. In benevolence and universal hospitality, he was preeminent. In the firm expectation of a future retribution, he was called from his ministry on the 2d of February, A.D. 1752, aged 54 years.

There is the story of Natick in the early years of the eighteenth century in the words: "needful learning," "aborigines," "hospitality" and "future retribution."

It might be expected that the other Olivers would stem from this line, but such was not the case. There was another Oliver, and like his father he was a minister, but he did not ever marry and he died only three months after his father, in 1752. The names of the Peabodys, besides, are so intertwined and so much used by all branches, as in scores of other old American families, that there really are no clues to be found in given names. Oliver appears several times in the first four generations among different branches, and Joseph appears six times in the first three generations. When a family starts out with fourteen children the population explosion is remarkable, and the incidence of favorite names is frequent.

For whatever reason, be it piety or love, this Reverend Oliver's brother John named his firstborn son in honor of the Reverend Oliver, adding to the confusion. This Oliver, born in Boxford, moved to Andover, served honorably in the Revolutionary War as a lieutenant, and then moved to New Hampshire, where *his* son, still another Oliver, grew up.

Lieutenant Oliver, as we shall call him, was a simple farmer, and yet he added to the Peabody influence in his own way. His way was not through politics, or in any manner calculated to bring his head above the crowd, for he had no ambition other than to carve as good a living as his harsh God allowed from the rocky bosom of New England. Yet so much are men the creatures of fate, that Lieutenant Oliver Peabody left his name engraved in history.

One night, while traveling through the wilderness of New Hampshire he was overtaken by darkness in the vicinity of an Indian settlement, and he spent the night in the rude shelter of an Indian host, on the edge of the village. In the middle of the night he and the others were awakened by a loud noise, and rushing out of the hut they looked, to see a wall of water come down upon them. Peabody escaped the flood, and when it was light he examined the new waterfall that came down the mountain, and discovered that it had burst forth that night from a place where no water had flowed before. Thus when he returned to civilization he marked it on a map, and it became Peabody's River, a branch of the Saco— and another Peabody was immortalized.

Lieutenant Oliver Peabody settled in Shelburn, New Hampshire, set up a farm, prospered, had great good luck, married, had four children, was able to educate them more than respectably, and lived to the ripe age of eighty-one, dying in his bed, serene and ready to meet his maker.

His son Oliver, born in 1753, was able to attend Harvard College, where he took his degree in 1773, in a spate of Republican sentiment so strong that this was the year in which the college for the first time democratized the degree list, placing the names in alphabetical order, instead of the old order of standing in the class. The feeling was a mark of the independence of spirit and rebelliousness against the old or English ways of doing things. Three years later the same spirit would lead to an irrevocable breach with the old country.

Oliver Peabody decided to study law, so he took service with Chief Justice Parsons of the New Hampshire courts, then a young lawyer who had himself graduated from Harvard in 1769. Oliver Peabody was lawyer Parsons' first student, and Parsons seemed to be a man of considerable acuity or vast practice, because at the same time into the office came Rufus King and Christopher Gore, both to be famous figures in New England history.

The Parsons law office was in Newburyport, one of the old Peabody centers, and Oliver stayed here during the War of Independence. While Joseph Peabody was stopping here on privateering expeditions, and perhaps rubbing shoulders with this cousin in the streets, Oliver was learning the law, going to balls and parties, frequenting the house of the Tracys of Newburyport—the town's first and most glittering citizens—and meeting many well-to-do families. He became especially well acquainted with a Dr. Swett of Newburyport, a fashionable physician who had married one of the daughters of Colonel Bourne of Marblehead. The Colonel had another very marriageable daughter, Frances, and in a short time Oliver Peabody, having been accepted as an eligible young man, courted Frances Bourne and married her.

Lawyer Oliver Peabody took no open part in the War of the Revolution—a matter in which he was far from unique. Unless men of education found commissions in the service they were loath to give up everything and risk their lives with the common herd, the ill-educated plowboys who carried muskets and bled in the fields. Oliver believed it far more important that he prepare for the years to come, and he did so. In 1781 he had completed his legal education, and even served a stint in Boston, where he worked as assistant clerk in a court, thus effectively protecting himself from a callup to the army. Two years before the end of hostilities, he moved to Exeter, then the capital of New Hampshire, and established a law practice that would continue for the rest of his life. With the debtor's prison located there, and the business of the government, he had plenty of opportunity.

When war ended, Exeter grew rapidly. Many business firms built factories there, and the market area grew, so that legal affairs also prospered. The young lawyer was personable and able, and in 1790 he was appointed judge of probate for Rockingham County. He served for three years in this capacity, and then was elected to the State Senate, coming into that body a few years before his cousin Nathaniel left it. In 1794 Oliver Peabody was reelected to the Senate, and was chosen President. Later, he was selected as State Treasurer by the House of Representatives.

Whereas Nathaniel Peabody's career was ending in the 1790s—as far as politics was concerned—young Oliver Peabody's was beginning. He allied himself in the legislature with the Federalist party of Washington and Hamilton, and when Burr and Jefferson began breaking away, young Peabody pledged himself all the more fervently to the more conservative Federalist cause. The Federalists continued in power in New England in 1796 and 1800, and Oliver Peabody continued to be State Treasurer. In 1803 the

Democratic-Republicans won control of the state legislature and he was replaced by Nathaniel Gilman, a Jeffersonian. But in 1805 a Federalist governor was elected, and Oliver Peabody was appointed sheriff of Rockingham County. He held the office for five years.

In the elections of 1796, 1800, and 1808 Oliver Peabody was a Presidential elector (the Federalists losing control in 1804) and he voted for Washington, Adams, and his old friend Rufus King in those elections.

Oliver Peabody continued in politics until 1813 when he was appointed a judge of the court of common pleas. He served thus until 1816, when the court was reorganized under new political auspices and a new set of judges was appointed. Oliver, then sixty-four years old, retired from the political arena. He was urged to seek a judgeship, to run for Congress, and to take other part in the political play of the times, but he chose to retire to his house in Exeter and maintain generous, even elegant, hospitality for his friends and their friends. His house was almost always open and almost always filled with guests. So in his own way, Oliver Peabody affected the course of American history, by his votes in the Electoral College (then a very much more independent and important organization than now) and his political maneuverings in the state legislature. In the fifteen years between retirement and death, he took no further open part in politics, but he mingled constantly with Governor Gilman, Governor Smith, Judge Tenney, Dr. Abbot of the Phillips Academy, and the other leading political and intellectual figures of Exeter, and his opinions had a way of becoming the opinions of the friends who came to his table. Thus was another segment of the Peabody influence formed.

CHAPTER 8

THE SONS—I

IN THE GRACIOUS big house at Exeter ten children grew up under the careful tutelage of Oliver and Frances Peabody. Eight of these children lived what might be called ordinary lives. Sarah, the first-born, married Stephen Pearse of Portsmouth and went off to live in his home city when she was twenty years old. Lucretia Orne, the second child, married, also at twenty, Alexander H. Everett, who eventually became the United States Minister to China, and she went off with him to live in faraway Peking and exert her own influence in affairs by what she did at the court of the Manchus. How much of American policy in China was made by diplomats on the scene? How much did Lucretia have to do with making policy? Was she aware of the basic threat to the Ch'ing dynasty in the growing power of Hung Hsiu-ch'üan, leader of the Society of God Worshippers? When Minister Everett died, and Lucretia spent the anxious weeks waiting for his successor, what influences did she exert on the conduct of the American mission? Here are secrets to be unveiled in the study of the dusty archives in Washington. Certainly these questions concern Americans, and Americans were concerned with Chinese affairs very seriously in the middle of the nineteenth century: an American named John E. Ward was the predecessor of "Chinese" Gordon in the leadership of the Ever Victorious Army of mercenary officers. Might some household gossip or some loyal servant have dropped words in Lucretia Everett's ear that changed the course of Chinese history, too? Perhaps, but for the purpose of this book it is enough to say that she *was* the wife of the American Minister to China in a delicate and vital period of Chinese history, when the foreigners were exerting their muscles and the Ch'ing dynasty was beginning to disintegrate.

Then came the third and fourth children of the family, twins, born July 7, 1799: Oliver William Bourne Peabody, first son, named for his father, and William Bourne Oliver Peabody, second son, named for his mother's father. There were other children, but except for Edward Bass Peabody, the others died in childhood, and Edward Bass died in 1830 at the youthful age of twenty-eight.

From their early days the Peabody twins were remarkably alike in every way. They looked alike and thought alike and acted alike, they were educated alike and they played alike. Their educator was Dr. Abbot of Phillips Exeter Academy, which they both attended as day students until they were thirteen years old, when they entered Harvard College.

At Harvard, the boys moved into adjoining rooms in the dormitory. Their furniture consisted of pine bedsteads, washstands, tables, desks, cheap rocking chairs (one to a room), and several other chairs. They brought featherbeds from home, but those were their single luxuries. There were no carpets on the floor, except in the rooms of certain southern senior students—all southerners were reputed then to be fabulously rich—but even the southerners waited to show such luxuriant display until their senior year and then rented threadbare carpets from a local secondhand furniture dealer who had a monopoly of the Harvard trade.

The students' rooms and several of the recitation rooms were heated by open wooden fires. Coal was just coming in and only a handful of rooms had a coal fire or Franklin's celebrated stove. Nearly every student had also, among the *transmittenda* handed down from one occupant to the next, a cannonball reputedly from the days of the Revolution (most cannonballs had stories to go with them), and these were heated red hot in the fire on very cold days and then put beside the bed on a skillet. In spring and summer the cannonballs also served, when sent down the stairs, to awaken and bedevil the dormitory's proctors.

Fires were a problem in the winter, because the boys did not have friction matches. They buried coals carefully in the ashes at night, nursing them to start the morning fire, and that failing, they hauled forth the awkward flint, steel, and tinderbox, to light shavings and kindling.

Life was not easy at Harvard in those days. Morning prayers were held at six o'clock during the summer; in the winter they came a half hour before sunrise—and in a chapel that was never heated except by human warmth. From chapel the young men passed into the recitation rooms which were in University Hall, and it was not until after the second recitation that breakfast was served in the college commons. Breakfast consisted of coffee, hot rolls, and butter. The students then studied until ten, when the next recitations were called and lectures were held. Dinner came at half-past twelve, then more recitation except on Saturdays, study, evening prayer at six o'clock or twilight, and supper, which consisted of tea, bread, and butter. The students were then free until eight o'clock when the study bell rang (nine in summer), and then the college became quiet, for there was the strictest adherence to the rule of silence for study in the evenings, and any offender was often publicly admonished in chapel.

Only on Saturday afternoons could the students leave Cambridge for any purpose and then the college emptied as they went off to Boston—it was almost a universal exit. There was a two-horse stage coach which ran twice a day, but few could afford that and most walked. The laws demanded that they be back in college by evening prayers, and if they were late they must register their names with the regent, and then expect heavy penalty. If they came in after nine o'clock the penalty was even more dire. Actually, however, the regent's book was kept by a freshman each week, and he could be intimidated or bribed very easily to falsify the time—it was an old Harvard custom.

In the commons, where board cost $1.75 a week, the college officers and graduates had a table on an elevated platform at the head of each room, and the students occupied the main floor at tables that held from eight to ten men.

There was very little intercourse between undergraduates and teachers; indeed, they regarded each the other as natural enemies and woe betide the student seen going to the room of a professor, or entering the classroom before the bell sounded, or remaining after class to ask a question of the instructor. Coventry was very real at Harvard, and some offenders were sent there so often that they could not bear the ostracism and left the college. Even to be uniformly first in class was regarded with suspicion by the mass of students.

The best feature of Harvard at that time was its lectures. Professor Farrar taught physics and astronomy; Dr. John Collins lectured on anatomy; Dr. Jackson on hygiene; Chief Justice Parker on law; Professor Ticknor on French and Spanish literature; Dr. Ware on the New Testament. Indeed, Harvard's fame between 1810 and 1825 was regarded by some of its old graduates in later years to have reached its zenith.

With his twin brother, Oliver William Bourne Peabody went into this heady atmosphere and prospered. He was an amiable boy and full of fun, so that he soon became a favorite among his college mates even though he was very young. He played the flute, which helped, and his singing voice was clear and pleasant. Life in his father's drawing room had given the youth a grave good manner, and this impressed all who met him, so he fared well in Harvard.

On leaving college, Oliver decided that he would be a lawyer like his father, and he began his law studies in the latter's office in Exeter. Then, he returned to Cambridge to takes courses at the young law school, and came back to New Hampshire to be admitted to the bar, with as much knowledge of the law as any young fellow could be expected to have.

For eleven years Oliver practiced law in Exeter, beginning in 1822, just after he had his LL.B. from Harvard. From 1824 to 1831 he sat as a member of the legislature, and at various times he wrote for newspapers or edited them. He was editor of the Rockingham *Gazette* at one period, and then of the Exeter *News-Letter*. He wrote witty articles, editorials, stories, and poems which were published in these pages, and which gained for him a reputation as a careful stylist.

In 1831, Oliver William Bourne Peabody left Exeter. That was the year in which his father died, and the dutiful son felt that he had fulfilled all his promises. Because he was his father's namesake the old man had set his heart on his son's following in his footsteps. For that reason only did Oliver choose to take up the law when all his instincts led him from an early age toward the ministry, and even as he attended Harvard Law School he yearned to be learning the tenets and practices of the preacher.

In 1831 he moved to Boston, where his brother-in-law Everett was editor of the *North American Review*, one of the most prominent of American literary journals. Oliver helped Everett with the magazine and contributed to nearly every issue for a time. The ministry was discarded, for he felt himself too old at thirty-three to begin a new set of studies. With the heavy heart of a man trapped into doing things he did not wish to do, he set out to make the best of his situation. He knew he wanted no part of the law or of politics; and literature, or journalism, seemed the best solution, so he worked on the *Review* and also took a job as assistant editor of the Boston *Daily Advertiser*, where he wrote editorials.

In 1836 Oliver William Bourne Peabody supervised the preparation of a set of Shakespeare's works for the publishing firm of Hilliard, Gray, and Company. His editing was largely based on the edition prepared in England by Samuel Weller Singer, but not totally. Peabody went back to the first folio of Shakespeare for some instruction and adopted some folio readings. The way in which he handled the task caused the *Dictionary of American Biography* to credit him with "showing thereby a certain awareness of critical principles and making himself in a sense the first American editor of Shakespeare."

He was asked by Jared Sparks to contribute to that editor-author's *Library of American Biography*, and he wrote a biography of General Israel Putnam, and another of General John Sullivan, probably without ever knowing that both men had at one time been close to his cousin Nathaniel.

Eschewing politics for literature, he was still drawn into the political scene, as most thinking men with any leisure were inclined to be in those days. He served as register of probate for Suffolk County for several years, a lucrative post with fees based on the value of the estates probated.

He had one brief interlude devoted to education when he accompanied Everett and his sister to the College of Jefferson in Louisiana, where Oliver was to serve as professor of English literature; but the climate proved too much for him, and he came back to Boston after only a few months of the damp heat.

At this time his original instincts prevailed, and he undertook the study of the Gospel with an eye to becoming a minister. He was helped by his twin brother, and he began the rigorous studies, sometimes working in Boston, sometimes in Springfield at his brother's house. In 1844, Oliver William Bourne Peabody was ordained by the Boston Ministerial Association, and in August of the next year he settled in at Burlington, Vermont, as pastor of the Unitarian church. At the time that the Reverend Mr. Peabody was serving in the Unitarian church, another cousin, Selim Hobart Peabody, was beginning study at the University of Vermont and teaching in the Burlington High School, but if these two ever met it is not recorded in their memoirs or the biographies written about them. Five or six generations is a long time in America, and cousins by that time have little sense of belonging to the same family branch.

So Oliver lived out the remainder of his life as Unitarian minister in Burlington, known there for the "saintliness" of his life and the vigor of his pen. He continued to be a literary man, wrote for the

North American Review, for the local press, and for other publications. Indeed, when he was ill toward the end of his life, he prepared a biographical study of his twin brother, which was to be his last work. He died July 5, 1848, leaving behind very definite influences within the Unitarian movement, in Burlington, in Boston, and wherever Shakespeare was read for many years.

CHAPTER 9

THE SONS—2

FORTUNATELY FOR William Bourne Oliver Peabody, his father's sense of dynastic succession extended to teaching only one son into the paternal footsteps, and William was allowed to go his own way after he graduated from Harvard College in 1816. His way was to return to Exeter Academy and teach for a year under his beloved old Benjamin Abbot. Thereupon William went back to Harvard, for, like Oliver, the calling to the cloth was strong in him, and there was nothing to prevent his following his own bent.

The college was beginning to grow, but it still consisted of a handful of buildings. Divinity Hall was being built, and the Divinity School as a separate entity would be opened soon. William studied theology under Henry Ware (the younger) and was ordained a year after the school opened its doors. He became a minister on October 12, 1820.

He was sent immediately to the Third Congregational Society in Springfield, Massachusetts, and after preaching there a few times was accepted as pastor. Thus began what the *Unitarian Review* was to call "the story of the original missionary enterprise that planted the Unitarian form of liberal Christianity in Southwestern Massachusetts, in the very centre of the ancient Calvinistic bigotry of New England. There can be no doubt that, in his own way, and that the highest way, his ministry of twenty-seven years was one of the most fruitful agencies for good in the history of this beautiful valley."

The Congregation of the Society liked its new minister. "He makes at once a strong impression in his favor—an impression that everything in his character is as it should be, and he inspires confidence that he will never disappoint any reasonable expectations." Quite an order for a young man not quite twenty-two years old.

Four years after coming to Springfield, William took a wife, Elizabeth White, in Rutland, Massachusetts, and brought her back to the pastorate in Springfield where she won the immediate approval of the ladies of the congregation.

All his life, William struggled with bad health. Very early in his ministerial career his eyes gave out for a time, which meant he could not read, make notes, or write proper sermons without the help of another, and his wife, for some time served, for all practical purposes, as assistant pastor. A daughter and four sons were born, and they, too, contended with bad health in the hard climate of Springfield.

The climate in Springfield was hard both physically and spiritually for the Reverend William Bourne Oliver Peabody. His parishioners had been elbowed out of the Calvinist churches of Springfield and had embraced the Unitarian church in their search for some affiliation. The Unitarians did not come into Springfield to start a church; William Peabody was sent to Springfield in response to a call from an already organized, if poorly so, congregation.

From the beginning he was harried by the other ministers, as were the members of his congregation. For a young man of frail disposition it was another cross to bear, but he bore it manfully, and never engaged in open disputation with the Calvinists of the Puritan church.

So William's was a lonely life. He had his parishioners, but he had no one with whom he could foregather to "talk shop" as ministers loved to do. So lonely was his lot that at one time he preached in his own pulpit, without relief, for eighteen solid months. This meant no travel and tremendous work. Each Sunday he delivered two sermons, and on Wednesday evenings he gave a lecture of some religious significance.

For relief, William turned to his brother Oliver (they were always very close). In the early 1830s, after Oliver moved to Boston, he brought William to the attention of the literary community, and William, too, began to write for the *North American Review*. He wrote book reviews, at first, then articles and essays.

He reviewed George Cheever's *Studies in Poetry*, giving special attention to the influences of Puritanism on English poetry. He gave the Puritans grave credit for their aspirations: "We look with admiration and almost with awe, upon these stern patriots and martyrs . . ." But he also saw further—that what the Puritans were trying to do and what they accomplished were entirely different: "While they labored to elevate the mind, the tendency of some of their efforts could be only to degrade it." What gnashing of teeth must there have been in the pulpits of Springfield when the ubiquitous *North American Review* found its way into the homes of the cultured folk of that town, bearing the Unitarian minster's unmistakable message!

He went on then to praise the poetry of Charles II's reign, the ideal of chivalry that came forth again. He spoke of the "genius of Pope," of the "essentially coarse and vulgar minds of Fielding and Smollett," and with love and admiration of Thomson and Cowper. It was fashionable among moralists to lament the talent gone wrong, morally, of Byron, and William Bourne Oliver Peabody did so. He was of mixed minds about Wordsworth: "In Wordsworth we see a gentle lover of nature, always simple and pure, and sometimes sublime, when he does not labor to give dignity to objects which were never meant to be poetical."

Therein, of course, the Reverend William knew whereof he spoke. He was a student of poetry all his life, and he was a student of nature. Indeed, he wrote as much about nature—perhaps more tellingly—as about literature. He was a friend of Jean Jacques Audubon, an ardent birdwatcher, a student and cataloguer of trees and other plants.

As community moralist, he must attack Byron, and of course he did so when he was asked by the *North American Review* to review Thomas Moore's *Letters and Journals of Lord Byron* (with Moore's own notes of Byron's life). How could the editors of the *Review* have expected anything else from a minister of the Gospel? Byron's peccadilloes had become common moral property of all the English-speaking world—and there was little enough common gossip about open sexuality. To talk about Byron, one must, of course, denigrate both man and author, but to talk about him at all, as the Reverend William sensed, was usually an exercise in sensuality, not because Byron was unworthy, but because these Victorians had so little chance to consider sexuality. But Byron must be unworthy, this seducer of women, this winer and diner and rake of all Europe: ". . . he was declared entitled to a place among the great; but, though he had the elements of a noble nature, no one, so far as we know, claimed for him a place among the good." He concluded the comment by noting, "we hold him up as a warning, not as an example," and declined to review the second volume of the work, which would carry Byron to his death.

Much less predictable, much more interesting, was William's writing on nature in the pages of the *Review*. This prose took the form of reviews and essays (and once of a special report for the governor of Massachusetts on the ornithology of the state in which he listed 286 species). He wrote learnedly on forest trees and on the habits of insects, accepting a new view put forth by an Englishman that students ought to spend more time in he field and less at their desks.

His review of Audubon's "ornithological biography" took note of the controversy then raging between Audubon and Alexander Wilson. The Reverend William knew both men well and was able to comment intelligently on the fine accomplishments of each and to review Audubon's book with the eye of an expert.

William reviewed many other books—volumes of science, history, biography, and even novels. He wrote poetry for the magazine and for other publications.

Brother Oliver also brought William to the fold of Jared Spark's *Library of American Biography*, and William found time to write of the lives of naturalist Alexander Wilson, Cotton Mather, David Brainerd, and James Oglethorpe.

He published sermons of his own, as well as a *Poetical Catechism* and a collection of hymns, and he wrote innumerable letters on public subjects.

He was one of the first to bring nature study into the church and relate it to Biblical matters in the Sunday school. He was the founder, almost singlehanded, of the big cemetery at Springfield; he planned it, he arranged for the money, he donated and planted many of the trees himself.

William's life was singularly happy despite his ill health; that at least drove him out of doors and caused him to take long walks, during which he composed his sermons. So he was happy, until 1843 when his beloved wife died, to be followed to the grave the next year by his daughter. After that William lived on only three more years, until May, 1847, when, having delivered his last sermon and declaring himself at peace with the world, he died at the age of forty-seven.

This Peabody's influence was strong and direct as a clergyman, for he brought Unitarianism and liberality to the town of Springfield, where it had not perviously existed. As a literary figure, who knows how many minds he swayed in his arguments about Byron and the merits of the Audubon-Wilson dispute, the virtues of Addison, and the importance of nature study?

PART III

Man of Affairs

___

If one advances confidently in the direction of his dreams, and endeavors to live the life which he has imagined, he will meet with a success unexpected in common hours.

Henry David Thoreau, from *Walden*

Of all the Peabodys who have come to the attention of American historians, George Peabody is by far the most famous. Perhaps, in the American tradition, that is because he was richest. But there is another reason: he was one of the first of the American philanthropists to give great sums of money for lasting purpose. One might almost say he was the innovator of the foundation. Although the term would have meant nothing to him, the concept would have been familiar. George Peabody spent his life in the pursuit of fortune. Then, having achieved wealth and fame, he discovered they were worthless, and he sought to immortalize himself and appease his New England conscience with good works carried out late in life. Here, in the following pages, is the account of the New England boy's odyssey into his private empire—for that is what his career became; he was the first American to become a successful international banker—and the story of his later years and his triumphant exit from the world.

CHAPTER 10

THE DRY GOODS MERCHANT—I

By THE END of the eighteenth century the Peabody name was well known in the infant United States. Six generations of Peabodys had come since the day that Francis emigrated from England to Massachusetts. The influence of the family strain had already been considerable on the pattern of New England life. Judge Oliver Peabody of Exeter was still remembered a hundred years after his death. His twin sons, William Bourne Oliver and Oliver William Bourne, had taken their places at the forefront of early American letters.

Several other Peabodys who had joined the ministry were recalled by their townsmen in Topsfield as instrumental in creating the growth and moral atmosphere of the community so that it prospered more each generation. A Peabody had been a professor at Dartmouth College, and Professor Silliman of Yale would count his descent from a Peabody with more than a little pride.

As noted, Peabodys had served the nation in every field, and not the least as citizen soldiers. A Peabody fought with Wolfe on the Plains of Abraham. Peabodys fought at the capture of Ticonderoga, at Louisbourg, and at the siege of Boston. Others commanded units, from platoon to company, in the Continental army; Nathaniel had even headed a regiment. Peabodys had served in Congress and had practiced law and medicine, and already, in 1795, the first great merchant of the name was well known to everyone in Salem.

But not all Peabodys were rich, famous, or even well-to-do. Altogether by this time more than four hundred children had been born to carry, at least for a time, the name of Peabody. As with any American family, the vast majority of these descendants of old Francis lived quiet, respectable lives without exceptional distinction.

The story of the second generation has been told: they were farmers, increasing the wealth of the family, and doing little else except what every man must do, fighting Indians and the French, even, for the right to live in North America. In the third generation, Peabodys were churchmen, soldiers, and one, Ephraim, son of William, was a madman, who became deranged in his forty-third year, and was kept forcibly in the house of a guardian. He was a brother of Oliver, Puritan minister at Natick, and he must have caused the good pastor to consider mightily the unknown ways of the Lord. Oliver carried the burden, and did so with such piety and success that the Peabodys of his generation were known in Essex County as "a wonderful family, possessing more virtues and fewer vices than could seldom be found in one family." *

It was true, the Peabodys were a good solid family without pretensions. Ebenezer Peabody had been a lieutenant at Bunker Hill. John, one of the fifth generation, had been a general in the Revolutionary army. Zerubabel, of the fourth generation, left an estate of more than 4000 pounds, but his brother Joseph left no more than 79 pounds. Poor farmer, rich merchant, middle-class lawyer—the tides of fortune rising and falling—this was the story of the family.

Among the less wealthy branches of the family was Thomas Peabody of the fifth generation. When Thomas was a child his family had first lived in Andover, then moved to Haverhill. He grew up, mostly, in Haverhill on the family farm, but when it came time for him to marry and settle down to the common life

* Genealogy, p. 8.

of farming, he was low on the list of children, and the family assets were not so great as to make him well-to-do. He went to Danvers, took up farming there, and made a respectable life for himself, his wife Judith Dodge, and eight children who survived.

Third of these children to live was George, born on February 18, 1795, in South Danvers, in a frame house on the road between Salem and Boston. The house was a New England saltbox, to which later was added a long back wing. It consisted of two stories and an attic and was heated by fireplaces and heat holes that went up into the second floor. George grew up in that house and was seldom out of it or the farm around it until he was seven years old, when he was sent to the village school. There he studied reading and writing, elementary geography and arithmetic, until he was eleven years old. Danvers was a large place for its time, with some three thousand inhabitants, two churches and two public schoolhouses. George Peabody attended the one just beyond the South Church on Lowell Street. The school was a tiny building, smaller than most modern-day classrooms, with three windows, a handful of desks, and a stove where teachers and children clustered for warmth in the coldest weather. The schoolmaster was ragged and poorly paid, and he was invited by the parents of the children to lay on with the rule and stick when necessary to preserve order.

George was not a very good student. He was particularly weak in arithmetic and sometimes his teacher quite despaired of getting the problems and solutions through his head. Yet George was shrewd even as a youngster, at least in the ways of the world. One Fourth of July he set up a stand in the town green to sell cakes and fruit to the villagers when they came to enjoy the celebration and the orations. He earned more than a dollar that day.

George did learn to write in a handsome hand at school, and forever after there was never a question about his statements or his bills. He drove sheep for neighbors to earn extra money and did other odd jobs.

When George Peabody was eleven years old he was apprenticed by his father to Captain Sylvester Proctor, who kept a general store in Danvers. He slept in the store and arose with the sun to sweep out the public rooms, lay the fire in the potbellied stove, change the flypaper, chop kindling and carry wood until his breakfast time. After breakfast he donned an apron and helped wait behind the counter. He carried groceries and other provisions out to the carts and wagons of the townspeople, and climbed high into the shelves to stack canned goods and bags of flour. He learned to do inventories and to sell yard goods, to cut hams and measure out spirits and calomel. Since he had so orderly a mind and so excellent a hand, Proctor gave the boy the responsibility for keeping the accounts with a minimum of supervision. He learned arithmetic, then, because he had to keep his books straight or suffer a whipping. He did everything from filling the lamps to braiding buggy whips.

At the end of four years of apprenticeship, Captain Proctor gave George Peabody a new suit of homespun and twenty-five dollars, stipulated in the contract of indenture. George had also managed to earn another five dollars which he had put away. So at the age of fifteen he was a man of the world, a journeyman storekeeper who could go anywhere in New England, find a store almost exactly like the captain's and keep it in order.

Captain Proctor urged George to stay on and offered him wages to do so, but the boy wanted to shake the dust of Danvers from his feet. He had been all but deserted by his family; the four years of apprenticeship, coming at the crucial age of adolescence, had pulled him away even from his mother, and there were no ties in Danvers which would not vanish as he walked away from the town.

Before he made up his mind, however, George took a trip to Thetford, Vermont, to visit his maternal grandfather, Jeremiah Dodge. Listening to gossip around the cracker barrel, George learned that a carter he knew was going up that way with a load of freight, and since he had an urge to travel, he asked if he might not have a ride in return for help with the work. The offer pleased the drayman, who undoubtedly wanted company anyhow, and the pair set off from Salem for Thetford.

George went for a visit, not knowing how long he might stay. It all depended on how he and his grandfather got on, for George Peabody at fifteen was a thoroughly independent young man.

In 1810, Thetford was a big Vermont town with few people in it. Off in the northwest corner was a tiny settlement that could scarcely be called a village but bore the name of Post Mills. It consisted of a grist mill, a sawmill, a schoolhouse, two general stores, a smithy, a tavern, and a physician named Dr. Niles.

It was then, as now, largely an agricultural community. The farmers raised a little grain for their cattle and their tables, sheep for mutton and wool, pigs for bacon and ham. They shoed their horses and went into the village to buy shoes and nails from the smith, perhaps to have custom shoes put on if they had the time and the spare cash. The smith was busy all the time, for he was to the rakes and threshers and wagons of the town what Doc Niles was to the people and the horses.

The citizens got together on good Sundays when they all trouped from near and far to Thetford Hill and the community church, where the Reverend Asa Burton held forth, offering fire and brimstone as a weekly dose for the weak-spirited. On bad Sundays, especially when the ice closed in after a winter thaw, the church went abegging for pewholders.

George's grandfather, Jeremiah Dodge, lived in a small two-story house on the outskirts of Post Mills village, five miles north of Thetford Hill, which made a good long cart or horse ride to church on Sunday mornings. There was a veritable colony of Dodges there. The old man lived on the north side of the road that leads to the Connecticut River and Oxford, New Hampshire. His son Eliphalet lived east of him on the south side of the road in a house of which the best that might be said was that it "once was painted." Eliphalet's fences were tumble-down, and he had never properly engineered his barnyard, so it was an ice pond in the winter, a quagmire in April, and a dustbin all summer long.

Like most New England properties, the "farm" of perhaps a hundred acres or so belonged to the old man, and his son lived on it in the small house and did his father's bidding. As long as the old man lived, the son was hardly better than a hired man and depended entirely on paternal good will for his money and his luxuries. Eliphalet and his wife had bred a small army of sons and daughters who kept the animals, tended the fires, and gathered eggs from the barns.

Eliphalet's brother, Daniel, had gone to sea at an early age, knowing that Eliphalet would have the farm, and knowing also that the hundred acres could barely support one farm family of the size of Vermont households in those days. At the time that George Peabody visited, Daniel was just returning from or just going on a voyage. He was a captain, a master mariner, and he sailed out of New York in the China trade, carrying sugar and rum and made goods to Canton. From Canton he ran down to Sumatra, picking up spices which he returned to China. More than likely he also dealt in opium, for Daniel was one of those suspicious traders who worked back and forth between Southeast Asia and East Asia for three years at a time, then picked up a final cargo of tea or spices or choice goods—possibly all of these—and headed home to New York to deliver his profits to his owners.

Although Vermont was a landlocked state, the only one in those early days, she had more than her share of sea captains, the second and third sons of independent settlers, who chose to go east rather than west to strike out for their forunes, who sailed the seven seas, and came home bearing scrimshaw to decorate the parlors of their big frame houses. So the villages grew, where there seemed no right for villages to be. Vermont then, as now, was a state of peripatetic citizens, many of whom earned their living abroad, then came back to their beloved quiet and their mountains to enjoy themselves.

Here in the wilds of Vermont, talking to his grandfather, to Uncle Eliphalet, and to Daniel and his kin, George Peabody learned more in a week about international trade, finance, and banking than he could have learned in five years in Danvers. One might say that in the Green Mountains he was exposed to China and foreign trade. It was an important exposure.

So George Peabody stayed with his grandfather, the white-haired, straightbacked old patriarch. They liked one another on sight, the tall, slender boy and the tall man. George was mannerly and quiet and thoughtful. His grandfather seldom raised his voice. He was an affable old gentleman, with a lively sense of Vermont humor. There was work to be done on the farm, but every evening the family gathered around the parlor and there was brisk talk about far-off places and strange peoples. George liked it, and he stayed on. He remained there a year, and when he left he was a man of affairs.

CHAPTER 11

THE DRY GOODS MERCHANT—2

AT THE END of a year, there was little more to be learned in Post
Mills village, and little enough to occupy a restless boy who wanted
to get on with earning his fortune in the world. Uncle Daniel had
gone back to sea and would not return for three years. With Mr.
Jefferson's manipulation of the right to trade in so scandalous a
manner, a sea captain was better off in the China trade, staying out
three years or so, than in coming home to fight the American revenue cutters. George had never heard of his cousin Joseph, already
a powerful figure in Salem and becoming more important in foreign commerce every year; but had he heard of Joseph Peabody,
it would have made scant difference, as they were a million miles
apart in attitudes and yearnings. All that Joseph Peabody might
have offered George was a place in one of his trading ships as super-
cargo, perhaps. George had no bent for the sea.

At the end of his year he headed south—east, first, really, stopping at Concord, New Hampshire, treading through ground where
other Peabody cousins had smoothed the way. He did not stop
overlong, else he might have learned of the currency of the Peabody name in New Hampshire and been tempted to remain awhile.
He stayed overnight in a Concord tavern, and to save money cut

a pile of wood for the innkeeper instead of paying in cash for bed and board.

Back home in Danvers, George Peabody visited and planned for the future. Shortly after his return the sixteen-year-old boy went to work with his brother David, five years older, in the latter's draper's shop in Newburyport. "David Peabody and Company" was the name of the establishment, the "and Company" being another young man named Samuel Swett and George, who ran the errands and did the dirty work, including, once again, the keeping of the ledgers, because of his fine hand. He earned extra money, too, by writing election ballots.

In the spring of 1811, the boys' father died, leaving them the farm, heavily encumbered with mortages, and little else. By this time the farm was really not a farm at all, but the big house and twelve acres only, scarcely enough to keep a cow for household milk and butter, and a few other farm animals to feed the family. Then, two weeks after the father's death, Newburyport suddenly erupted in flames, on a howling windy day when the wooden structures passed the fire from roof to roof until 250 buildings were burned. The Peabody draper's shop, located at 3 Cornhill, opposite the old Town House, was not touched, but the general depression that set in was as effective as fire. Knowing the town had burned out, people of the market area went elsewhere to make their purchases. Consequently, in a few weeks the brothers were out of business. They were no worse off, however, than their uncle, Colonel John Peabody, who kept a dry goods store at the corner of State Street and Market Square. He had been burned out in the fire, and he never recovered, declaring bankruptcy in a few months.

In a way, the fire and its aftermath were lucky events for George Peabody. The draper's shop had been prospering, and limited as might be the horizons of a draper, present profit is hard changed for future wealth, and George Peabody might have been persuaded to forget his Uncle Daniel's exhilarating lessons about foreign trade.

The Colonel's bankruptcy was also all in George's favor, because it disgusted the older man with the future in Massachusetts. Washington, in the District of Columbia, had been made the actual capital of the United States in 1800, and ten years later it was apparent that the town would grow and prosper. For a time there had been fears, but the swamps and the muddy streets had been improved, people were beginning to flock to the center of government, and Colonel Peabody convinced himself that here was a chance to recoup his burned-out fortune. George Peabody heard of the plan and joined in it enthusiastically.

During his months in Newburyport, George had exerted himself to be friendly with the other young men in business. He had an open face and a pleasant manner, and soon he had a number of friendly acquaintances. Most of these youths were well connected or were the sons of merchants, and they had far more money than George. But the lack of capital or income never seemed to stop his mingling with the others, and he said later that they often paid his way into various amusements because they knew that oherwise he could not attend, for which he was duly grateful.

One of George Peabody's friends was Prescott Spaulding, a man fourteen years older than himself. Spaulding knew of the circumstances of Colonel Peabody and George, and when they decided to move south, he lent them his good name, which was lucky for Colonel Peabody, because after his bankruptcy his own friends turned completely against him. The Colonel and George went to Boston with letters of credit from Spaulding, and there they managed to secure two thousand dollars' worth of merchandise. With this small supply they set sail from Salem in the brig *Fame* on May 4, 1812, bound for Georgetown, District of Columbia.

Bankruptcy was the next thing to a crime in those days, and so the dry goods business was to be conducted in the name of George Peabody, the seventeen-year-old nephew, although the management was actually in the hands of the uncle. They set up shop in a wooden building on Bridge Street, selling blankets, leather gloves, shoes, cotton cloth, thread, haberdashery, laces, and perishables.

Scarcely had the new firm gone into business, when the nation

was plunged into war with Britain. George Peabody joined a volunteer company of artillery formed in Georgetown under Colonel
George Peter, and went into training at Fort Warburton, for in
the spring of 1812 it was rumored that the British would attack
the national capital. After a few weeks, however, the threat diminished and the volunteer company was disbanded, so George Peabody put down his ramrod and brush and went back to selling dry
goods.

The Peabody business was profitable enough, and George had
many experiences. He spent some time in the beginning as a pack
peddler, carrying his goods to the outlying villages on foot and
stopping before he came back to dispose of the unsold wares at
a smaller profit in some general store along his route.

George worked hard. He helped support his mother and sisters
in Danvers, and he went home to visit them once or twice in the
next few years after his coming to Washington.

About two years after arrival in Georgetown, George became
worried about the business relationship with his uncle. The Colonel
was a high liver; he spent money freely and was not careful in his
contracting of debts. As the business was in George's name, the
young man was responsible for the old in a way, and because they
had a partnership, George was also legally responsible for his uncle's
obligations. He came to fear that these debts were growing too
large, on a personable basis, and that he might be called upon to
meet them.

George's one recourse was to resign from the firm, and he did
this in 1814, to go into partnership with a man named Elisha Riggs,
who was around thirty years old. So mature was George Peabody
at this juncture, that the partnership was made before Riggs discovered that his new partner was still a minor of nineteen years.
Riggs did not mind, but he was thoroughly astonished, for he believed George to be very nearly his own age.

The firm of Riggs and Peabody was formed, with a capital of
about $7000, most of it supplied by Riggs. George put together all
his resources, about $1700, but he offered something else—un-

limited energy. He became the road salesman, the peddler, for the firm. He bought a horse and began traveling through New York, Pennsylvania, Maryland, and Virginia, selling their goods. Soon the orders were large enough so that it paid to hire delivery wagons. The farmers and businessmen he met liked this tall, active young man with the ready smile, and soon they were asking him to carry out commissions for them. It was not long before he found himself acting as shipping agent for his customers. This became so important a part of the affairs of Riggs and Peabody that they decided to move to the sea, so they deserted Washington and went to Baltimore. It was a good move, and their business increased even more rapidly. Soon they were as well known on the coast as any firm of merchants, and as well trusted for the quality of their goods and the honoring of their commitments. In 1822 they started branches in Philadelphia and New York.

In 1829 Elisha Riggs retired to go back to Washington and engage in other affairs. He built an office building, a banking house, and a hotel which was in its time the most luxurious in the national capital. On Riggs's retirement, as was then the practice, the name of the company was changed. (It was not until considerably later in history that the practice of keeping a firm name through several generations became customary.) Riggs and Peabody became Peabody, Riggs, and Company, with the Riggs respresenting the young nephew of George Peabody's original partner. George Peabody, by this time, was thirty-four years old, and wealthy by the American standards of 1829.

From the business of buying and selling, it was not a hard step into international finance. In a way George Peabody acted as banker to his customers, the farmers of the midlands, when he arranged their purchases at the same time that he arranged to handle their goods in the marketplaces of Baltimore, Philadelphia, and New York. He had made his first buying and selling trip to England in 1827, selling cotton and buying machinery for customers in Maryland and the south. Soon he was making annual voyages to England, and when that became known he was quickly entrusted with commissions. The firm of Peabody and Riggs was known for its ready ability to meet commitments and was trusted by businessmen up and down the coast. The authorities of the state of Maryland asked George Peabody to carry out certain commissions for them, too, and he obliged.

It became apparent to George Peabody that there would be a profitable business for some American who was well connected at home if he would make his headquarters in London, cultivate the British, and find ready sources of investment and purchase of American goods. England was emerging as the banker of Europe, and certainly the banker of the Western Hemisphere, where her citizens were streaming in search of empire and profit. As George Peabody continued to make excursions to London, he cultivated the banking families there, made himself useful to merchants and to diplomats, and began building a stout reputation as a man of worth who could be trusted.

Meanwhile, he continued his interest in the New England of his family. He supported his mother until she died in 1830, and then took on the continued support of his sisters.

By 1835 the American pride in nationality had grown so that various New England communities were erecting statues to commemorate their roles and the roles of their sons in the War for Independence. Danvers was one of these towns, and the citizens chose the sixtieth anniversary of the battle of Lexington to propose a memorial which would stand at the corner of Main and Washington streets. Enthusiasm was high, but when seven hundred dollars had been raised, more enthusiasm could not be found locally, and the committee of businessmen who had backed the plan began searching afield. George Peabody was well-enough remembered, and now known as a successful southern merchant, so an appeal was made to him for old times' sake. He responded with a typical gesture; he wrote out a blank draft to his old townsmen and instructed them to make up the difference on his account. So they did, and he ended up as largest contributor with a gift of three hundred dollars for the Revolutionary monument of Danvers.

At about this time, Peabody became involved in an affair that tested his abilities and was to determine the course of his future. The state of Maryland found itself in serious financial difficulties because of the War of 1812 and the twenty-year depression that followed. The various states had scarcely been created and the federal government established when the war came. After the war there was an extended debt, and the Maryland government found itself in the position of needing funds for expansion, to carry out many tasks entrusted to each state. Some states defaulted on their obligations to their citizens, and the legislators of Maryland considered following the same course. Now many of these obligations were held by rich men abroad, and some of them were in England.

The strongest possible pressures were brought by responsible bankers in America and abroad to prevent default, but the final position of Maryland continued in doubt. In 1835 the state needed men of financial security and great ability to consider this matter. The legislature went into session and chose a commission of three to settle the state's financial problems. One of these men was George Peabody.

After his appointment, Peabody sat down with his fellow commissioners to determine what might be done to help the badly depleted state treasury. A long-term loan was neeed with provisions elastic enough to encompass the usual difficulties in which basically agricultural economies often found themselves. George Peabody knew where such loans might be found: in England. Maryland's credit was not very good. It was not as poor as the credit of several of the other states, which had already defaulted, but the general credit of American states was hurt by every failure, and it was known in England that even Maryland legislators were talking irresponsibly of failing to pay the state's obligations.

Peabody soon sailed for England, first cautioning his friends in the legislature that they must stop talking "default" if they expected him to be able to raise any money for them. They agreed, and soon he was in London.

In the English capital, George Peabody used the connections he had cultivated so assiduosly in the past and gave a splendid dinner for a dozen of England's merchant bankers. After the port had been passed, and King William IV and the President of the United States had been toasted, and the amenities had been met by various introductions and brief remarks, George Peabody arose and stated the problem of Maryland and the solution he sought. Several of these English bankers already held Maryland paper. Before that dinner the bankers were calling for payment of their loans and bonds that were overdue. Afterward they subscribed eight million dollars more to Maryland's account, so well did George Peabody convince them of his probity and thus of the good will and credit of his adopted state.

"He borowed the money on his face," said George Owen, the radical English political leader who was also George Peabody's friend.

Back home in Baltimore the news of George Peabody's accomplishment arrived long before he came home, and he was honored in Baltimore as were few men of that day. More was his honor when, after his return and the normal payment by the treasury of his brokerage commission of $60,000 for the sale of the bonds, Peabody returned the state's draft for this amount with his compliments.

George Peabody was not a millionaire, and he could not afford to pass up this commission. But in the bigger game he could well afford it, and indeed, it was essential that he make some such mark, for he was playing for the highest stakes. From his visits to England he knew that the British financiers regarded their American counterparts as little higher than confidence men or sharpsters. Too often they had seen how the Yankees tried to turn every transaction to make the most personal profit, no matter the cause at hand. Yet no British banker would have refused so high a commission in a legitimate bond sale, and the British bankers were much impressed by the probity and gentility of a man who would not take advantage of the straitened circumstances of his state government. By that gesture was George Peabody's reputation made in England.

He was no longer a merchant; he was a merchant banker whose name might be spoken in England in company with the Baring Brothers, who were emerging as the strongest of a large group of investment banking houses.

Joseph Peabody
by James Frothingham

Mrs. Joseph Peabody

Joseph Peabody's House, 134 Essex Street, Salem, Massachusetts

Ship *Glide*

Ship *New Jersey*

Two of Joseph Peabody's ships

Peabody Arms

William Bourne
Oliver Peabody

George Peabody

George Peabody's Birthplace

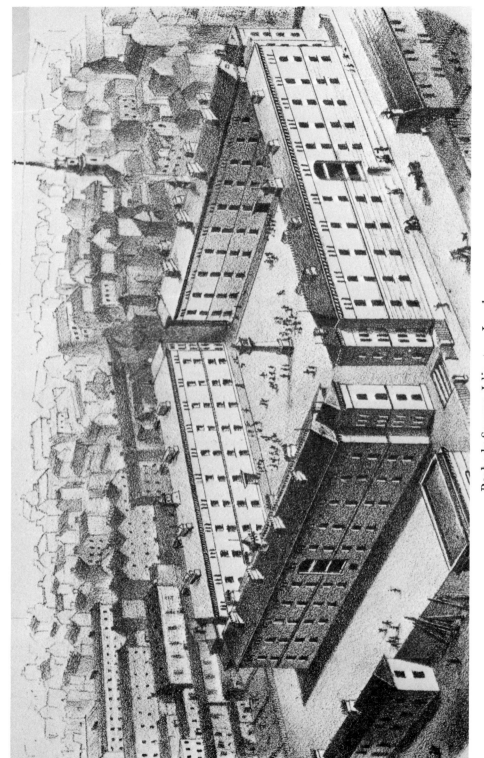

Peabody Square, Islington, London

Elizabeth Palmer Peabody in 1887

Mary Peabody Mann, soon after her marriage to Horace Mann

Sophia Amelia Peabody, who later married Nathaniel Hawthorne. Probably painted by Harding in 1830

Josephine Preston Peabody, at the age of thirty-seven, with her daughter, Alison, and her son, Lionel

Endicott and Fanny Peabody on their honeymoon

Tombstone, Arizona in 1881

The Protestant church in Tombstone for which Endicott Peabody raised funds and
where he served as the first minister

Brooks House in 1884, the original building of Groton School

Henry Peabody's Yacht, *Halcyon*

Henry W. Peabody

George Foster Peabody

CHAPTER 12

MERCHANT BANKER

By 1837, George Peabody had outgrown the dry goods business and was buying and selling such commodities as cotton on his own account and on the account of various customers of his houses— which must be regarded from about 1830 as an investment banking house. He had made a number of trips to England following the negotiation of the Maryland bond sales and was so well regarded in London that he decided his future lay as an intermediary between American and British interests.

Following the War of 1812, trade between the United States and Britain had revived slowly, but there was a good deal of ill-will on both sides. The British aristocracy was inclined to be anti-American for obvious reason: we always look down on our wild and uncontrollable relatives.

So many American states and municipalities had defaulted on their obligations that British bankers tended to regard the new republic with the eye that Americans would later bestow on the "banana republic" south of the United States border.

In Baltimore, Peabody, Riggs, and Company was doing better than expected. This year, 1837, was a depression year in the United States, but the panic that struck the business community did not threaten Peabody, Riggs. A year earlier, correctly reading the signs of coming crisis, George Peabody put down his assessment:

> I am confident that the rage for speculation which has character-
> ized the last two or three years must produce disastrous results.
> Accordingly, I have written to my partners to keep everything
> snug and without reference to new sales or profits, to get in out-
> standing debts and prepare for the emergency.

For five years speculators had been trading recklessly in lands and futures. Land sales jumped from $2.5 million in 1832 to ten times that by 1836, and the land was bought with cheap paper money. So was everything else, and loans were easy to get because the banks loaned paper money, which they printed themselves according to an elastic schedule set up by an incompetent banking system.

In February, 1837, the storm broke, as predicted by George Peabody. The price of cotton fell 50 percent in one week in the New Orleans market, and dropped almost as severely elsewhere, more so once the facts were known. The sale of public lands almost stopped, the circulation of money came to a quick halt. In New York, where the panic hit investors hard, the banks stopped payment of gold and silver. Peabody, Riggs was ready, as was nearly no other house in the area.

By that time George Peabody had seen the handwriting on the wall and had realized that the opportunity he had created in London was too good to pass. He had entree and trust where other Americans met closed doors and suspicion. He moved to London early in 1837 and was in residence there, with his offices in Warnford Court in the city when the trouble came. Peabody, Riggs, and Company was solid as a rock, and when the British bankers discovered it, their respect for George Peabody grew once again.

Peabody, Riggs continued in business until 1843. Peabody insisted his partnerships be dissolved every five years so he could reassess his position, and in that year when the partnership was dissolved it was not renewed. George Peabody preferred to continue in business alone on the eastern side of the Atlantic and give up his share of the business he had built from Baltimore, so he withdrew from the American firm and kept the London office as his own enterprise.

By this time Peabody was forty-eight years old and still a bachelor. There are several stories as to the reasons for his continuation in the single state, and each of them involve a "true love" by whom he was smitten. One story has her in Georgetown, a poor but honest girl whom he took as his ward, educated, raised, and hoped to marry, when she fell in love with one of his clerks, whereupon he stood the cost of the wedding and promoted the clerk. Another story has her in Baltimore, where she pledged herself to him and wed someone else, a friend. Still another tale has her in England, where he met her while she was on the grand tour. She had broken with an earlier love in America and was engaged to Peabody by the time she returned to the United States. Having promised to come back to marry George, she encountered her old love, the flames engulfed her once again, and she wrote tearfully to ask his forgiveness and release. He released her, but was so smitten that he forever after remained a bachelor.

But the facts indicate that perhaps George Peabody was too busy to get married, too occupied with his banking affairs to lavish attention and affection on a wife. He began as a merchant, buying and selling goods, scouring the English markets for manufactures that would sell well in America and sending them back to the United States, then bringing in American cotton and other produce (largely agricultural) for the British markets. But since there were so few American merchants, or even British merchants with American connections, in the city of London, he also became a banker. He would make advances of cash against goods to some merchants, and would hold deposits for others. As the reserves of deposit became higher, he invested the money in various enterprises and secured new returns on this money. Other British bankers charged 10 percent interest on American paper, or discounted American bills at an even higher figure—all because of the trouble American money caused them, the fluctuations of the American market, and the innate distrust of America that was a result of the defaults of so many government entities in the payment of their debts. But George Peabody charged only 5 percent on American paper, so he soon became the repository of most business done between America and Britain. It was not long before Peabody became as much the financial ambassador of America in Britain as the American minister was the diplomatic representative.

Business was George Peabody's life. He cared nothing for liquor, he did not smoke, he cared no more for courtly entertainments, unless he was the entertainer—that is, unless he was footing the bill. He entertained lavishly but, oddly, while his guests were eating expensive truffled dishes and enjoying the finest of wines, Peabody was gnawing on a mutton chop, for that was his almost invariable fare.

The Peabody house was nothing, for he lived in furnished rooms kept by a minimum of servants, and almost invariably he chose to entertain at some inn or grand hotel dining room of the city. When visitors came singly or in small groups, he might take them to one of his clubs or to the house he kept at Richmond almost entirely for entertainment purposes.

The offices and his rooms were fixed up in a purely American style, with American furnishings, American paintings, American handicrafts, and sporting American books, magazines, and newspapers. His place, it was said, was a little enclave of America. Coupled with the reputation he built for solid financial security, this emphasis on things American did more than anything else done by anyone else to raise the position of the United States among the British upper class and the men of government. Peabody was popular because he entertained Englishmen lavishly, yet he could never be accused of being self-indulgent, and people on both sides of the Atlantic could say no worse of him than that his mind was constantly occupied with business. Yet even here he was not a dullard. The English liked him because he took to their ways, and even became adept at that favored English gentleman's sport, angling. He also possessed gentle manners, by English standards, and never failed to salute Her Majesty at one of his public dinners. The practice, in fact, got him into a serious difficulty because of the almost fanatic Republicanism of the Pierce administration and Secretary of State William L. Marcy.

In the 1840s and 1850s the United States was expanding its activities abroad, and as the nation grew, more was expected of American ministers than in the past. Congress, however, proved reluctant to endorse ample expenditures by Americans in the for eign service for the entertainment of royalty and others in foreign climes. Consequently American ministers and other foreign service personnel found themselves often in difficulties in carrying out their diplomatic duties.

In England a sore point during the Pierce administration was the courtly conduct of the American minister, James Buchanan, who would later be President of the United States. Buchanan was enjoined by the Secretary of State to wear a black frock coat and trousers at all times—including at court functions. The idea was to appear as a simple Republican, representative of a great nation of people who believed in social and political equality. Buchanan did as he was told, although he was an amiable creature and would have been more at home, under the circumstances, had his government allowed him a resplendent diplomatic uniform with silver sword, gold and silver threads in his cloth, lace work and even precious stones, to be worn at formal court appearances in the manner of the Russian, the French, the Austrian, and other distinguished ministers. Even so Buchanan was practically persona non grata to the court because so much fuss was stirred up about his appearance in simple clothes—the lords chamberlain took the position that such simple Republican dress was a studied insult to royalty.

As the peers of the realm bridled and insulted Buchanan, so did all Americans attached to the diplomatic mission become sensitive and annoyed with British manners, and determined to show their Americanism at all costs. For a time notes flew thick and fast from chancery to mission, and had not Queen Victoria herself chosen to regard Mr. Buchanan with a tolerant and friendly eye, diplomatic relations between the nations might have been seriously endangered.

On Independence Day, 1851, George Peabody gave a special dinner in honor of America's national holiday. Considering where he was, and the conditions under which nationhood had been secured, even in 1851 it was a bold gesture, and a sign of Peabody's position in the London community that he might dare so much. He first prepared his guest list with extreme care. Leading all was that greatest of Englishmen, the Duke of Wellington, the man who had brought Napoleon down. Wellington was then eighty-four years old, but spry, and he consented to be the guest of honor at the first American Independence Day banquet. With Wellington there, no one else could refuse, nor could the newspapers or the guests complain of the American celebration of the occasion. It went off grandly, the custom was established, and there was never a better, more effective public relations gesture. Peabody had succeeded in bearding the lion in his den, getting way with it, and making the lion like it, as well.

But such daring behavior was possible only by a man who knew the British way of doing things and was willing to sacrifice a small point to gain a great one. A simple illustration is the matter of toasts: in any well-run English household the first toast is always to the reigning monarch; whatever toasts follow it in procession might be adjustable, but the monarch is always first.

The postprandial toast in America was a custom inherited from the English parentage of the country, and although toasting was not always observed at American functions, when toasts were given in the United States, the President's name led all the rest. No king or queen would come before the chief magistrate of the nation; and in 1854 in American quarters, the name of Franklin Pierce, President of the United States, led all the rest.

On July 4 of that year, as was his custom, George Peabody planned his Independence Day dinner. It was a sign of his continued prestige in the community that he should give it, not the American minister, and that the minister and his diplomats should attend gladly and without thought that they, not Peabody, ought to be representing their country thus.

But before the dinner was held this year, First Secretary Daniel E. Sickles (who would later be famous as a Civil War general) came first to the minister and then to Peabody, protesting. It was not fitting that Peabody should give the dinner, he said. The American minister should be in charge.

This was a change in attitude by the United States government. Only three years earlier, when the first International Exposition was held in London at the new Crystal Palace, and when other governments sent magnificent displays of their products and inventiveness to the exposition, the United States government had refused to send anything or anyone, and America was quite the laughingstock of the Western world, until George Peabody had stepped in with a saving gesture. He had organized an American exhibition of sorts from among the products of his own clients which he could scare up within the British Isles. He had a reaper from Cyrus McCormick and several other farm tools, a number of Samuel Colt's revolvers and rifles, and one of the marvelous Hoe automatic printing presses which were revolutionizing the newspaper industry. He had other goods and he hired people to show them off. In all, George Peabody laid out $15,000 of his own money without a word, to save the honor of his country when his government would not do so; and at the close of the exposition he had given a grand dinner for all the Americans who had come and all their British friends and the officials he hoped would be their friends. It was a fine affair and most successful. As always, George Peabody's first toast had been to Her Majesty, Queen Victoria, and American Minister Abbott Lawrence had risen and drunk the toast with the rest, gentlemen that they were.

But in 1854, when the punctilious Mr. Sickles insisted that the American mission should undertake the entertainment and celebration of the great American birthday, George Peabody was not offended. He might have pointed out that he, and not the American mission, had made friends of English officialdom for America and

Americans. But he was too well mannered. He simply insisted that the cost of the affair be his, and he let Mr. Sickles take over the invitation list and the arrangements. Secretary Sickles was only too pleased at Peabody's generosity, for the American mission had little enough money for such entertainments.

But George Peabody's status as holder of the bill also made him host of the party, and even Secretary Sickles could scarcely have dislodged the banker for his minister, Mr. Buchanan, without embarrassment.

So at the end of the dinner, as was usual, George Peabody got up smiling and offered his first toast.

"To Her Majesty, Queen Victoria," he said.

All the British and almost all the Americans arose.

Secretary Sickles stood up in wrath and marched out of the room, angered that the Queen of Engalnd should be placed before the President of the United States at an American function. Minister Buchanan, a better-tempered, more mannerly man, refused to rise, conscious of what was happening, but realizing as only a Presidential aspirant can how much more damage it would do him at home to rise than it would do him in England to sit.

The room became noisy with hisses and catcalls as the toast was drunk, and very shortly afterward what had been an impressive and pleasant occasion dissolved in friction and upleasantness. The fruits of the bad behavior of Mr. Sickles lasted for many years, and George Peabody, for one, never quite got over the insult of the insular, undiplomatic diplomat. In future he would have no more to do with the official mission in terms of joint entertainments. Instead he gave his own dinners, and comported himself as he would, letting the mission do its entertaining. At George Peabody's dinners, the Queen continued to be saluted in her own country first of all, while at the mission, which was considered to be American territory, the President always had the first salutation of the evening.

CHAPTER 13

PUBLIC RELATIONS EXPERT

GEORGE PEABODY possessed what would be known in the twentieth
century as a knack for public relations that quite surpassed the
diplomacy of any other Americans abroad, official or unofficial.
He also had the great advantage of being a millionaire, in control
of his own funds, who could do with them what he wished. What
he chose to do was make Britain pro-American, no matter what
the politicians at home might ordain or attempt. He did so by a
constant stream of favors and generosities that were scarcely
matched by any Briton.

In 1854 Sir John Franklin sailed off on his second expedition
to the Arctic regions of North America, attempting to find the
Northwest Passage. In July he met a passing whaler, and eventually
that ship came back to England to report to Lady Franklin that
Sir John had sent his regards. But then there was silence. Not another word came from the *Erebus* or *Terror*, the two ships of the
expedition. They had vanished off the face of the earth. Several
search parties were sent out by the British Admiralty to try to
determine the fate of Franklin and his men, but none succeeded.
In 1852, Dr. E. K. Kane secured the loan of a ship, the *Advance*,
from a New Bedford owner, and asked the United States Congress
to support his efforts to solve the mystery of the expedition's dis-

appearance. Congress would no more do that than they would support the American exhibit to the Crystal Gardens, and they were rude about it. So George Peabody personally subscribed the total cost of this Ameircan attempt to find the British explorer. The Kane expedition failed in its primary mission, but the British people were grateful nonetheless for the kindness shown by Peabody, and his great prestige was further enhanced. Nor could anything Congress might do destroy the growth of pro-American feeling with so ardent an exponent of brotherly relations on hand.

Peabody was never an expatriate in the usual sense of the word. He loved his country, and remained in England only because this was where his fortune and his ability to increase it lay. When his native town, Danvers, celebrated the centennial of its independence from Salem in the spring of 1852, Peabody sent messages to the officials of Danvers saying he wished he could be present, recalling the days of his schooling in South Danvers. Although business prevented him from going home for the affair, he managed to have himself represented. The banker asked that his first employer, Captain Proctor, be seated at the head table at the banquet as the Peabody representative, and he sent Captain Proctor a sealed envelope which was to be opened at the end of the dinner.

Captain Proctor attended the fete, and as the speeches were made he broke the seal on the envelope, arose, and presented George Peabody's surprise. It was a hot June day with the air standing still and rank around Crowninshield Pond, the clusters of party-goers uneasy in their chairs, sweating a little in the sun and eager to be off for a walk or an afternoon nap to ease the fulsomeness of the huge meal just consumed.

Captain Proctor arose a little self-consciously and read George Peabody's words: Peabody was donating $20,000 to his native town for the purpose of education. He asked that a building be put up in the South Park which could be used as a lyceum, giving public speakers a place to perform and teachers a place to gather students for lectures. Here, then, was George Peabody's first venture in educational philanthropy, awarded fittingly enough to the hometown that had given him so little.

As the years passed, George Peabody began to feel the tiring effects of constant entertaining, which was the key to the success of his business. He would not give up his business way of life, but neither did he feel up to the round of entertainments that life imposed. The answer, he saw with growing clarity, was to find an amiable and intelligent man of affairs who could relieve him of some of this responsibility and would be willing to do so for a chance at great fortune.

In 1853 when Commodore Vanderbilt had made millions in the steamboat trade, he built a handsome steam yacht called the *North Star*, brought his family, sons-in-law (he had a dozen children), and even a minister of the Gospel on a grand tour of Europe. They came to London, and as was George Peabody's custom, he entertained them as royally as if he had been the King of England and they his visiting relatives.

He secured their hotel accommodations—no mean feat for so large a crowd. He lent them his box at the Covent Garden opera house. He lent them his boxes at the theaters. He brought carriages around and took them driving in the countryside. He dined them at his country house at Richmond, along with Stephen A. Douglas, the senator from Illinois, who was in London on a fact-finding tour.

The Vanderbilts provided a grand case in point of the problems George Peabody faced in Anglo-American relations. Queen Victoria was a sociable lady who gave all the suggested public functions to honor her courtiers and the scions of the realm who distinguished themselves in her service. But Americans were practically never invited to such events, although Continental visitors of rank were nearly always asked when they were in town. The problem was, again, this innate condescension by the royal courtiers to the ultrademocratic ways of the homespun Americans.

Nor did money help a bit. In 1853, Commodore Vanderbilt was probably worth about fifteen million dollars, not a huge sum by his own later standards, but a healthy fortune. Instead of welcoming the Commodore as a visiting dignitary or upper-class citizen of the United States, however, the British well-to-do discovered that he had been an ordinary steamboat captain and, worse, that he was the son of a Dutch ferryman on Staten Island, and could scarcely read or write. The noses went up, the sniffs in Pall Mall were audible, and the Vanderbilts were thoroughly snubbed by the court. The Lord Mayor of London entertained them—but this was obviously George Peabody's doing, and even Peabody could not persuade the peers to dignify this nouveau riche family in their flashy steamer by any attention. The closest the Vanderbilts came to Victoria and Albert was when they saw them from George Peabody's box at the opera, during a performance of Meyerbeer's *Les Huguenots*. The crusty old Commodore, who was a big man with a big nose, sniffed audibly at the dumpy Queen and the fat balding prince, as he so termed them. He was miffed, and he let the world know it, not even deigning to give the British credit for producing decent horseflesh—another field in which he was an expert. Driving around Hyde Park in carriages laid on by George Peabody, Vanderbilt remarked that he would not buy the nags those "dooks and barons" used even to haul groceries to his house on Washington Square.

By the time the Vanderbilt party left for Russia, George Peabody had to admit to being a little tired; he had been entertaining the Douglases also, and keeping account of his business dealings with Cyrus McCormick and half a dozen other burgeoning manufacturers who were expanding into the world markets. When a Boston merchant named James Beebe came to town, Peabody unburdened himself enough to declare his ennui and the need for a competent assistant. Beebe knew just the man, a partner of his own in his merchandising business in Boston, a youthful but settled and mature merchant named Junius Spencer Morgan. This Morgan was descended from a respectable Hartford family which traced its lineage back as far as Peabody's own, if that had been a consideration. Peabody considered, and then offered Morgan a partnership in his London banking house. Morgan was to move bag and baggage to London, to undertake primarily the entertainment and satisfaction of American customers in England, and then to act as he would. He was to have an entertainment allowance of $25,000 a year, and was expected to spend it all.

Junius Morgan came to London as a Peabody partner, and so admirable was the selection, so amenable the man, so agreeable the circumstances, that it was as if old George Peabody had a son who was joining him in business. Peabody was able to take more and more time off to enjoy his hobbies, which were walking and planning for future charities. Morgan settled in a big house at Prince's Gate and the business life of the firm flourished without the slightest disturbance. Thus was begun the rooting of the great international banking house of Morgan, for Junius S. Morgan was the father to a young man named J. Pierpont Morgan, who was then studying at the University of Goettingen in Germany, and who would soon return to the United States to learn the banking business and become a banking associate of his father. For many years Junius Morgan would manage the banking house's activities in London, and Pierpont would handle affairs in America. As time went on, after the Civil War, the balance of economic power in the Western world would gradually shift, until the positions of the United States and Britain would be reversed; the United States would cease to be the debtor nation and become the great creditor or banker nation to the West.

In 1854, however, when Junius Morgan came to London, that city was the banking capital of Europe, challenged only by Paris, for the German bankers were more or less out of the competition. Beginning in the 1840s the burgeoning of American industry and railroads had brought big securities business to England, and much of this came through the hands of Peabody and Company—more every year until the Civil War began.

George Peabody probably purchased most of the rails for the early railroads of America, as they were mostly fabricated in England. He financed the expansion of the McCormick reaper company of the Middle West into the world market, and for several summers part of his time was spent as a sort of traveling show-man, accompanying a reaper around England while the operator demonstrated its abilities.

Two years after Junius Morgan came to London, George Pea-body indulged himself in a trip home to the United States. He had been in England for nineteen years, and he had entertained every American of any consequence to come to London. As a result he had as huge a reservoir of good will for himself as any American since the days of James Monroe and the Era of Good Feeling. When it was learned that he was coming home, the mer-chants of New York, Boston, Philadelphia, and Baltimore all of-fered to give him receptions, testimonial dinners, and the keys to their city if he would come to participate in the ceremonies. But George Peabody was a wise and understanding man, as well as a naturally modest one, and he knew that the best manner in which to dissipate a reservoir of good will was to take advantage of such offers—to drink it up, as it were. So with great regret publicly expressed, he said his energies were not up to such a tour, that he was unworthy of receiving so much attention, and he confined himself to acceptance of a public reception by the citizens of his native Danvers.

In the summer of 1856, George Peabody planned his trip home, hoping to make a tour of the country and see just what changes time had brought since his early manhood. He went to Boston, and then to Georgetown, where his sister lived. He went from there to Danvers on October 9, for the grand reception planned in his honor. A barouche drawn by six black horses was brought up outside the town for him to enter, and he got in, to receive the salute of a hundred guns from the artillery that accompanied the parade. It was as good a day as could have been prayed down, it was New England Indian Summer, the first frost had come and gone, and the sun was friendly and warm in a light blue sky.

The barouche was escorted through the streets of Danvers by a cavalcade of more than 300 ladies and gentlemen on horses, fol-lowed by 250 carriages, the whole marching order preceded by a band that announced the coming and raised the spirits of the people who lined the streets and cheered their hero, the banker of London.

From the Danvers line down through South Danvers, the way was decorated with flowers and bunting, and they met and joined another band (Gilmore's Famous Band) and five thousand paraders, led by a corps of cadets from a military school nearby. A group of lady riders (sidesaddle) came by the carriage, dressed in splendid silks and carrying a big bouquet of flowers done up in ribbons. As each lady passed the barouche of honor, she tossed her bouquet in to banker Peabody, who gallantly caught it, bowed, tipped his hat, and smiled.

The procession was a mile long and to buoy the spirits of the marchers and amuse the watchers, half a dozen bands were scattered along its snakelike course, each playing briskly. Eventually the line of march reached Main Street, and the Peabody Institute, which had been built with the original gift and other gifts of money from George Peabody. The Institute was eighty-two feet long and fifty wide, consisting of two stories, the lower given to a library and the upper to a lecture room.

Before this imposing, churchlike structure, the paraders halted, and the guests of honor filed onto a wooden platform in front of the building, where brief exercises were held, under the direction of the Honorable Alfred A. Abbott, one of the town's leading citizens. The students of Holten High School sang a hymn of welcome, and George Peabody responded with a brief address.

"Mr. Abbott and Fellow Townsmen," he said, arising and beginning the oration expected of him.

> "I have listened to your eloquent words of welcome with the most intense emotions, and return you for them my warmest acknowledgments. My heart tells me that this is no common occasion. This vast gathering, comprising many old associates, their children and their grandchildren, to welcome me to the home of my childhood, almost unmans me. . . ."

There were perhaps ten minutes of it, for that is how speeches went in that pre-Civil War day, long on rhetoric and short on facts. He spoke of his declination of other hospitality, and the impossibility of resisting his old friends. He spoke of the many changes in the scene before him ("the hum of busy labor . . . has even converted Foster's millpond into solid ground"). He marked the passing of those who were old when he was young, and the presence of so many scholars. He spoke of the grand opportunities awaiting the youth of the nation ("not a youth within the sound of my voice whose early opportunities and advantages are not very much greater than were my own"). He reminded them that all was possible to him who would work.

He called on all his listeners to exhibit "steadfast and undeviating truth, fearless and straightforward integrity, and an honor ever unsullied by an unworthy word or action." He reminded the girls, in an aside, that there was room for great women in the world as well as great men, and ended by blessing the assemblage in God's name. Then they all marched away to a big open field on Washington Street where a banquet for fifteen hundred people was laid out on long tables.

So the guests ate, and when they were finished there were more speeches. Governor Henry J. Gardner of Massachusetts had come for this joyous occasion, and he spoke of the glittering career of this grand citizen:

> . . . a young man, with no other capital . . . but his hands and his integrity, going abroad across the waters unheralded and unknown; by his own industry and integrity distinguishing himself among his fellows, and, in the good gifts of Providence showered upon him every hour of every year, seeking how he might benefit his countrymen at home [cheers] . . .

Edward Everett, statesman, author, teacher—the senior citizen of Massachusetts, who had been minister to England during some of the years when the Peabody reputation was abuilding—reminisced about that, lauded his fellow traveler, and joked a little with him in a superior sort of way, and called him the "dutiful and grateful child and benefactor of Danvers."

Oh, it was a glorious occasion, and George Peabody's heart

truly swelled at the bounty heaped upon him in testimonials and praise. Their stomachs full of food and their ears full of ringing phrases, and their hearts full of good will, the assemblage moved back to the Peabody Institute for a reception, where every man, woman, and child might shake George Peabody's hand and have a moment of speech with him.

Peabody was really overcome with it all. He gave $10,000 to a jealous Danvers, for location of a library of its own on Danvers Plain. He gave money for the purchase of library books at the local high schools.

Then George Peabody moved on, traveling quietly about the country, seeing changes and making mental notes of areas of American life in which he might one day wish to contribute to the common good.

The matter of contributing very nearly left his mind, however, before very long. He had stayed in the United States until late summer of 1857, when he sailed back to London.

The offices of George Peabody and Company were then located at 22 Old Broad Street in the heart of London. Peabody had scarcely set foot back in the offices after his American trip when he discovered a financial crisis brewing in London which made that of 1837 in Baltimore seem like child's play. It was bound up in difficulties that extended all the way across the world. British firms were heavily invested in South American railroads, and the Crimean War costs had drained away much capital. American firms were heavily invested in railroad stocks and bonds; Peabody and Company had dealt widely in these securities in London, assuring their British investors that they were as good as gold, and the house itself held millions of dollars in railroad stocks and bonds on its own account.

For Peabody, the crisis began in America, with the failure of several investment houses in New York. The New York City office of the Ohio Life Insurance Company, a heavy holder of railroad securities, had closed its doors late in August and refused to pay out debts. This failure immediately led to others, and like a house of cards the New York financial market, which had few safeguards, began collapsing.

In the summer, when the crisis began, George Peabody hastened home to London to protect his interests. He was perfectly confident of the abilities of Junius Morgan, but he wanted to be on the ground in case of trouble.

The trouble was not long in coming. The prices of railroad stocks and bonds began to fall on the American market, and when the newspaper reports and exchange reports reached London, the prices fell there, too. Actually, the problem by October was to keep a market at all in American railroad securities. No English house would buy them from a stock or bond holder. Had George Peabody and Company not bought the securities, the holders would have been forced to dump them on an overloaded New York market, and depress the prices still further. Since nearly all these securities had been marketed in England by Peabody and Company, the result of such action would have been the ruin of the Peabody firm with its loss of the trust of the English buying public.

Peabody, then, had to buy the railroad securities that were thrown on the market, to keep up the price. As the securities came back to him, week after week, the drain on the bank's resources was phenomenally large. On one day, November 27, he was called on to pay out eight hundred thousand pounds, or about four million dollars. But by the time that particular blow came, Peabody was already a very worried man.

". . . all is gloom and affliction," he wrote his niece in America. "Nearly all American houses in Europe have already suspended, and nothing but great strength can save any. You will understand that it is the loss of the credit of my house that I fear."

No one in America was of any assistance to Peabody. He could not ship the securities back to the United States for sale, because there was only a declining market; the railroads were oversold and overcapitalized, and it was becoming frighteningly apparent.

The situation was desperate but not hopeless. British purchases of American railroad securities had been made because of interest drummed up by the Peabody company, for the most part, and if the British investors could be sure that Peabody was solid, they would begin to calm down. If Peabody could weather the storm for a few more days it might blow over.

The trouble was that his cash reserves were nearly exhausted, although he had been the most conservative and provident of bankers. He turned to other private investment houses, British merchant bankers who were the counterpart of himself. They had been hard hit, some of them, but not as hard hit as he. Yet they were always sensitive to the competition that Peabody and Company gave them, and in this hour of need, some of his brethren in London decided they would get rid of him. They offered him a purse of the four-million-dollar loan he sought, but only if after his affairs were cleared he would agree to close up his house and quit the banking business in London.

Peabody had sent Junius Morgan off to make the request, and when his junior partner brought back the answer of the British merchant bankers, Peabody literally quivered in anger. He would be damned if he would yield to such blackmail, he said. He would have no more to do with the British merchant bankers, would not even reply to their offer. If he was going down, he would go down, but he would not quit or be blackmailed out of England.

In this dire hour, Peabody had yet one place to turn. Many years earlier he had befriended a young Englishman married to an American girl, and now this Englishman, Thomson Hankey, Jr., was the governor of the Bank of England, the Little Old Lady of Threadneedle Street, the agency that set Britain's financial policies. The Little Old Lady had millions of pounds in these days, if the authorities could be persuaded to give them out.

The request George Peabody made of Thomson Hankey was no ordinary one, and Hankey was wise enough to see that more depended on his action than the salvation or destruction of a single American banking house. If Peabody failed, there was no telling what might happen in London—his house was that highly regarded. But more than that, if the market in American securities failed—

and this particular house was the control factor in American securities—then what might not happen to British-American trade for years to come? Peabody was an honorable man: he told Hankey that all he needed was a temporary loan to tide him over, and Hankey believed him. After several days of meetings the Bank of England made the unprecedented loan; the word that Peabody was backed by the Bank of England stopped any run that was coming on his bank. He bought the railroad securities as they came in on the basis of current prices, but always kept the market moving, and soon the crisis was over. He repaid the loan to the Bank of England, and the House of Peabody was stronger than ever, because it had the unlimited faith of English investors in American securities.

Throughout the crisis, while talking of borrowing a million pounds, while watching the investors come to his bank's door bearing their silver and gold bonds and stock certificates and asking for their money, George Peabody, grown a little stout in his sixty-third year, sat at the simple desk he used in one of the front offices at 22 Old Broad Street and worked at his banking. When it came time for lunch he pulled out a small leather box, which he brought every day from his rooms, and extracted from it the two little tin boxes which contained his lunch. Then, usually alone, but sometimes with Junius Morgan, he sat quietly and ate in the office before going back to work again until the middle of the afternoon. Crisis or no crisis, it was nearly all the same to him.

CHAPTER 14

PHILANTHROPIST

GEORGE PEABODY was really ready to retire in 1860, but with the impending crisis caused by slavery he saw that it was impossible and stayed on. Then he was caught up in the strangeness of being almost a national asset to a Union at war, and he gave no thought to quitting his banking business during the struggle across the Atlantic.

Even before Peabody's trip to the United States in 1856-57, he had begun considering what he might do with his large fortune. The riches were somewhat reduced by the Panic of 1857 and the concomitant decrease in values of railroad securities, but George Peabody was still very much a multimillionaire. As an expatriate who was very far in every way from members of his family, he possessed a detached view of the United States; he rather looked upon the whole nation as his family and the coming generations as his children. It was easy to adopt so Olympian a view from the distance of London in the 1850s.

In 1857 he committed himself to the support of a large educational institution, the Peabody Institute. Eventually he would give more than $1,500,000 to that institution, and before the war he financed the building of the original structure. Even the setbacks of 1857 did not trouble him in this regard, and as he slept in his lonely rooms, George Peabody gave much thought to other manners in which he might serve the best interests of Americans at large. The Peabody Institute would serve Baltimore, the adopted city which had been so kind to him, very well indeed. It consisted of a marble façade on Mount Vernon Square, into which were built a public gallery, an academy of music, an art gallery, halls, and lecture rooms. The building connected with a preparatory school where music was taught. But what about the rest of the nation? Peabody pondered.

As he considered what was to be done with his fortune, the clouds of war descended and broke across the Atlantic. Immediately Peabody aligned himself with the Union—not an easy decision, since he had his loyalties in Baltimore and southern allegiances from the cotton brokerage days, and since the sentiment in England was very strongly pro-Confederate. But there was never a tremor in the House of Peabody: the Union was the United States and the United States would be a union. He bought even more heavily for the house's account in United States government bonds and northern railroad securities.

Again, detachment was the key to George Peabody's attitude toward his native land. He had been away so long—twenty-four years in 1861—that he found it impossible to beocme emotionally aroused by the Civil War, and he played no role in London as agent. He did not help the Confederates in their efforts to raise support and money, but neither did he use his important position in a political way on behalf of the Union.

Because he was cut off from his homeland by the events of the Civil War, George Peabody turned his mind to the people among whom he had lived for so long, and to whom was attributable part of his fortune, the people of London. With Sir Curtis Lampson, one of the architects of the Atlantic Cable, he went salmon fishing from time to time (once paying $2500 for a fishing preserve on some lord's estate for a six months' period). Otherwise he lived his frugal, one might say almost miserly, life, subsisting on cheese and mutton chops for the most part, and pondering the best use to which he might put his fortune.

In March, 1862, he began a series of gifts to the city of London, with an announcement of the men he wished to administer this fund for the benefit of the poor. They were American Minister Charles Francis Adams; Junius Morgan, his junior partner; Sir Curtis Lampson, his friend; and Lord Stanley and Sir James Emerson Tennent, two English friends who were also men of great standing in the London community.

Peabody's income was at this point about $300,000 a year. He was beginning to feel the aches and pains of rheumatism that come with age, reminding him how mortal he was. He was also guided by his New England conscience, which gave him a feeling of guilt because of his wealth. He could look around him in nineteenth-century London to see the vast gap between good fortune and bad, for the London poor were ubiquitous. It was the same conscience that had led him to report a railroad conductor who cheated him of a shilling on the fare of his train ride from some upcountry spot back to London one day. Peabody claimed that the shilling meant nothing, but that he saw the conductor cheating others who could ill afford it, and the thought that the man might get away with it disturbed him.

Peabody was not by nature given to philosophizing, but in these years as he pored over the backgammon board with Curtis Lampson, his boon companion, he considered his blessings. As every millionaire everywhere, he was the recipient of a constant stream of personal requests for money from those who felt ill used by the world.

Out of all these considerations, over a period of years, came the first program of philanthropy of this sort ever established by an American. Others were giving to universities and to needy relatives. George Peabody never stinted there; not having sons, he was generous to his nieces and nephews, but in a canny sort of way. Boys, for example, were told that he would see to their educations (which he did for a half-dozen young Peabodys) and start them in business. He would not give them vast chunks of money, but they might get anywhere from $20,000 to $80,000 from him, depending on their needs and behavior. They must never marry until in a financial position to support a wife and children, and to do so meant to be cut out of Uncle George's will. Often, too, George Peabody combined his philanthropy in public and private ways: Yale University was to have $100,000 for establishment of a museum to promote the natural sciences—and one of the trustees was O. C. Marsh, who would be Yale's premier professor of paleontology, and who was also George Peabody's nephew.

Now that Junius Morgan was bearing the entertainment load of the company, George Peabody spent little more than $3,000 a year of his $300,000 annual income. He often stood out in the rain, walking from his club, because he would rather ride a public horsecar than take a hackney coach, and he did not keep a carriage.

"It is not easy to part with the wealth we have accumulated after years of hard work and difficulty," he once told an acquaintance of similar means, "but I advise you to try, for if you do, you will find it very pleasant."

Having decided to donate his money, Peabody sought the best method of doing so. He considered a large gift to Lord Shaftesbury's Ragged School Union—an attempt to bring education to the poor. With great public spirit and presence of mind, Lord Shaftesbury dissuaded Peabody from this course. He described to the American millionaire in grimy and bawdy detail the manner in which London's poor lived. He spoke of the crowding of whole families into single rooms or shacks, the sickness and the wretchedness of people who froze in winter, roasted in summer, who had no medical attention, not enough food, and no privacy. From his own experience, Lord Shaftesbury had come to the conclusion that nothing could be done for the London poor in the way of education until something had been done to relieve the tribulations of their daily lives.

So the trustees of the Peabody fund in London were advised that the donor would like to have them consider using the money to build housing for the poor. The concept was revolutionary. When complete—the work took half a dozen years—the Peabody housing project was one of the new wonders of the civilized world.

Designated Peabody Square, in Islington, the first project consisted of four blocks of buildings, joined around an open plot which was to serve as a public garden. All in all there were 155 apartments, accommodating about 200 families, or 650 persons. Not only was this a revolutionary concept in charity, it was revolutionary in architecture as well, a huge square tenement, light and airy, four stories high, built at a cost of 31,690 pounds. Many were the wonders. Refuse shafts which connected with basement bins meant that trash and garbage could be disposed of easily and neatly, to be then carted away rather than burned on the premises. The halls were lighted with gas lamps, and every apartment had running water provided from cistern on the roofs. Free baths were provided for those who wished to use them. Each block had its own laundry with wringing machines and drying lofts.

Each kitchen was provided with cupboards (a new idea) and with a boiler and an oven. The number of rooms in each apartment varied according to the size of the family occupying it. Mothers in particular were thrilled by the enclosed garden where they could go with their baby carriages and their children could safely play.

Peabody's first gift toward this project was 150,000 pounds, more than a million dollars in purchasing power. The first tenements cost 31,690 pounds, so there seemed to be plenty left over for maintenance. But it soon became apparent to Peabody and his trustees that the poor were far greater in number, that helping 650 people would not solve any problems. When the applications for the housing began to come in, the trustees were staggered. They went to Peabody, and the result was a series of gifts to be in the aggregate more than 500,000 pounds, perhaps $3,000,000 or more.

The Peabody housing plan never gave away apartments entirely free of rent. The idea was to help the poor, not totally support them. The trustees also wanted to set an example for private capitalists to build more such houses, and so they tried to show how the tenements could be profitable to the owners as well as light and airy.

They took the going rate, say two shillings sixpence for a single tumbledown room without water or sanitary conveniences in London's poorest areas, and they used that as their guideline. In other words, here was what landlords were getting for their rotten shack housing, and they set out to prove that the landlords could make money by providing decent accommodations. So the residents of the Peabody buildings paid two shillings sixpence for one room, four shillings for two rooms, and five shillings for three rooms.

When the committee of trustees got down to work, they set qualifications for entrance into the housing project. A person must be poor—and of good character. He could not be a drunkard or someone convicted of a crime. Otherwise the doors were open to all the poor.

Almost immediately the trustees were flooded with applications from charwomen, nurses, basketmakers, butchers, carpenters, firemen, laborers, porters, omnibus drivers, seamstresses, cobblers, tailors, and waiters. So great was the demand, the need, that another block was constructed and opened at Spitalfields; other tenements went up quickly, until there were six squares of these five-story buildings, with their four floors of apartments and upper floor, given over to the baths, washrooms, and drying lofts. Colonel J. W. Forney, a contemporary observer, had this to say:

> In evidence of the improved salubrity of the buildings, the superintendents report that ill health is rare; and that the number of deaths since the first buildings were opened, three years ago, have been one man aged thirty, who died of a chronic complaint, and four children, one of whom was under five, and two under two years old. The social contentment of the tenants is freely expressed. No complaints have been made of any of the arrangements provided for their comfort; and they all speak approvingly of the unaccustomed advantages they enjoy. Among these, they particularize the security of their furniture and effects, which are no longer liable, as they formerly were, to be taken in distress, should the landlord become a defaulter.

As regards the moral conduct of the tenantry, the superintendent reports that habitual drunkenness is unknown, and intoxication infrequent; and where the latter does occur, to the annoyance of others, it is judiciously dealt with by giving notice to the offender, that, in the event of its recurrence, he must prepare to leave. There has been but one person removed for quarreling and disturbing the peace, and one expelled for non-payment of rent. These exceptions out of a community of eight hundred and eighty persons, speak strongly for the self-respect and moral principles by which they are influenced.

There are four other squares, two of which have already received occupants; and the other will soon be completed. . . . I conversed with many of the inmates: they were all clean, healthy, and happy. The men were off at work, and the women seemed to be industrious and tidy. The contrast between their condition and that of the poor in the miserable houses around us was painful in the extreme. In some of the rooms of the latter, as many as seven people were crowded.

But not everyone in the world approved of George Peabody's gesture, nor did everyone believe it was in the best interests of society to build such tenements. There came charges that Peabody wasted his money, that the real poor never got into the apartments, that the builders and the trustees were so extravagant the inhabitants were overcharged for accommodations, that the houses were like prisons.

One day in the middle 1860s a writer for the *Boston Journal* visited the tenements, and reported to his readers:

I must tell you of my visit to Mr. Peabody's model buildings near Islington; or, rather, to the buildings which the trustees of his fund built according to their own ideas. Told that Peabody Square was the most favorable specimen of these groups of workmen's homes, I drove down there on a recent Sunday and a foggy one. My route lay through Islington; and, long before coming there, we drove through one of those interminable streets called roads in London, where one sees only immense museums of trade and horrible poverty. . . . But the neighborhood was more respectable towards Peabody Square. The fog, however, was of the consistency of cream, and seemed to strike us in the face as we cut through it. At last cabby showed me up a narrow and dark alley, which finally opened on a square, around which were ringed four fine five-story stone blocks, each exactly like the other. . . .

Here the reporter's preconceptions began to show. He had come expecting to find the Peabody houses overrated, and he looked about him suspiciously, then was puzzled by what he found.

Here were no quarreling or fighting children, no drunken women, no discouraged-looking men. There were flowers in the windows, and bright, happy faces looked out from among them; but the blocks had a prison-like appearance, nevertheless. There was not a blade of grass, or a twig, to be seen in the stone-paved yard; and the fog settled down into the area worse than outside. The outer doors were open; and I soon made the acquaintance of a brawny Englishwoman in the porter's lodge of one of the blocks.
How many families were there in each building?
"Forty-two; and p'raps six in a family, sir."

The writer went for a look at the buildings.

We looked into some of the rooms. It depended on the taste, more than the resources of the individual tenant, how comfortable he made himself. There were neatly tiled floors, whitewashed walls. The rooms were small, but planned as economically, as to space, as a travelling jacket. I noticed, especially, that each room was well-lighted and ventilated. Some families had three rooms, so planned as to avoid any of the lamentable lack of decency which large families crowded into small tenements sometimes exhibit in London and New York and Boston. Each floor is divided into lettered sections, which are traversed by spacious corridors. Each tenement, or suite of rooms, has one door, numbered, opening on these corridors. There are iron traps in the halls in each story, into which the dirt and rubbish from each tenement is swept. . . .

So impressed with the tenements was the writer, who had arrived with a chip on his shoulder, that he believed he must have come to the wrong place.

Are these workmen, living here, of what you would call the better class? I asked.
"I rather think not, sir," was the answer. "Most o' them does common sort o' work; 'n sometimes they hasn't any in the dull

season: but they all manages to stick by the square, in any case. Me'n my man does all the hirin' rooms; and we never has any disputes. All pays, allers."

The reporter came away convinced.

So in this square, here are one hundred and sixty-eight families, averaging six members each, renting comfortable rooms, in a clean, airy, and respectable quarter of the city, for about five dollars per month, per tenement. Their condition is much improved by the arrangements made for them; and any drunkenness or fighting in the building is never known. I saw, in many of the rooms, the men at home, evidently enjoying the society of their families, instead of swilling beer at the public-house. I should give my testimony in favor of the success of Mr. Peabody's money as a most practical beneficence.

The most sincere flattery was imitation, and one of the early imitators was Alexander Turney Stewart, a Scotch Presbyterian boy brought up in Catholic Ireland. Stewart's story was almost the reverse of Peabody's, for Stewart had gone from the Old World to the New to make his fortune, and had done equally as well as Peabody. In 1869, following the Peabody pattern, Stewart purchased a 7000-acre tract from the town fathers of Hempstead, Long Island, and cut it up into housing developments, ranging from expensive $17,000 houses to tiny homes for workers.

After the Civil War, many in America pressed George Peabody to come home and enjoy his declining years in the warmth of the adulation of his countrymen. As a millionaire and a philanthropist he was sure to receive the admiring attention of the nation's press. And among those who pressed were the trustees of the Peabody Institute in Baltimore, who had delayed the formal opening of the Institute until after the war.

So Peabody in 1866 made plans to return to the United States, although too late for the opening of the Institute named for him in Baltimore.

One reason for the delay was the flattering attention bestowed on George Peabody by no less a personage than Her Majesty, Queen Victoria. She wished to show the gratitude of England in some fitting way, and suggested a knighthood or the Grand Cross of the Order of the Bath. Unlike his friend Curtis Lampson, Peabody refused the honors—perhaps it was that old Puritan conscience again, or it may have been simply a republican soul that kept him from taking monarchy's awards.

If he would not have honors which other men coveted, then what would he have? asked the royal court.

A letter from the Queen, said George Peabody, "which I may carry across the Atlantic, and deposit as a memorial of one of her most faithful sons."

Queen Victoria was quite beside herself because a letter was simply not enough for her to give to a man who had bestowed millions on her subjects in one way or another, but she wrote:

> Windsor Castle, March 28, 1866

> The Queen hears that Mr. Peabody intends shortly to return to America; and she would be sorry that he should leave England without being assured by herself how deeply she appreciates the noble act, of more than princely munificence, by which he has sought to relieve the wants of her poorer subjects residing in London. It is an act, as the Queen believes, wholly without parallel; and which will carry its best reward in the consciousness of having contributed largely to the assistance of those who can little help themselves.

> The Queen would not, however, have been satisfied without giving Mr. Peabody some public mark of her sense of his munificence; and she would gladly have conferred upon him either a baronetcy or the Grand Cross of the Order of the Bath, but that she understands Mr. Peabody to feel himself debarred from accepting such distinctions.

> It only remains, therefore, for the Queen to give Mr. Peabody this assurance of her personal feelings; which she would further wish to mark by asking him to accept a miniature portrait of herself, which she will desire to have painted for him, and which, when finished, can either be sent to him in America, or given to him on the return which she rejoices to hear he meditates to the country that owes him so much.

It was to be no ordinary miniature: the royal dignity insisted that this gift to the man who would accept no honor be of princely quality. The Queen adorned herself in robes which she had not worn since the death of Albert five years earlier. All the more remarkable was this tribute because since 1861 she had been withdrawing more and more from public functions. She put on a black silk dress, with a dark velvet train, trimmed in ermine. She wore her favorite Mary Stuart cap, surmounted with a demicrown, and wore the Koh-i-noor diamond and a jeweled cross. A London artist named Tilb painted the miniature, a half-length portrait, fourteen inches long and ten inches wide, and when the color was transferred to the enamel all was taken to a furnace specially built to manage so large a piece of porcelain. There it was fired and finished.

In this way did the Queen demonstrate her high regard for a man who had subjected himself to her although not a subject, and whose loyalty to the Empire was as great as his loyalty to his own nation. He had done more than any other to re-cement the bonds of brotherhood between nations torn asunder by revolution and the War of 1812. George Peabody, quite aside from his gift to the London poor, was the most effective advocate of British-American friendship in the history of the two countries. No expense was spared, and when finished, the miniature was mounted in an elaborate and massive frame of chased gold. All in all, it cost the Crown somewhere around $70,000 to fulfill Peabody's simple request in a fitting manner.

The people of England also honored this benefactor in many ways. The merchants of the city raised a fund for erection of a statue, and the officials of the city itself first elected Peabody a freeman and liveryman of the Ancient Company of Clothworkers, then granted him the freedom of the city, embossed on a document, encased in a box which was valued at 100 guineas. A similar box, of gold, was presented by the Ancient and Worshipful Company of Fishmongers. Oxford University conferred the degree of Doctor of Civil Laws on this adopted son of England.

When it came time for the unveiling of the statue of George

Peabody in the city of London, the drape was pulled aside by no less a figure than the Prince of Wales. The crowd filled the area about the Royal exchange, and jammed Threadneedle Street and Cornhill to overflowing. The high and the mighty had tickets to a special enclosure, and they came in full regalia, while the less lucky stood in the streets and jeered at them. The cordons of police were harried, and finally a troop of the Honorable Artillery Company was called up to quiet the restless crowds. There were speeches after the Prince pulled the cord—the Lord Mayor made one, so did Mr. Story, the sculptor, who was also an American, and so did Mr. Motley, the American minister. The Prince called Peabody that "great philanthropist" and "citizen of the world." Peabody did not speak, for he was on his way to America.

CHAPTER 15

END OF A PHILANTHROPIST

IN 1866, George Peabody, at seventy-one, was feeling his age. He was still interested in the distribution of his wealth, but the strain of accepting the gratitude of men and of nations was telling on him, and his rheumatism bothered him mightily.

He went down to Georgetown, Massachusetts (New Rowley before it changed its name), to visit his sister, Judith Peabody Daniels. There he gave the money to build the Peabody Memorial Church, which was to be in memory of his mother. He also gave the town $25,000 for a library.

There were many such gifts. Thetford, Vermont, received one. The Peabody Institutes at Baltimore and South Danvers (which later became Peabody) were given more attention. He gave the money for the establishment of the Peabody Museums at Harvard and Yale universities, and he donated $140,000 to pull together the collections of items important in study of natural history owned by the Essex Institute and the Salem East India Marine Society, to make one grand natural history collection, known for a time as the Peabody Academy of Science, and now as the Peabody Museum of Salem. He also gave money for the library at Newburyport.

Altogether not a place that had housed him was forgotten in the benevolences of George Peabody. Each gift was given for the advancement of education (except the housing for the London poor, which was indirectly concerned with their education), and when it was all finished—or so the people of America believed—George Peabody unveiled his master stroke. Early in 1867 he picked a list of prominent Americans, including several governors, as well as General U. S. Grant and Admiral Farragut, the heroes of the Civil War. He called the men together at the Hotel Willard in Washington, and he gave a grant to the people of the South that would amount perhaps to two million dollars. His concept: to better the educational opportunity of white and black, and particularly to fit the American Negro for the full citizenship the Unionists were demanding that he enjoy immediately.

It was a grand gift, and if there was a catch to it that was not of George Peabody's making. A million dollars was in cash, another million and more in the defaulted bonds of the state of Mississippi. Peabody believed that those bonds would be paid off in time, because he had experienced defaults of other bond issues, which the states ultimately paid rather than injure their credit permanently. Later Peabdoy gave more to the fund, including nearly half a million dollars in defaulted bonds of the state of Florida.

For this munificence, George Peabody was granted a signal tribute from the United States government; a special medal was struck in his honor by Congress, which recognized the vast generosity of this man.

Peabody's final gift appealed to many in the nation. As a result of it, the D. Appleton publishing company provided a hundred thousand books for the southern schools, and the A. S. Barnes Company provided thirty thousand. Under the leadership of Robert C. Winthrop, who had been Peabody's friend for many years, the committee guiding the spending gave over the largest share of the income from the gift to the public schools. Thus sparked, the southern states began to take responsibility for their own educational systems, and the committee gradually could change the nature of its benevolence to support the normal schools, where teachers were taught.

Having indulged his taste for philanthropy so thoroughly, having been honored by the governments of the two nations to which he belonged in nationality and spirit, having even seen the town of South Danvers change its name in his honor to Peabody, the banker took his aching frame back to London. There he watched with a careful eye the growth of the Peabody housing project, and approved by and large of what he saw happening to London because of it. He continued, also, to send money back to America. The Essex Institute was given a substantial gift on its own account, and the Massachusetts Historical Society received a gift of $25,000. Since a friend, a bishop, was president of an obscure college in Ohio called Kenyon College, Peabody gave that institution $25,000, too.

By this time, Peabody was bedeviled with requests from every sort of money seeker and crank—an English gentleman who had fallen on low estate wrote him thirty-six pages of complaint. But he preferred to give his money for public purposes, such as a new organ for the church he had built at Georgetown. Although there were a thousand letters of requests each month, he did not reply to most of them and granted assistance to practically none of the individual seekers. He provided for the members of his family, he gave $25,000 to Phillips Andover Academy in Massachusetts, and he planned more, but always in the public behalf.

In the spring of 1869 George Peabody returned again to the United States for a visit. He attended meetings of various of his established charities, and then he headed south. He announced the gift of a second million dollars in cash to the Peabody southern educational fund. By this time, when it was all totaled, he had given more than eight million dollars away, and was prepared to give more. Still he was as judicious as in the past.

In July, Peabody was in White Sulphur Springs, West Virginia, having gone to the spa in the hope that the baths might help his painful rheumatism. He arrived coughing, and doubled up with his pains. Oliver Wendell Holmes, who had seen him that spring, wrote a friend about Peabody, referring to him as "the Dives who is going to Abraham's bosom, and, I fear, before a great while."

So other friends believed as well, for he was seventy-four years old and very infirm. He took a cottage on Balitmore row, near his friends: W. W. Corcoran, the Washington banker, and Johns Hopkins, the Baltimore banker. Peabody's influence on these two men was supreme, and both were to make substantial charitable contributions in following his example. Hopkins, in particular, founded the first graduate university in the United States after seeing and hearing his old friend Peabody discourse on the values and pleasures of philanthropy.

Here at the resort came a historic meeting, between Peabody and the ailing Robert E. Lee, then president of the little Washington College (later Washington and Lee) at Lexington, Virginia. Lee was unwell, and he came to the springs seeking health, too. To honor him, the people of the area held a reception at an inn called the Old White, raising $605, whereupon Corcoran gave another $100 and so did Peabody.

Peabody and Lee became friendly in this brief visit, and before he left White Sulphur Springs, the philanthropist made a gift to Lee's college. Many years earlier, Peabody had purchased $35,000 in bonds of the state of Virginia and had them shipped to England. But off Newfoundland, the ship had sunk with all hands. There was no doubt about the sinking; the place and date (September 27, 1854) were known, but the legislature of Virginia was loath to hear the Peabody petition, and the money was not refunded. Therefore, with interest, the bonds should in 1869 be worth $55,000, and that was the gift made by Peabody to Washington College. All Lee had to do was try to collect it.

Having made this shrewd grant, Peabody prepared to go home, and on August 30, two frail old men walked along the platform waiting for the train that would take Peabody back to Washington and Baltimore, chatting, and shaking hands as the engine came hooting into the station. Peabody boarded and was off, as his friend Robert E. Lee waved after him.

Before he left the United States, George Peabody completed his will, giving $300,000 to nephew George Peabody Russell, who served him well on several of his boards of trustees; $300,000 to another nephew and to his sister; and dividing the rest of his fortune among other relatives, leaving none who had been loyal to him less than $100,000, quite enough to make each of them wealthy in 1869.

He had great hopes for his charities. The gift to the London poor, for example, he expected to be so great in two hundred years as to amount to a sum sufficient to buy all the property in London. (Banker Peabody forgot that land values in London and everywhere else would rise with the growth of population.)

So George Peabody went to New York, boarded the *Scotia* (for he always believed the British steamers were safer than the American ships, and with good reason), and steamed back to England. He had no intention of remaining long, he was bound for the south of France to winter over, and intended to remain in London only long enough to see a few friends and then head for Nice.

He went to the house of Sir Curtis Lampson in Eaton Square, where he had been living these last few years, and he settled in for a brief visit. But his health worsened, and on November 4, without ever being able to start for the south of France, George Peabody died, muttering, almost as his last words, "Danvers—Danvers, don't forget." Eventually, on consulting the old man's will, those close to him translated this to be a reminder that he wished to be buried in Harmony Grove Cemetery, near the line of the town once known as South Danvers, the town that became Peabody.

London could not have mourned him more sincerely had he been one of her own children.

"The news of Mr. Peabody's death will be received with no common sorrow on both sides of the Atlantic," said the London *Times*.

"Mr. Peabody was one of the few whose private virtues are followed by public fame, and whose virtues may be cited as examples," said the London *Post*.

"The inscription on his mausoleum may tell, with unquestioned truth, of the man who loved his kind and served two countries," said the *Telegraph*.

"Merchants, in passing his statue daily, do not need to learn from the consummate man of business how to gain money; his career may teach them how it may be wisely spent," said the *Daily News*.

How strange it was, the mourning for this man. He never held a public office; he never sought the acclaim of his fellows. And yet, when he died, the respects paid him were greater than those paid any American up to his time. Others had been greatly honored in death at home, but none had been so honored by the governments and people of two nations as was George Peabody. In London, a funeral of state was prepared, although it was known that his body would be taken back to America for burial.

In the United States, the doors of the Peabody Academy of Science in Salem were draped in mourning. The legislature of Massachusetts passed resolutions in his honor. Salem declared its regrets. The town of Peabody mourned officially. Congress authorized a state funeral for him. Funereal portraits, edged in black, were printed by the thousands and sold in the cities and in the towns of America, for not since the death of Abraham Lincoln had a man been so mourned. Indeed, unlike Lincoln, Peabody had alienated no section of the country, and the South, if anything, declared him to be a firmer friend than did his native Massachusetts.

In London, it took nearly a week to prepare for the funeral of this distinguished man. There was a solemn procession, starting at Sir Curtis Lampson's house and moving slowly along the streets, carriages in procession, to Westminster Abbey. Among the mourners were the Queen, the Prince of Wales, the Prime Minister (Mr. Gladstone), the Secretary of State for Foreign Affairs, the Earl of Clarendon, the Lord Mayor of London, and the sheriffs in their official robes.

At the Abbey, the interior was crowded, and outside in Broad Sanctuary and Victoria Street stood scores of workmen's wives who came to pay their respects to the man who had done more to ease the lot of the London workman than any other.

The coffin was covered in black velvet and on top lay a wreath of immortelles. It was carried by ten friends of Peabody's and deposited on a brier in front of the steps leading to the altar. The mourners then took seats on each side of the sacrarium, while the high officials sat inside the rails of the communion table.

The funeral included the "sentences" of the Church of England service, "I am the Resurrection," the ninetieth Psalm, and the lesson was from 1 Corinthians xv.

After the lesson the procession resumed and an anthem began. The pallbearers picked up the coffin and carried it into the nave, where they placed it by the side of an opening three feet deep. There it was lowered, and a graveside service was read by a sub-dean, the Reverend Lord John Thynne. The Dead March from *Saul* was played while each mourner stepped forward to pay last respects to the coffin. After these ceremonies, the body lay in state in Westminster Abbey for the next month, and the Bishop of London preached a funeral sermon there on the first Sunday.

Knowing that the body must go home to America, the editors of the *Daily Telegraph* suggested that it be conveyed there in a British warship, and the government and public took up the plan with enthusiasm.

Among the tributes from far and near came one from the French writer and humanist Victor Hugo, which was remarkable in its depth of feeling for a man so far-removed from its author in every apparent way:

> Yes, America has reason to be proud of this great citizen of the world and great brother of all men—George Peabody. Peabody has been a happy man who would suffer in all sufferings, a rich man who would feel the cold, the hunger, and thirst of the poor. Having a place near Rothschild, he found means to change it for one near Vincent de Paul. Like Jesus Christ, he had a wound in the side: this wound was the misery of others. It was not blood flowed from this wound: it was gold which now came from a heart.

On this earth there are men of hate and men of love: Peabody was one of the latter. It is on the face of these men that we can see the smile of God. What law do they practice? One alone,— the law of fraternity, divine law, humane law; which varies the relief according to the distress; which here gives precepts, and there gives millions; and traces through the centuries in our darkness a train of light, and extends from Jesus poor to Peabody wealthy.

May Peabody return to you, blessed by us! Our world envies yours. His fatherland will guard his ashes, and our hearts his memory. May the moving immensity of the seas bear him to you! The free American flag can never display enough stars above his coffin.

Then, when the appointed time came, the British man-of-war, H.M.S. *Monarch*, a nine-gun ship, Her Majesty's most modern ironclad, was chosen to escort the body home, together with an American warship, the *Plymouth*, and a French man-of-war in attendance.

Aboard the *Monarch* the draped coffin was placed in the wardroom, and candles burned throughout the voyage.

The escort arrived off Portland, Maine, on January 25, 1870, in a heavy fog that soon turned into squalls of sleet and rain. The ships could not come into harbor, and lay offshore that night. Next morning, the vessels entered through the heavy weather, and thousands of citizens flocked to the shore at the signal of the city's fire alarms, coming down in a heavy snow to see the body landed. The revenue cutter *Mahoning* went out to the harbor entrance to escort the warships in, accompanied by the American ironclads *Miantonomah* and *Terror* and the steamer *Leyden*. There were many salutes, fired in honor of Peabody and the visiting British and French vessels, as they came into the inner harbor. For three days the body lay aboard the *Monarch*, and Americans came to pay their respects, led by Admiral Farragut, the hero of Mobile Bay. On Saturday, January 29, although it was still snowing, the body, guarded by British and American officers, was moved to the *Leyden*, the admiral's flagship, which came up the bay under the escort of the

U.S.S. *Iris*. The Fifth United States Artillery band played a dirge as the procession advanced, and Admiral Farragut transferred his flag to the U.S.S. *Cohasset*.

The cortege passed through an honor guard fleet of twenty-two boats drawn from the various warships, filled with seamen oars apeak, each line drawn by a tugboat.

On the wharf stood Governor Chamberlain of Maine with his staff and nearly all the members of the Maine legislature, attended by two companies of militia, presenting arms. A steady, slow salute of the guns in the harbor, in the fortresses, and the arsenal began to boom out across the harbor, as the body removed from the *Leyden* and taken to the city hall.

On Monday the city hall was opened to the public to pay honors to George Peabody, and as this occurred, various delegations from all parts of the United States were moving toward Portland to join the special train that had been laid on to take the remains and the mourners to Salem. All the cars were new-built from the Salem shops of the Boston and Maine, and the locomotive was named the *George Peabody*.

On Tuesday the funeral was held in Portland at the city hall, enhanced by the three hundred voices of the Handel and Haydn Society. The ceremony was complicated by the onslaught of a severe snowstorm, which hampered the progress of the horses and marchers during the half-mile-long procession which was escorted by the Germania Orchestra of Boston. Preceding the cortege were two huge snowplows, each drawn by six horses, followed by a group of shovelers who cleared the way. Then came the marchers, and the coffin, guarded by soldiers bearing reversed arms.

At the railroad station the engine was puffing in the cold, and the coffin was put aboard the heavily draped special train, guarded then by four companies of the Fifth U.S. Artillery. The mourners followed, and the train moved out of the station for the solemn journey south.

Crowds came out to every platform, and the majestic cars steamed by, black crepe fluttering in the wind and snow. At

Beverly the Mayor and City Council of Salem boarded, and at Salem, the train stopped for a salute from guns fired on a wharf on the North River. From Salem station to Peabody the tracks were lined solidly with crowds.

At Peabody the casket was removed and taken to the Peabody Institute where it remained on display until Tuesday, February 8, when services were held at the South Church. Prince Arthur, the Duke of Connaught and Queen Victoria's youngest son, came from Boston with the British Minister to Washington, on a special train, to attend the services as representatives of Her Majesty. The governor of Massachusetts was there, and so were many other dignitaries from state, local, and federal government, and from educational institutions, such as Harvard College. Again it stormed, again the soldiers and horses slipped and staggered in the ice and sleet and snow, but finally, after the longest and most impressive parade of all, the body was taken to Harmony Grove Cemetery and placed in the tomb of Joseph Peabody, the other merchant, until the George Peabody tomb could be completed.

The remarkable story of the man who invented American philanthropy had come to its end.

PART IV

The Literati

He who would write heroic poems should make his whole
life a heroic poem.

Thomas Carlyle, *Life of Schiller*

Although many Peabodys were concerned with literary affairs in the early days of the United States, and even before the states were united, the flowering of the Peabodys as literary figures came in the middle of the nineteenth century. Oliver William Bourne Peabody and William Bourne Oliver Peabody were both literary men, and yet not primarily so; Oliver was a lawyer, newspaperman, master of jurisprudence, and finally a clergyman. William was a clergyman who took to literary affairs as an escape from the trials of a liberal minster in a closed community which he and a handful were trying to pry open. Nevertheless these twins, who contributed in a literary way after the first quarter of the century, served as precursors to others who would make the name Peabody in the nineteenth century synonymous with good breeding and good taste.

CHAPTER 16

THE EDUCATION OF AN AUTHOR

LITERARILY SPEAKING, the most productive of the Peabodys was Andrew Preston Peabody. In the last twenty years of his life, when his other activities had quieted down, he wrote 120 books, making a lifetime total of 190 published volumes.

The young Andrew could read a book when he was three years old, and thereafter bedeviled his mother, a widow by that time, with requests for suitable reading material. At some time in the learning process someone put a book in front of him upside down, and he found he could read it that way, or indeed if it were sideways. He possessed a photographic mind that could simply take in a page at a glance and digest it.

One time after he had been studying German for a few years he was riding in a stagecoach, leafing through a German work, and when the ride was over one passenger scoffed to another that this student was trying to impress them.

"Why," said the scoffer, "he was holding that German book upside down."

And so he was.

But the habit helped in some ways. When he was teaching, he did not have to have an extra copy of the book from which his students were reciting, because he could simply look down at one held by the boy in front of him and read upside down quicker than the student could read rightside up.

From the beginning of his life in school, Andrew Preston was troublesome to his teachers. At Middleton in the church Sunday school one morning, the teacher of his class decided to put the noisy seven-year-olds to work doing something useful, so they were told to begin reading the Bible, to memorize what they read, and to be ready to recite at the end of the class time. The teacher then went on to instruct older students in the ways of the Lord.

At the end of the class session the teacher began calling on selected pupils to recite what they had learned, and one after the other they stumbled through a few lines of the book of Genesis. They would falter, halt, and he would go on to the next boy.

And then the teacher called on Andrew.

"In the beginning God created the heaven and the earth . . ."

The teacher nodded approval, and little Andrew continued.

"And God said, 'Let there be light . . . ,' " recited the child as he go to the beginning of the second page. The teacher assented, smiling. My, how bright a boy to manage so much!

Little Andrew charged on.

"And God said, 'Behold I have given you every herb . . . ,' " and the student repeated the rest of *that* page.

The teacher nodded. A child prodigy. No less.

The boy continued. "And the Lord God said, 'It is not good that man should be alone . . .' "

And the teacher nodded. A little grimly this time.

The pages flew on.

"And Cain came out from the presence of the Lord . . ."

The teacher looked at the hourglass. It was run out, cold and still.

Little Andrew droned on.

"And God blessed Noah and his sons," he continued, reaching page 15 without yet pausing for an extra breath.

Finally the teacher bravely stepped in.

"Yes," he said. "Very good, Andrew. But it is time to close the school."

So Andrew Peabody stopped reciting, but the story was quickly out through his awe-struck companions, who had heard him moving on like a talking machine. The Minister of the Middleton church stopped Andrew before he left the house of God that day and asked just how many pages he had memorized.

Most of the book of Genesis, replied the boy (in the old version the book of Genesis occupied 96 pages). Did the minister wish to hear him recite?

"No, no," said the minister hurriedly, for although he was a true follower of the old faith, even with a Puritan there was a limit.

So little Andrew was excused from reciting what he had learned every Sunday. Almost immediately he had memorized the whole Bible, Old Testament and New. No one questioned him, for they knew that if they did, they might have to listen to proof of how well he had memorized—and there were crops to plant and weeds to weed, and harvests to bring in during the year to come.

Little Andrew was something of a thorn to the minister.

"Which would make the better fire—a fool or a philosopher?" the minister shot at him one day, when he and the lad were discussing affairs.

"I think an intermediate person would succeed best," said the boy, and the minister had to grit his teeth and commend him for that.

When little Andrew was nine a letter to his cousin Robert Rantoul, Jr., then a student at Phillips Andover Academy, described what he was up to:

Dear Cousin,
 I write this letter, that I may receive an answer; therefore I hope that you will answer it at the first opportunity. I hope before many years have passed that I shall be at the Academy. I have now under my care a class in Colburn's Arithmetic. I take them into the library room in the afternoon, and seat them at the round table,

wherefore I style them "knights of the round table." I am perfectly satisfied that Colburn's Arithmetic is founded on an excellent plan, and that will be of great use in instructing those who know nothing of Arithmetic. . . .

Two years passed, and Andrew began to show impatience with his studies:

As Saturday afternoon is the only leisure time I have, I take this time to write to you. I am writing exercises from Dana's Latin tutor. I began Virgil yesterday. I never, since I was five years old, studied so much or read so little as I do now. . . .

So Andrew struggled on. His nose was forever in one book or another. When there was no school, he took advantage of the free time to visit a lady who gave him lessons in botany. She also taught him French, which soon he was able to read as easily as English, whereupon he tackled German and began studying German literature, becoming so fluent that before he went to college he was an apt student of the subject.

By the time he was ten years old, little Andrew was a master of Bowditch's *Navigation* and had been on top of the paradigms of Greek grammar for some months. For pleasure other boys played ball or with hoops or marbles. Not Andrew Peabody. He read Hume's *History of England*, Mosheim's *Ecclesiastical History*, Rollins' *Ancient History*, the novels of Walter Scott, Mungo Park's *Travels in Africa*, Milton's *Paradise Lost*, and for really light work dipped into Milton's sonnets of a late afternoon.

So mammoth an amount of literature and knowledge did he memorize, and so quickly did he learn, that he was admitted to Harvard College at the age of twelve. His teachers and guardians, however, decided he was too young to go to college, so he spent the next few months studying with his old teacher Bernard Whitman (later minister of the Second Religious Society in Waltham).

That study consisted of more memorization, more delving into the catechisms and musty Roman Christians such as Grotius. The eager lad was never tardy, never absent, never played hooky, and never seemed to have a boyish thought in his head. Except for the merchants and politicians among them, few Peabody males who rose to prominence could be accused of boyish thoughts. Indeed, the Peabodys were Puritans among Puritans, and Andrew Preston was the prime example.

Andrew Peabody whirled through his Harvard studies without going to Harvard to live in the cold dormitories and mix with the hard-hearted students, who would not hesitate to haze so small and serious a youth. At the end of 1823 he passed the examinations which the Harvard freshmen had to pass for advancement; in the spring of 1824 he passed the sophomore examinations, and in the fall of 1824 he entered Harvard for the first time, but as a junior in class standing. He was thirteen years old.

During his studies under Whitman the youngster had worked twelve to fifteen hours a day, took no vacation, and begrudged even an hour for recreation. At college, he kept the habit, which enabled him to keep up the furious pace of his studies.

In 1826 Andrew Preston Peabody graduated from Harvard, the youngest in his class and the second youngest ever to graduate up to the turn of the twentieth century. He was fifteen years old.

Not many job opportunities were available to a fifteen-year-old, even in days before child labor laws, but he found a post teaching at the district school in Middleton, where he instructed some youngsters older than himself. This situation did not work well, so next year he was a private tutor to a family in Meadville, Pennsylvania. The third year, at the age of eighteen, Andrew Preston Peabody was made principal of an academy in Portsmouth.

His pedagogical experiences, however, were fairly miserable. He ran constant danger of being thrashed by his students, and few of them deigned to learn anything from him. One day somebody asked him how he liked teaching.

"I enjoy my vacations," he said.

At the end of three years, it was apparent to Andrew Preston that he was not for this world, and to escape it he entered the Harvard Divinity School. For the next three years he buried himself in the protective cloak of the university. He was proctor in the college—one of those hated men who made the undergraduates go to bed and prevented horseplay from developing into mayhem, stopped "feeds" in the middle, and generally made of himself a nuisance to red-blooded young Americans in residence. He taught Hebrew to anyone who wanted to learn, and mathematics as a tutor. In his later years he preached on Sundays in various vacant pulpits.

He received offers to take over as minister from three congregations, but was afraid to assume the responsibility, although many young men of twenty-one were doing so. Too many years spent in libraries and not enough in human company had made him unsure of himself.

But one offer was for a lesser opportunity: Dr. Nathan Parker of South Parish in Portsmouth was feeling poorly and needed a rest. The congregation, however, wanted him to stay on. So the answer was an assistant, and this post was offered to Peabody. He took it eagerly; here was task without responsibility, opportunity without problems. On October 24, 1833, he was ordained at the church. Three weeks after Andrew had come to Portsmouth, Dr. Parker died, leaving his young assistant to preach his funeral sermon and take over the parish.

South Parish in Portsmouth was hardly the place where you would expect to find a shy young minister in 1823. It was a busy well-to-do place, the Brookline of its day, where lived the wealthy merchants and ship captains of the West Indies trade. Its wharves and warehouses bustled with goods and men moving them; the old triangular trade (rum, sugar, and slaves) was still going on, although serious efforts were being made to stamp out the slave trade, and in 1817 international ordinances had outlawed the practice in northern waters. Some captains were engaged in the secretive, lucrative opium trade in China, too, and some were moving to the spice islands. The people knew a good deal about the world around them, and the knowledgeable parishioners could hardly expect to be instructed by a boy who had just come from divinity school, and before that had scarcely set foot abroad.

Dr. Parker had been knowledgeable in the ways of the outside world, and was held up by his parishioners as the finest minister in the country. He was dignified and simple, but he could tell a port from a sherry. Suddenly now, here to take over the grand stone church so newly built to honor Dr. Parker, was a stripling whose hand shook as he balanced a teacup in the parlors of the big white houses and who was visibly embarrassed at conducting Bible class for young ladies on Wednesday afternoons.

But the parishioners of the South Parish were good-natured and willing to abide by their own bargain, so they taught Andrew Peabody his duties and gave him the polish he needed to carry them out. He quite won them over in the first three weeks because he was so ardent a preacher. They could forgive much in a young fellow who could make them squirm a little in their pews and send them forth determined to be better men for the coming week.

Andrew Preston Peabody satisfied those who supported his church, and that was all that was necessary. He prepared two sermons every Sunday, his talks for the Bible class, and every Thursday night he gave an Expository Lecture to those (mostly ladies) who chose to come to the church to hear a more worldly discussion.

It was good that Andrew Preston had practiced abstinence and had overworked most of his young life, because now he discovered that the only time he could devote to his writing was late at night when the house was still. He arose early, and spent the forenoon in his study. Then after midday he went out among the people, finding themes for his preaching in making calls on the sick, the aged, and the wealthy old ladies. He also took a small boat on decent days across to the Isles of Shoals where lived poor fishermen whose souls fell in his parish because there was no other nearer. He helped them, soliciting support from the rich parishioners across the water, and the fishermen did not forget him, although few of them came regularly to his church.

After some years of this regimen, Andrew fell sick—like most of the Peabody preachers he was a slender, ascetic young man who was prey to rheums and mysterious fevers all his life. He took a trip then to recover his health, voyaging in one of his parishioners' ships to New Orleans and then coming back up the Mississippi by riverboat. The geography and the sounds and smells would have attracted any man, and one might have expected the Reverend Peabody to dwell on the virtues of travel, but true to his calling he interested himself in the slave question rather than the scenery, and wrote *Slavery, As It Appeared to a Northern Man in 1844;* then he turned the material into a year's supply of lectures and sermons.

The next year, flushed with success, he went to Europe. He wrote a series of letters back to the parish, and so well received were they that he was asked to give the Lowell Lectures at Harvard, which he did, publishing them afterward. The fact was that the Reverend Andrew Preston Peabody wrote a lively travel article.

Soon he became a trustee of Phillips Exeter Academy, and eventually served forty years, eighteen as chairman of the board. In the 1840s he began his dazzling literary career, with *Lectures on Christian Doctrine,* and other tracts which sold widely. His *Lectures* went into several editions and flourished for twenty years on the market. His social work *Conversation: Its Faults and Its Graces,* went into any number of editions and earned the minister a considerable sum of money.

After a few trips to Europe, the South, and other areas the shy young man was timid no longer and actually sought adventure, within, of course, the confines of his calling. By the time he was forty he was bored with his existence, and the next year, quite to the shock of parish, relatives, and friends, he went into wordly business by buying up the *North American Review* and becoming proprietor as well as editor-in-chief.

That project did not sit comfortably with the good merchants of South Parish, and it was not long before Andrew Peabody had moved to Cambridge to carry on his affairs, taking a testimonial silver fish-knife from his friends on the Isles of the Shoals, and a good deal of grumbling from the parishioners who had sent him to visit the slave states and then around the educational spas of Europe.

As always, Peabody was a demon for work. When he settled into the editor's chair of the *North American Review,* he took charge of the book reviews in the beginning, and then moved on to other subjects, writing an average of 160 pages a year for the magazine, or 1600 pages in the ten years during which he was editor. Besides that, of course, he continued to preach here and there, to write tracts, books, and to read hundreds, thousands of works written by other people. In the eyes of his own day's literati he was regarded as one of the important figures of American letters. He wrote on history, biography, archeology, moral philosophy, theology, travel, poetry, art, science, and literature. He said that the wide range of his interests kept him fresh and observant, and that he did better work for doing so much of it.

In 1845, Andrew Preston Peabody was the first to propose a graduate school for Harvard, and he wrote some oddly prophetic words:

> Why might there not be instituted at Cambridge a course of studies for students of much higher attainments than those now admitted,—a course on which the graduates of other colleges might be just qualified to enter? If pupils were received at Harvard at nearly the point of literary acquisition at which they are now sent forth, the institution would become at once and long continue without a rival the University of America. Studious young men from all other colleges and from every part of the United States would be drawn together there.
>
> The studies to be pursued, the books to be read, might with propriety be left in a great degree to the option of the student. Recitations might for the most part be superseded by lectures or by critical expositions. The attainment of a degree might be made to depend on a series of thorough, searching examinations.
>
> An institution thus organized would be of incalculable benefit to the whole country. Its influence would be at once most sensibly felt in the so-called learned professions. It would remove the reproach of juvenility. [How the memories must have smarted when

Andrew Preston Peabody recalled his own uncomfortable youth as a prodigy.] It would prescribe a thorough basis of liberal culture for those who aspire to eminence in professional life. It would fix the scholary habits of its graduates and make them reading, thinking, improving men for life; whereas now half our graduates can exhibit, ten years after leaving college, no marks of a liberal education except its parchment testimonial.

But all this, desirable as it is, is more than we can at present expect, although we believe that Harvard University is destined at some future time to assume this position; and we cannot but trust that, by calling the attention of our readers to the need of higher means of culture than are now enjoyed, we may have done something towards the ultimate supply of such means.

That article appeared in his own magazine. Besides writing for the *North American Review*, its editor thought nothing of contributing elsewhere. In 1837 he began writing for the *Whig Review*, and continued until 1859. He was an editor of the *Christian Register* from 1849 to 1852. And sometime he wrote on topics that specially interested him for the *American Monthly* and the *New England Magazine*.

Obviously, Andrew Preston Peabody stood high in the estimation of the churchmen of New England, because he accomplished so much so tastefully. In 1852 Harvard gave him an honorary degree of Doctor of Divinity. Eight years later he was chosen to be Preacher to Harvard University and Plummer Professor of Christian Morals.

So began Andrew Peabody's third career—as educator—for which he is possibly known best of all. During twenty-one years he taught at Harvard, and every year there arose a raft of stories about him, many concerning his manner of dealing with moral turpitude.

One time, during the summer vacation, two students wrote improper letters to two young ladies, and when these letters came, the girls showed them to their parents. The shocked parents sent them to the college, and they came to the hands of Dr. Peabody so he might deal with the problem.

In the fall, when the young men returned to the campus, he called them in. He asked if they knew the young ladies, and they said they did, whereupon he showed them the letters and said no more.

The young men read their own words, and became confused and uncomfortable.

Dr. Peabody simply looked at them, calmly.

They became more ill at ease.

"Young men," said Dr. Peabody, "I see by your looks that there is something in these letters which disturbs you. But I have not read a word of them. My sense of honor forbade my doing so. I am entirely ignorant of what they contain, except by inference. But if they are of the nature which I infer from your embarrassment, they had better be disposed of at once."

He threw the letters into the fire and spoke again.

". . . Never write anything which may come back long afterward to bring to your faces a sense of shame. Good morning, gentlemen."

So he dismissed two thoroughly chagrined college boys, and turned back to his work.

The terms of Dr. Peabody's association with Harvard called for him to teach ethics, conduct morning prayers, and preach at the required service on Sunday mornings in the college chapel. But, of course, this was not enough work for Andrew Preston Peabody, and at various times he taught logic, political economy, astronomy, Hebrew, and supervised the senior forensics. Twice, in 1862 and 1868, he was acting president of Harvard.

Wherever he was and whatever he was doing, he was soon known to the college as Dear Old Doctor Peabody, or Old Doc, and on Class Day no man received such hearty cheers as Old Doc. The reason was apparent: Doc Peabody was the silent intercessor between the students and the faculty; whenever possible he ameliorated the harsh discipline that still marked Harvard; he defended the students in faculty meetings; and when they were sick he went to call on them when their other professors did not even notice their absence.

At Harvard, Dr. Peabody continued to publish on a wide range of subjects. *Christianity, the Religion of Nature* came out in 1864, and went into several editions, also becoming Lowell Lectures. Then came *Sermons to Children*, in 1867, and *Reminiscences of European Travel*, 1868, another tangy travel book by this bright observer. He wrote on moral philosophy, Christianity, and science, a matter that some Christians did not like to consider in the days of Darwin, and he went to London to lecture on this subject. He also went to Rochester in the spring of 1863 for a Doctor of Laws degree.

Old Doc was a man of many parts, and of faultless character. When he took the job at Harvard, he decided that if he lived that long he would resign as a teacher at seventy, on the principle that a man grew too old to do a good job. So at seventy he retired and set off on another trip to Europe, writing furiously all the while.

The university was not enthusiastic about the resignation, and some officials even tried to talk him out of it, but Old Doc said he had too much to do, so it was agreed that he would become Professor Emeritus. He agreed, and then spent a solid year in Europe, effectively destroying any attempt anyone had considered to use his services. As to the college, it was an expensive exchange, because in no time at all they had six different ministers occupying the jobs that Old Doc had carried on his shoulders, besides his writing.

With a little more time Andrew Peabody got down to work again in earnest. He translated five ethical treatises of Cicero and Plutarch and for amusement knocked off a volume of *Harvard Reminiscences* and another called *Harvard Graduates I Have Known*, which became big sellers in the New England trade. He kept on preaching and published his sermons from time to time. In fact, besides reviews, books, articles, sermons, and letters, he also wrote and published some two hundred pamphlets.

On his return from the reinvigorating year in Europe, Dr. Peabody was elected to the Board of Overseers of Harvard and served with great gusto for ten years. He preached all around the Boston community, and in the summers at Nahant where he went for relaxation between books.

He became engaged in a number of enterprises more common to the twentieth century than the nineteenth. As noted, he was vitally interested in graduate education. He was also interested in ecumenicalism when the word was scarcely known by those who were not Roman Catholics or students of Greek. He was chairman of a committee of Catholic and Protestant clergymen who worked together for the good of the city of Cambridge. He was head of the school committee, and a school was named for him. He was vice-president of the American Academy of Arts and Sciences, and when he was asked to become president he said he would do so if he were younger and able to make all the changes he wished. He was vice-president of the American Antiquarian Society and of the American Oriental Society. He was a member and worker for the Massachusetts Historical Society, a manager of the Perkins Institute for the Blind, and vice-president of the American Peace Society.

At eighty he was still writing and still preaching. He used to spend a day on his social work, and then go home and write a sermon because he liked to write sermons at night.

"It rests me to write a sermon," he said.

Although he was always busy, Dr. Peabody was never in a hurry. He never minded interruptions, and he seldom appeared tired or irritated.

Generally speaking, after those early years in Portsmouth his health was good. He went walking every day and particularly enjoyed mountain climbing, because he discovered that it employed one set of muscles to go up and another set to come down. As he grew older he grew more stalwart, rather than weaker, and sometimes walked seven or eight miles a day.

He could and would talk on nearly any subject. He once spoke to the Harvard Medical School commencement on *What the Physician Should Be*. He wrote a paper for the Smithsonian Institution,

The Scientific Education of Mechanics and Artisans. He lectured on mathematics and once said that "to undervalue mathematics were blashpemy, did not the stupidness of the offender cancel his guilt."

Finally, Old Doc ran down, although he outlived by more than thirty years the wife he married in Portsmouth. (They had three daughters, no sons, so produced no more Peabodys.) In February, 1893, he suffered a fall. He lingered for a month and then died on March 10.

Eulogies were received from all over the world. An English writer said that what Arnold was to the boys at Rugby, Peabody was to the boys at Harvard. The college, which had represented one of his lives, put a marble bust of him in Gore Hall, commissioned a portrait, named a building for him, and put up a bronze tablet in his honor on the wall of Appleton Chapel.

Among the tributes was one from the rector of an Episcopal church in New Jersey who said, "You could not compare him with Isaiah or Paul. But you could not help likening him to Saint John, the beloved disciple, who was so near to his master."

And Old Doc was equally mourned at the Boston Wednesday Evening Club, where he was an honorary member, for his sparkling reminiscences and even spicy anecdotes.

One of the most fitting eulogies was that of Edward J. Young, teacher and writer, who spoke of Old Doc before the Massachusetts Historical Society three years after his death:

> Of course he was not an expert on these several subjects, and did not possess a minute knowledge of all their details. But he had a wide learning, sagacity, and experience, a comprehensive and well-furnished mind, and his addresses were profitable and interesting. Undoubtedly if he had concentrated his talents and his energy, he might have produced some great work, which would have given him rank among thinkers and scholars, and perhaps have secured for him fame in future generations. But he then would have sacrificed the influence which he exerted on his contemporaries. . . .

And, of course, that was just the point about Dr. Andrew Preston Peabody, for as his students at Harvard said on their bronze plaque in Appleton Chapel:

> . . . while for thirty-three years he moved among the Teachers and Students of Harvard College, and wist not that his face shown.

CHAPTER 17

THE MISSES PEABODY

ONCE UPON A TIME a young teacher at Phillips Andover Academy in Massachusetts courted a young praeceptress at the North Andover Academy for young ladies, won her hand, married her, and settled down, after a fashion, to raise a family. He was Nathaniel Peabody, and he was a fifth-generation descendant of old Francis Peabody of Topsfield through the fourth son Isaac. She was Elizabeth Palmer, daughter of a gentle but impoverished family.

Since neither party brought money to the marriage, it was a struggle. Nathaniel began studying with a local doctor in Billerica, became a physician, and then went to Harvard and studied dentistry. But as doctor or dentist, or even as a figure in society, Dr. Nathaniel was not to leave his mark directly upon the future. His share of the Peabody influence was to come through his three daughters, Elizabeth, Mary, and Sophia.

From their father, the girls inherited all that has been chronicled in these pages: an old American lineage, a sense of belonging to history, awareness of the intense respectability of the name. From their mother they inherited a feeling for family and a regard for social position. But in passing along this regard, Elizabeth Palmer also imbued in the girls the virtues of gentility, the regard for art and accomplishment and education that was to mark the careers of all her daughters. Yes, careers they were to have, of one kind and another—a sure sign of the changing ways of the nation.

The first of the girls, Elizabeth Palmer Peabody, was born in Billerica on May 16, 1804. The second, Mary Tyler Peabody, was born in Cambridgeport on November 16, 1806. The third, Sophia Amelia, was born on September 21, 1809. Three other children were born to the family, two boys and a girl, but they were to be totally eclipsed by their sisters in the story of the Peabodys, and two of them were to die young.

During the childhood of the girls, Dr. Peabody moved to Salem, and there the name was a door opener, for who in Salem did not know the Peabodys? Obviously, no matter what the relationship, the Nathaniel Peabodys were connected to that great shipping magnate Joseph Peabody, and so if the doctor was not as successful in his profession as he might be, still Mrs. Peabody and the children went to tea at the best houses and to entertainments when they could afford them.

In order to raise money that was badly needed in the family, their mother Elizabeth kept a school for young ladies. Daughter Elizabeth entered that school when she was four years old, and soon was outdistancing the other girls, although one, Elizabeth Hawthorne, had entered with a considerable knowledge of Shakespeare at the age of six.

So rapid was Elizabeth Peabody's progress, and so great the need for family assistance in a material way, that when she was sixteen years old she was virtually running the school for her mother. It had changed location several times, as the family moved from one Massachusetts community to another. During this period when Elizabeth was sixteen, the Peabodys were living in Lancaster. And when the dowdy, bright Elizabeth was not teaching, she was studying Greek.

When she was eighteen, Elizabeth (Lizzie, she was called) decided that she would go to Boston. Not right away, of course; in the first quarter of the nineteenth century such matters must be planned by a young lady, no matter how great her yearning or her spirit. But she would go.

So she did, to visit friends and to try to establish a school for young ladies, as well as to continue her Greek studies. She secured a Greek tutor whose name was Ralph Waldo Emerson, then nineteen, a year older than Elizabeth, and about to enter a theological seminary. She did well in Greek, and Emerson soon told her, in his tongue-tied way, that she knew so much he could not teach her. She did not do so well in her conquest of the city, and soon secured a position as governess to the family of Benjamin Vaughan in Hallowell, Maine. The Vaughans were an old family, English in descent, and extremely cultured by Boston or Salem standards. When Vaughan had come to America he brought with him a library of 10,000 volumes. Harvard College Library had only 12,000 volumes then. So in Maine, Lizzie had available to her literary resources almost as great as those of the nation's finest educational institution, and plenty of spare time in which to peruse them. Furthermore, the Vaughans—and there was a tribe of them living on this grand estate—were wordly people who knew Edinburgh, London, Paris, and Rome as well as they knew Boston, and better than they knew rude New York. In consorting with them, Elizabeth developed a polish that was quite unknown to her but quite apparent to the people outside this little community.

In a few months there was an opening at the estate of Robert Hallowell Gardiner (a relative by marriage of the Vaughans), and Elizabeth decided to take that job and bring her sister Mary up to the Vaughans to replace her as governess. Elizabeth was a managing person: she managed her sisters, she managed her mother, and she tried to manage her father, which resulted in many fierce arguments and much raising of the paternal voice. He did not manage, but the others did, and on the call that came by letter from Elizabeth, Mary packed up her bags docilely and went off to the Vaughan estate to become a governess, while Lizzie moved on to the Gardiners.

There Lizzie suddenly discovered that she was a young woman

and took pains with her person for a change: "I rigged myself in my black bombazeen which is trimmed with a very handsome crimson and black merino trimming. . . ."

Then she went to a meeting of the Reading Club which had been formed, and as it was her turn to read, she selected a piece from Frisbie's *Fragments:* "The gentlemen were very polite and I took the greatest pains to please them. I went and sat down by each who had formerly considered themselves neglected by me and made myself as agreeable as possible. . . ."

By such manners, Lizzie acquired a beau, and entered into an experience which would affect the course of her life. The beau was serious. He talked to Lizzie of love, and he asked her to marry him. She hesitated and refused to talk about it. She was frightened and fascinated. But one thing stood out in her mind—she would not be caught in the wilds of Maine for the rest of her life. There was only one place to live: Boston. She told her suitor that she could marry him only if they would live in Boston.

He, poor fellow, could not take her to Boston, at least not right away. Why, she never explained, but she turned him down, and when she did so, he committed suicide. The tragedy was to stay with Elizabeth Palmer Peabody for the rest of her life.

This shock and disagreement with the lordly Gardiners brought Lizzie back to Boston for a second attack. She and Mary started a school for girls in the quiet countryside of Brookline. Elizabeth was twenty-one and Mary was nineteen, but they were good teachers, better by far than most who taught young girls in those days.

While all this was going on, in 1825, Sophia, the youngest, was being made into an invalid by her mother. She had problems, no doubt about it: she suffered from headaches that in a later day would be termed migraine. But perhaps they were nervous headaches brought on by her mother, who wanted desperately to keep Sophia at home and kept telling the girl how sick she was. Dr. Peabody was called on to dose his daughter with drugs until he began to worry about the quantity—and then there were arguments, which he could not abide, so Sophia was dosed some more.

Sophia was the artistic member of the family. She had studied drawing with one of her aunts, and also became quite expert at Latin and French. She pursued her course, painting and drawing, quarreling with her mother, but returning home as a dutiful daughter and lapsing into the role of an invalid.

Lizzie, when her school in Brookline was successful, came back to reopen the assault on Boston, and bearded Dr. William Ellery Channing, the greatest preacher of the day. The fact was that she had fallen in love with him—or the man she thought he was. Although he was a quarter of a century older than she, and married to a rich cousin, she insisted on being near him. She established herself in a room in a respectable Boston boardinghouse, made herself acquainted with Dr. Channing's parishioners, and urged him to have his sermons copied and printed, saying she would copy them. He demurred but there was no escaping an aroused Lizzie, and he did not get away.

Channning was the lion of Boston's literary society, and when the respectable Miss Peabody went walking with or copied for Dr. Channing, in a most respectable way, her career was made. Soon Dr. Channing's daughter was in her school, along with thirty others.

So the school prospered, and Elizabeth became better and better known in Boston. Finally she moved her family to Boston in 1828—father, mother, and children all came to take a house, and only Father groaned at giving up at least part of his Salem dental practice. But Elizabeth would have her way, and he was not strong enough to oppose her.

In Boston, Elizabeth continued to work miracles. The better art teachers charged twenty-four dollars an hour for lessons, but Lizzie pushed and pulled Boston artists until they came to teach for nothing. Francis Graeter came, and then Thomas Doughty, a famous landscape painter of the period, then Chester Harding, quite the rage for his portraits and the object of Gilbert Stuart's envy. Harding, who came in 1830, painted Sophia, showing her as a wide-eyed girl, with perhaps too much nose to be beautiful, and her hair cut short and set in ringlets that swept away from the middle part of her head.

Having the family in Boston made life easier for Elizabeth because she could pursue her intellectual friendships without worry about wagging tongues. Bronson Alcott and his wife came to the house for dinner—but Lizzie talked all the time they were there, and so Sophia and the others learned little about him. Lizzie was an intellectual, there was no question about that—she shared Madame de Staël's attitude that brains were an international and bisexual commodity, that genius knew no sex—and she was out to prove it.

But intellectual as she might be, Lizzie was not a good business manager. She took into partnership, because of his stunning manners, an educator named William Russell, and in a few months he had spent so much of their money on his wardrobe and dinners that the school was insolvent. So Lizzie went to New Bedford, and all the other Peabodys went back to Salem, except Sophia, who decided to escape by going to visit a friend in Dedham. While there Sophia caught the attention of Washington Allston, popular painter of the period, and was properly impressed by his attentions. (She was really a promising young artist; not all these painters could be simply flattering.) She visited the young George Flagg, and he visited her and pontificated about her talent. And then she went home to Salem, as everyone knew she would do, and painted and played semi-invalid again.

In the spring of 1833 Elizabeth returned to Boston again. She brought Mary and set up a school in a room in their boardinghouse, which was run by a Mrs. Clarke. Here Mary met Horace Mann, a young lawyer, legislator, widower, and crusader for help for the mentally ill.

Back in Salem, Sophia wanted to come and teach art in her sister's school, but Mrs. Peabody said she was much too weak, and Sophia subsided, painting to ease the tension she found in living at home. In Boston, Elizabeth took over young Mr. Mann, as an intellectual exercise, in between her teaching and her writing of books—for she had begun writing for young scholars about the history of the world.

Elizabeth was brave as well as indefatigable, or she had unlimited confidence in herself. She undertook her book—the first—raising the capital for the printing, and agreeing to take a 10 percent royalty. She proposed that Sophia illustrate the book for her; it was to be *Grecian Theology and Mythology*. Lizzie insisted, with the insouciance of the completely uninformed, that Sophia should make lithographs—and Sophia tried, although she did not know how. They were terrible. Lizzie said they were fine, but Sophia said they were just as bad as they really were (she really knew) and she began dreaming of Elizabeth dead and having serious nightmares.

Lizzie knew what to do, she always did. She arranged for Sophia and Mary to go to Cuba where Sophia was to recover her health and Mary was to be governess to a planter's family. Sophia would live with the family, too.

So off they went in December to Havana. Sophia took up with a rake named James Burroughs on the trip aboard the brig *Newcastle* and threatened to disgrace the family. They went to the Morell hacienda, a day's journey from Havana, where they were to live and teach the children, and immediately (beginning the moment she left her mother) Sophia began to improve. They rode forty-five miles to the hacienda over bad roads, and Sophia slept that night as soundly as a baby. Soon she had ensalved a young Spanish don. She went thundering about the hacienda on horseback, her ringlets falling over her eyes, and then went dancing!

Her mother, back at home, trembled in fear for her daughter's health and warned her sternly against waltzing and riding. But Sophia's health so improved that she was soon quite scandalously involved with Burroughs, and everybody back in Boston was talking about it. And Mary, poor Mary, not hearing from Horace Mann, her appetite grew slender and she seemed pale and wasted.

But eventually matters took a turn for the better. Sophia was persuaded to stop being so flamboyant in her relations with men, and Mary heard from Horace Mann!

It was fortunate, in a way, that Mary's correspondence with Horace Mann began when it did, because in her own fashion Elizabeth was showing more than friendly interest in him. It was all very intellectual, of course, discussions of eternity and the existence of an almighty being, and theories of education, but it was very frequent; and in years to come, when Mary saw the letters that Elizabeth had saved, she realized that her sister was more than mildly interested in the young lawyer.

The spring of 1828 brought Mary and Sophia back from Cuba, and soon the family was ensconced in a big three-story frame house on Salem's Charter Street, where Dr. Peabody had his office, Mother Peabody had her parlor, and the girls had the garden.

Two years later Nathaniel Hawthorne began coming to the house to call. There was some acquaintance between the families dating back to the years when Mrs. Hawthorne had been persuaded to send her Elizabeth to the first Peabody school, but Hawthorne was now a successful author (*Twice-Told Tales*). At first Sophia would not even go down to see him, but soon she was fascinated when Lizzie reported that Hawthorne was "as handsome as Lord Byron"—and she found that he was. The moment she saw him, she was electrified, and so was he with this pale wraith of a girl. It was love at first sight.

Soon Hawthorne was inscribing books to Sophia, and then he was so bold as to dedicate *The Gentle Boy* to her. The reason: Sophia had made a drawing of the character Ibrahim, and to him that drawing became the character, and in words he built around what she had imagined and drawn. So here was the Peabody influence at work again.

Sophia's health, aided by the stay in Cuba and encouraged by love, became remarkably good and she ceased to be an invalid altogether; one could sense in the long walks she took with Hawthorne that she was growing robust. Mother Peabody was insistent

that Sophia never marry, so when the young couple became engaged, they kept it secret from her for a long time.

Sophia worked at her art, took up sculpture, and Hawthorne
struggled with the economics of writing, trying to secure enough
money in hand to get married. Finally, in 1842, they wed, after
several false starts and much opposition from Mother Peabody. She
finally succumbed to all the rest of the family, insisting only that
Sophia must never, never have a child.

The Hawthornes went to live in Concord in a big old house he
called "the old Manse." Their gardener was Thoreau, who was
sent over to them by the Emersons. The naturalist and philosopher
had taken up gardening as part of the simple life just that year.
Sophia quite won his heart by lending him her favorite music box.
Another touch of the Peabody influence? Thoreau liked the Hawthornes, and one is influenced by the people one likes—so the influence was there, an influence for gentleness, love of beauty, and
joy in the world—that was Sophia in the summer of 1842.

They lived in a world of ideas and letters, with Margaret Fuller
coming to call, the Emersons, and Elizabeth Hoar. Sophia soon
was delighted to learn that she was pregnant; she had some anxious
moments about her ability to conceive, but then in March, 1844,
Una Hawthorne was born. The happy family settled down to an
idyllic existence, troubled only about the shortage of money, which
at that moment was not so severe as to make them miserable.

Mary was married, too. She and Horace Mann married suddenly
in 1843 after he had taken a position as Secretary of Education,
the first to hold the job in Massachusetts.

And what influence had the Peabody women on Horace Mann?
For one thing, he went around the state holding what he called
"revival meetings" in which he discussed the future of public education. He talked of the superiority of women over men as school-
teachers, and some of that feeling he must have secured in his talks
with Lizzie and Mary Peabody at the boardinghouse and in his
observations of Mary over the years of their acquaintance and
courtship.

They were married and went rushing off aboard the *Britannia*, to Europe, where Horace studied educational systems, finding as many schools of which he disapproved as otherwise. It was in Germany that he found the best of the school systems—and he discovered this through his interpreter, Mary, who spoke the language of which he knew not a word. When they came home, she spent many weary hours translating German documents and books for Horace's report on European education. The report, when delivered, was to cause a ferocious controversy, but eventually to lead to the reformation of the Massachusetts public schools and to influence American education everywhere. Not a small part of it was the Peabody influence.

As far as Sophia was concerned, the rest of her married life was happy. Hawthorne wrote and he took a job as American consul in Liverpool to support his writings. In his writings his wife often appeared, and so did his inlaws.

Mary's influences were more overt. In 1848 on the death of U.S. Representative John Quincy Adams (influenced in his lifetime by Stephen Peabody), Horace Mann was appointed to fill the vacancy. And when Horace took the boiling Drayton case in Washington, Mary backed him to the hilt. The case involved a master of a schooner who had carried fugitive slaves into free territory, and it had aroused the South. As an ardent abolitionist, Mann was really in physical danger during the conduct of the affair, and had his wife said no, he might not have continued to the end. In 1852, Horace Mann went to Antioch College in Yellow Springs, Ohio, and Mary went with him. He was to be president of the new liberal college, where women were to be educated as well as men.

The influence was here dissipated, as Antioch did badly by Horace Mann, and Mary objected. They parted, really, the summer of 1859 when she went back east to recover from a bout with typhoid. Mann died in Antoich, and then Mary lapsed into the quiet life of a widow, raising her children.

In 1858, after the stint as American consul in England, Nathaniel

Hawthorne took Sophia and the children to Rome. Sophia was the central female character in Hawthorne's *The Marble Faun*, written that year. They met and mingled with the Brownings in Italy, and discussed art and literature. In the sense that intimate circles always show the influence of one person on another, Sophia was an influence of light and beauty on the ebullient Browning and his dark, strange wife. Elizabeth Barrett Browning really *liked* Sophia, and she really liked very few women. When one of the Hawthorne children was very ill, Mrs. Browning came around like a true small-town American friend. Then, when Hawthorne died, Sophia lapsed into difficulties, struggling with a careless, indifferent, and dishonest publisher over the cheating of the author in the accounts rendered on his books. She died in 1871, saying at the last that she had lived out her life after Hawthorne's death only for the children, because she wanted nothing more than to be with their father.

CHAPTER 18

ELIZABETH

ELIZABETH PALMER PEABODY's course had separated from the lives of her sisters on the day they went off to Cuba aboard the brig *Newcastle* in 1833. Until then they had been inseparable, or at least their affairs had been inseparable, and the strongest and oldest of them Elizabeth dominated the others. But when they went to Cuba, and Sophia discovered her beauty, her attractiveness to men, and her health; and when Mary found her love for Horace Mann and had it reciprocated (by mail), then the younger girls began to move away from the shadow of their older sister. But the change was definite and recognizable only in 1840, and that was the year Elizabeth acquired a house at 13 West Street in Boston, established it as a home for her family and a shop for herself.

After many years of teaching, Elizabeth had gone to work for Bronson Alcott, the pedagogue and preacher, who had shocked all New England with his ultraliberal approaches to life and education. (He would most certainly have been called a Communist in the twentieth century, and he probably would have *been* one.) His Temple School failed in disgrace, and as his assistant Elizabeth, who had never been paid a penny by the irresponsible Alcott, was in the sad position of being unemployable.

With the doors of other schools closed to her because of her association with Alcott, Elizabeth Peabody decided to go into business. She would open a bookshop.

The world of books had fascinated her for a long time. During her association with Alcott, almost her entire income had come from the books she had herself written. She produced three volumes of ancient history for youngsters and a Christmas book called *The Casket*. She also wrote innumerable articles for the "little" newspapers and magazines, which brought much praise within the intellectual circle and nearly no money. Her book about the Alcott experiment, called *Record of a School Exemplifying the Principles and Methods of Moral Culture*, actually cost her money. Elizabeth had signed the usual publishing contract of the day with the publisher, James Monroe. One night all the unsold copies of *Record of a School* were burned up in a warehouse fire, and reading the fine print of her agreement, she discovered that she had to pay for the publisher's loss, which caused her real financial problems.

Elizabeth Peabody's idea of a bookshop was unique, even revolutionary, and utterly charming. She looked at books from the viewpoint of author and reader, not that of businesswoman. Books were written by people about people, and for people, she said, and a bookshop, then, should be a meetingplace for the exchange of ideas. She would encourage authors to come there to speak and readers to come to listen and buy books.

So the bookshop came into being. Shelves were constructed in the front parlor of 13 West Street, and a big rocker was put in the front window. Here Mrs. Peabody would sit as principal custodian. Various English magazines, *Punch*, *Blackwood's* the *Illustrated London News*, and ladies' magazines, were available for sale or on loan for a small fee. Works in German, French, and Italian were stocked—one could hardly learn botany, for example, without studying the Germans because they were by far the leaders in the field, and most of the works were not yet translated.

Soon the intellectuals of Boston were, indeed, coming to the bookshop. Dr. Channing came often, as well as the Emersons and Dr. Holmes. On Wednesdays, Margaret Fuller held Conversations there. Chairs were brought up from the basement and set up in every nook in the house (including the doctor's upstairs office, to his indignation), and ladies of all ages and conditions came from Cambridge and Brookline and Beacon Street to listen to the lady who considered herself the greatest of all female orators.

So the bookshop flourished. Under Mother Peabody's eagle eye, few of the ladies escaped a session without buying a new book. She quickly learned their tastes and the extent of their collections, and she, the mother, became the champion retailer of the clan. Elizabeth, having pioneered and started the bookshop—having gone into trade to the shock of much of the Boston business world— exerted the now-famous Peabody influence in a new and startling direction. She became Boston's first lady publisher.

Elizabeth was wise enough to know that there would be preju- dice against a lady publisher, so she referred to herself as E. P. Peabody. Few women in Boston would have considered such a career in a business that was as cutthroat as any in the world. Bio- grapher Louise Hall Tharp put it this way:

> . . . Elizabeth imagined that she was cautious, good at arithmetic, and sure to make money. She thought that honesty could be made to pay in a business which was unscrupulous to a degree at a time when business ethics were almost nonexistent in many quarters.

Elizabeth would have also become the first lady printer, had she thought she could get away with it, but she knew every one of her acquaintances would have turned against her—a woman meddling with machinery! A woman directing men! A woman with ink on her face!

No, as she told Dr. Channing, she was resigned to jobbing out the printing of the books she would publish, and would confine herself to assembling the editorial material and selling the printed and bound result.

Elizabeth's very first publishing venture could have earned her fortune. Dr. Channing submitted his pamphlet on Emancipation— the burning issue of the day in New England. He offered to *give* it to her, let her take all the profits from publishing. He knew, and she knew, that the pamphlet would sell many hundreds of thousands of copies in North and South, that it would cause the northern Abolitionists to smack their lips and the southern slaveowners to gnash their teeth—but it would be bought and read. The Anti-Slavery Society came to Elizabeth, and in one of her typical bursts of generosity she promised to sell them the pamphlet at cost. Thus, out the window went a best-seller and the strong beginning of a new publishing venture.

Elizabeth was a very happy woman in these years. She was one with the Transcendentalists (the name given the Emerson crowd of intellectuals by their enemies because of Emerson's *Nature*). This group of poets and writers of prose flourished in Boston. There was William Ellery Channing, not well known to the twentieth century, but very well known indeed to his own. There were Thoreau and Emerson and Dr. Holmes, and a dozen lesser lights, including, of course, Sophia's Hawthorne, who even went so far as to *invest* in the communal Brook Farm, live there, and become manager of finances before Brook's marriage!

Bronson Alcott had started a publication called the *Dial*, and the Transcendentalists took it over as their literary magazine. The hallmark of the *Dial* was a search for a new freedom in poetry, and it slashed its way through tradition and hoary lines of thinking, shocking the traditionalists with every issue and livening up the American literary atmosphere.

Lizzie joined in with a fine flourish: attacking the established order of religion in a contribution to the magazine called *A Glimpse of Christ's Idea of Society*. As much later Bernard Shaw was to do, she suggested that there was not much wrong with Christianity except that nobody practiced it. She came right out with the communal ideas of the Reverend George Ripley—destroy the family as a unit, establish the community, to each according to his need, from each according to his ability. Communism, no less! The clergy dropped their Bibles and picked up the *Dial*, and one could hear the indignant rustling of their beards from the north shore to the south, as they mouthed their indignant protests.

In that one article Lizzie provided the stricken fundamentalists with enough material for six months of sermons.

In 1841, Lizzie became publisher of the *Dial* with Margaret Fuller as editor. But there were no profits for the editor's salary, and so Miss Fuller resigned and Emerson became editor.

The *Dial* established Lizzie as one of the Transcendentalists and secured her place in the literary history of America. As to Peabody influence, here was a distaff member of the family in the forefront of the most influential literary movement of the years before the Civil War. She became famous as a publisher, too. Hawthorne gave her his *Grandfather's Chair; A History for Youth* and his *Famous Old People* and *Liberty Tree*.

The bookshop became the headquarters for Ripley's communist movement which would culminate in the establishment (and total failure) of Brook Farm Institute of Agriculture and Education. But Hawthorne left Brook Farm to be married and then go abroad, and in the fulfillment, the dream lost its golden lining, and the Transcendentalist movement drifted away from West Street, away from any headquarters at all. Like any literary movement, it had its brightest hopes and most shining hours in the days of promise, and those days could almost be counted in moments.

The decline of the shop began with the death of Channing in 1842. Then Elizabeth's friend the painter Allston died. A few months later Margaret Fuller took her ideas about womanhood and strength to New York to become literary critic for Horace Greeley's *Tribune*, and although she took a share of Peabody influence with her, it was out of sight, out of mind, and there was too much new and different in New York for Miss Fuller to remember back to the dear dead days in Boston for long.

By 1845 business at the bookstore was at a standstill. The literary movement had lost its currency. The not-quite-suffragette female movement was dead, with Miss Fuller's passing, and there were no more meetings in the parlor at 13 West Street, no more scurryings about for chairs from dining room and kitchen. In 1848, Mother Peabody, the shopkeeper, remarked ruefully that they had not taken in even half a dollar in a two-day period. Time having healed many breaches, Elizabeth was back to teaching school again, in an academy for boys opened by a Hungarian educator, Dr. Kraitsir, who claimed to have a theory of teaching languages that would unlock all doors to all students. Lizzie printed a pamphlet on the theory; Harvard students flocked to public lectures to learn the secrets and thus get passing marks in their German and French; and the enthusiasm remained until the students discovered that all Dr. Kraitsir was selling was an unusually hard course of study.

Eventually Kraitsir went back to Hungary to become a revolutionary, and that little flurry died down.

In 1849, Elizabeth decided to start a new magazine. She had really gone out of the publishing business in 1843 when she quit publishing the *Dial* because she was losing too much money on it, but she was hopeful again. This periodical was called *Aesthetic Papers*. It lasted one issue, and small wonder! Elizabeth's own contribution was an article suggesting that prancing Bostonians go about the common arrayed in sheets and dancing in bare feet. She quite forgot about the climate of Boston in her enthusiasm. But there was much more to it than that, if we consider the Peabody influence, for here was one of the first open declarations for the teaching of the arts in public schools. Lizzie came out for music and dancing and art, and as educators have been doing since the dawn of time, she looked at the cost of the Mexican war, and lamented the fact that Americans had so much to spend on bullets and so little to spend on pencils.

Never one to quit, and as creative as ever in developing new ideas, Lizzie soon came upon a plan for the coloring of charts to make the learning of historical dates easy. Her biographer, Louise Hall Tharp, remarks that "anyone with sufficient patience to work out the meaning of the colored squares must have found the memorizing of dates mere recreation," but Lizzie spent many, many hours coloring her charts because she could not afford to have them printed. She tried then to sell the idea to the Boston and then to the Massachusetts school systems, and Horace Mann, the Secretary or Superintendent of Education for the state, tried to help her. But the educators were not like the educators of the twentieth century; they looked on new ideas with suspicion rather than embracing one after another, to the exclusion of Lizzie's charts.

In November, 1850, Lizzie was off west in Great Barrington, selling charts and lecturing. For nearly a year she followed this course, touring New England, making enough money to support her mother and father and herself.

Then, by the end of 1850 it became apparent that the West Street house was expensive and not very useful. The shop was not paying its way, and the neighborhood was becoming full of business establishments; there was still the view of Boston Common from the end of the street, but that was no longer enough. The parents were taken to live at a farm in West Newton, and Lizzie went back to selling her historical charts on the road.

For ten years she continued to play will o' the wisp, and then Elizabeth came upon an idea which further extended her influence on American affairs. She became enamored of the theories of a German educator named Friedrich Froebel. Froebel was the father of the idea of permissive education. He did not accept the use of the ruler or the switch; he advocated the training of the child's five senses, and the enjoyment of youth rather than the development of fear of God and man.

On this theory, Elizabeth started the Pinckney Street Kindergarten. It was 1861 and she was fifty-seven years old, but just as filled with energy as ever. She had adopted certain ways of her own—when she traveled she never carried baggage any more but wore her nightgown under her dress and took her toothbrush in her pocket. So she was happy and carefree as a summer's faun. Father and mother were dead by this time, Sophia was gone, too, and Elizabeth and Mary were partners again in everything, including the new school. They published a *Moral Culture of Infancy and Kindergarten Guide*, and it was successful in the educational field. The kindergarten succeeded, and in 1867 Lizzie went to Europe to study foreign ways, heading straight for Germany

(*Kindergarten* is a German word, of course), armed with letters from Carl Schurz, the German-American Republican politician, and other friends. She visited kindergartens much more advanced than her own, modeled on the Froebel plan. She became responsible, too, for the wide spread of the kindergarten in America, returning from Europe with the expanded idea that she would establish kindergartens from coast to coast. In 1870 she founded the first free public kindergarten in the United States. Kindergartens were then part of the New York schools, and had extended to Philadelphia, St. Louis, and San Francisco.

At seventy-three, in 1877, Lizzie suffered a slight stroke and was told to slow down. But she recovered sufficiently to take up her old stride. Six years later she was still going strong, and espoused a new cause. The Princess Winnemucca, an Indian lady whose real name was Sarah Winnemucca Hopkins, interested the Peabody sisters in the cause of the Indians, particularly her own Paiute tribe, and they took up the cudgels to right old wrongs. Mary wrote a book, *Life among the Paiutes; Their Wrongs and Claims* and Lizzie spoke about it and promoted it. Thus Princess Winnemucca was able to begin raising money for schools for the Indian children, to start them on the long, tortuous road of entrance to American society. One success begat another, and soon the Princess in full Indian regalia, and Lizzie in an old, once chic dress covered with laces and figured silks that had been given her by a wealthy actress friend, hired halls and gave the lectures, during which the Princess sang sad Indian songs and looked mournful about the plight of her people.

Unfortunately, the schools the Princess was to start were never really established, and she could not account for the money—so the cause collapsed, even though Lizzie went to Washington to speak firmly to President Grover Cleveland about the plight of the Paiutes.

Mary wrote a romance about her old days in Cuba, and as she finished it in the first weeks of 1877 she put it aside. On February 11, she recalled her own words when her beloved Horace had died so long ago—"My beloved, I will come and we will go on together" —and now, this day she kept her promise.

So Lizzie was alone at seventy-three, and she sat down to write her *Reminiscences of William Ellery Channing*, which sold fairly well. She also published *Last Evening with Allston, and other papers*, including materials she had written for the *Dial* and other magazines.

In 1882, Lizzie accepted an invitation to lecture at the Concord School of Philosophy and was so popular that she was asked back for a second series. She took up the cause of women's suffrage, and was so successful as to rouse the ire of proper Bostonians. Henry James made her an important character in *The Bostonians*, calling her Miss Birdseye and transforming her into an outrageous person, shabby-genteel, altruistic to a fault, and absolutely out of her mind about women's rights. The facts were more or less correct: Lizzie had been all these things, but she was very much more, a great human being who at the age of eighty-four asked Longfellow after a dinner party if he could tell her the best books to study to learn Chinese.

Early in January, 1894, Lizzie's ample, grandmotherly figure ceased to be seen marching up and down the Boston streets, on the way to this meeting, or returning home late from that one. She was confined to her bedroom, never to come forth again. On January 4, she died, in her ninetieth year, having become in those ninety years a Boston institution, leaving a mark on American letters and education that would never be erased.

There was something a little awesome about the lives of the three Peabody sisters, almost as if their careers were preordained. Sophia was precisely the right wife for the sensitive Hawthorne, and their love match enhanced his creative powers, besides making his life an inordinately happy one for a writer. Mary kept the feet of the idealistic Horace Mann on the ground, and although he refused to listen to her when she saw more clearly than he that the businessmen who had promised so much in Yellow Springs were not living up to their promises, still she forgave him everything, and carried on his works and his memory. But Elizabeth, Lizzie, was the strongest and the most dedicated of all to the cause of humanity and the education of people. Without Lizzie, Bronson Alcott would never have succeeded in shocking Boston. Without Lizzie, the Transcendentalists might never have become a coalescent group. Without Lizzie, the idea of the American kindergarten might have foundered. Without Lizzie, the cause of women's suffrage would have been a little further behind schedule. Elizabeth Peabody had an enduring influence upon the American scene.

CHAPTER 19

THE UNIVERSITY PRESIDENT

DOWN THROUGH THE FAMILY of Oliver William Bourne Peabody in the Vermont branch came a line of hardy intellectuals and adventurers, into which was born one man who would journey far afield and add a chapter to the story of the influence of the Peabody family in the affairs of the United States. He was Selim Hobart Peabody.

In 1829 when Selim Hobart was born, his father was the minister of the established church—which meant Puritan, or Congregational as it later became—in the village of Rockingham, Vermont.

The family lived in the minister's residence provided by the townspeople, a big white Vermont barn of a house where they were cool in summer and cold in winter, heated only by the fireplaces. The townspeople supplied wood for the fires and the salary of the minister, much of which was paid in kind. So during the harvest season the Peabodys were busy hanging bags of potatoes and stacking bushel baskets of apples and corn and rutabags. The farmers brought them grain, which the children took down to the mill in the village to be ground into flour. They had hams and sides of bacon, and when a family butchered beef almost always the parson and his family received a chunk of it.

The tawny gold-headed boy had little time to enjoy himself as a child, for the Reverend Charles Hobart Peabody believed in a strict regimen for the young. When Selim was four years old his lessons began, and they were no-nonsense lessons—absolutely nothing like those Lizzie Peabody would institute in Boston and across the country half a century later. The first task was to teach little Selim to read and write so he could learn his Bible. And so the lessons began, for two hours every afternoon in the parson's study, with Walker's dictionary as the basic book; and then as the boy learned to make out the letters, pronounce them, and move onto sentences, the Bible became his text.

As he grew, the lessons became longer, and he spent more time with his father. He studied Weems's *Life of Washington*. He also chopped the wood for the fires, milked the cow, carried the slops, burned the trash, and hoed the gardens in the summertime.

The parson owned a chaise, a one-horse vehicle with a cloth top for protection against the weather, which seated one passenger beside the driver. It was similar to "the wonderful one-hoss shay" immortalized by Dr. Oliver Wendell Holmes in his poem "The Deacon's Masterpiece," a favorite of preachers and physicians who spent much time on the road. By the time he was six years old, little Selim spent the afternoon driving with his father on the parson's calls, to learn the ways of the world, provide companionship, and receive the lessons which were taught him on the road.

By the time he was seven years old Selim had read Milton's *Paradise Lost* with enjoyment, and when he was twelve he was familiar with Greek and Hebrew and was beginning Latin.

All this education was marvelous for a boy who would be a preacher like his father. But Selim had no intention at all of becoming a minister. At seven he thought he might be a farmer, but as the chores grew harder he decided against that course; and then one day he saw a Concord coach, and he decided then and there that he would be a stagecoach driver, with a span of six under his hand, careening along the high road by day, traveling to the far corners of America—maybe even as far west as Albany.

As a boy, Selim had no toys—not one, except those he made for himself. His father believed toys were the instruments of the devil, and Selim was warned daily against the work of the devil and was exhorted to follow the ways of the Lord and expect his reward in the country beyond death. But within his limits, the father was a kind man, and on one trip to a nearby town, when Selim admired a china pitcher they saw in a store, the father bought it for him.

Life in this Peabody household tended to be grim. Although some of the old Puritan ways were changing, the Reverend Charles Hobart believed his family must set an upright example, and so even when his parishioners began relaxing the food laws, he did not. Consequently from sundown on Saturday night until sundown on Sunday night no fire was lit in the kitchen, no food was cooked, and they ate the cold provisions that Mother Peabody had put away for the holy day when no one was to work. In winter the cold meals were miserable, a piece of bread and a chunk of cheese or meat did not warm a small boy for the two long sermons he must undergo every Sunday. But luckily, Sunday came to an end at the time of the three stars that could be seen on a clear night, and then there was a hot meal, the liveliest of the week, and much rejoicing around the table. On Selim Hobart's part, although his father never suspected, the rejoicing was that Sunday was ending.

During the last year of his life at Rockingham, Selim was in trouble a great deal. On April Fool's Day he became so immersed in the spirit of the unofficial holiday that he planned a great joke on his father. The minister was partial to apples and ate them from the early ripening of the summer and all through the winter, as long as the supply lasted. Knowing that his father ate an apple regularly in the afternoon, Selim got a big red one, hollowed it out, and filled it with ashes, replacing the cap so that to an unsuspecting nibbler the fruit seemed quite whole and sound. When his father took a great bite from this apple, his mouth filled with ashes, his jaw dropped, he spat, choked, and seized his handkerchief, and the next few minutes were confusion as he cleaned his mouth and cleared away the debris. Selim scarcely had time to laugh and say April Fool before he was speared by a reproachful,

hurt, and angry glance from the old man. Selim was not punished—
the Reverend Charles Hobart recognized April Fool's Day—but he
never forgave his son for playing the trick on him.

Selim was punished, and harshly, for violations of the Reverend
Charles Hobart's code of conduct. One day, when guests came to
the house, the boy was playing with a little music box, which he
kept hidden in his room without the knowledge of his father, for
a music box was an instrument of the devil. When the guests arrived, Selim stuffed the box under the covers of his bed and rushed
downstairs to greet them as was demanded of him. Then, horror
of horrors, the music box slipped out from under the covers, rolled
to the floor, and began playing. The Reverend Charles Hobart
looked at his son angrily, and Selim rushed upstairs to clap the
top on the box and stop the unseemly noise that was poisoning the
atmosphere. He spent the rest of the evening in torture and for
good reason, for he knew what was coming. He was thrashed
soundly with his father's heavy belt for breaking God's law and
exhibiting levity.

In any village of youngsters, the minister's son was always regarded with a certain contempt as a goody-goody because he was
forbidden so many boyish activities by the nature of his father's
occupation. Selim was no exception. His father was also president
of the local board of education, and as such the main giver of laws
about the operation of the schools. Many of the strict rules governing scholarship and scholars were resented by the local teen-agers,
and some of them determined that they would take it out on the
son. The town bully—was there not always one?—began harrying
Selim on his way to and from school, and Selim did not like it. He
asked his father for support, and the minister sternly abjured him
against violence. If he fought he would be thrashed.

The teacher at the school observed this situation and sympathized
openly with Selim. He even went so far as to try to persuade the
Reverend Charles Hobart that his son be allowed to protect himself. But the father said that Selim must bear the cross of ignominy
as one of his Christian duties.

So the harrying went on—tugged coats in school, inkpots upset on his hands, chairs pulled from beneath him—all the petty violence that youngsters can muster was practiced on Selim, until his patience would stand no more.

One afternoon, when the bully began picking on him in the school yard, confident that the minister's son would not fight back, Selim lost all restraint, and unleashed with the fury of a whirlwind, fought off his larger opponent, knocked him down, and caused the bully to cry "uncle." The village tattletale went rushing to the school door to tell the story to the teacher—so that all the town would know—but the teacher firmly shut the door and locked it from the inside. He had seen nothing.

It made no difference. The bully had left his mark on Selim's eye, and when he returned home, his mother saw it and shook her head sadly; both knew what would come. His father saw, asked the question—fighting?—and Selim went to the woodshed to lower his trousers and be thrashed again.

In one way the Reverend Charles Hobart Peabody was a particularly callous father. He simply assumed that Selim would be a minister and never once asked him his preferences. So after this year in which so many untoward occurrences had passed, it was decided that Selim should be sent to Boston to the Boston Latin School. He could go cheaply, and such an education would fit him remarkably well for Harvard College and the ministry.

It was 1841 when Selim went to Boston Latin School. His father died that year, and he was supported there by a friend of the family who was also an admirer of his mother.

At that time the Boston Latin School was precisely what its name implied: a school for the study of Latin. When Selim appeared before the headmaster on his arrival at the school, that gentleman looked him up and down and asked him if he thought he could become a Latin scholar. Hesitantly Selim said he thought so.

Could Selim memorize this, asked the master, pointing to a thick Latin grammar?

Selim did not answer.

Could he memorize the grammar so that he could, on request, recite the precise facts from any given page?

No one could do that, Selim said.

The master smiled. He opened the door and called, "Everett, would you please come in here," whereupon a small boy, about Selim's own size, came hesitantly into the room and stood up straight as a stick in front of the headmaster's desk.

"Page six, line five, Everett, if you please," said the headmaster, opening the grammar so Selim might look on it with him.

The other boy opened his mouth, and out of it, as if by magic, came the words that appeared on the page.

"Page nine, line three," was the order. And again the performance was repeated.

Everett was dismissed, and he went away like a little soldier. The headmaster looked at Selim.

"Now," said the headmaster, "it has been established that it can be done. If it can be done, can *you* do it?"

Selim's courage returned. If it could be done, he could do it. He said so.

The headmaster nodded, satisfied, and like the other boy, Selim was dismissed, leaving the room with a new set to his shoulders.

The headmaster was not fooling about the difficulty of the work. Selim was assigned to a class of boys, and his new master called him aside on the very first day and explained the class procedure.

They would work with the Latin grammar at hand, he said. A boy came to class in the morning, prepared to recite the first assignment. The master would listen to the recitation and then give a grade.

"One" meant the work was satisfactory. "Two" meant the work was passing. "Three" meant the work was on the verge of failure; it was a warning. "Four" meant failure—and a caning. "Five" meant total failure, upon which the boy would be sent home from the school.

So Selim set out on his rocky road of education. His first recitation earned him a three and a warning. His second earned him a four and a caning—but then he caught hold, and thereafter the vast majority of his recitations were met by ones and twos.

Each morning Selim arose in the room where he boarded and broke the ice in the pitcher so he could wash his face in the basin on the dry sink. Then he dressed, shivering, and went down to his breakfast of porridge. Afterward it was off to school, to meet the first recitation, followed by a study period and a second recitation. In all there were four recitations a day, each subject to the harsh system of grading.

No other course was taught. It was all Latin. But then, when spring came, and the green buds began to thrust their tendrils out of the brown ground and the ends of the tree branches, the headmaster, too, felt the need for a change. Algebra was introduced as a mental relaxation for the boys. And then English was taught Selim, too, but he would not forget that first dose of Latin, and all the rest of his life he could sight-read Latin the way other men read modern languages.

There was only one year at Boston Latin School. The rich suitor did not win Mother Peabody's hand, but instead she decided to marry the poor but attractive Deacon Daniel Alden. The change meant that there was no further place in the family for Selim Hobart, and he was sent out to work for a farmer in exchange for his board and clothing. He milked the cows, tended the sheep, fed the chickens, and cleaned the barn. He also helped with the haying and stacking and the plowing, planting, and reaping of the food grains. He learned to lamb and calve. On some such farms the boys who worked out were allowed to keep chickens and sell the eggs for pinmoney. In the severe and ungenerous household where Selim found himself, however, this was the prerogative of the farm wife. It was the obligation of the farmer and his wife to give Selim warm clothes and good shoes. But they begrudged him every penny, thinking perhaps that his work for them was ordained by the Lord, but his living with them was the work of the devil. So Selim spent much of his time in what were virtually rags, his shoes unsoled, and his hands cold and frostbitten in the winter freezes.

He lived in an unheated loft above the woodshed on the side of the house. His meals were salt pork and salt cod, milk, and potatoes. This was a poor farm, and the food was poor; the beef and the eggs, the chickens and the butter that one would expect to be on the table were not there because they could all be sold at market. It was quite enough for the farmer, his wife, and the hired boy to have salt meat and fish to sustain life.

But boys and men will find a way to make money for themselves, and Selim did so. He was told that he could grow a little garden for himself in the summer, after he was finished with the farmer's market garden. He bought seeds, and he tended them with great care, and he took his produce to market. He also tried to persuade the farmer to listen to the general storekeeper who kept up on the best seeds and feeds, and who was advocating slightly higher-priced seeds for vegetables, because, he said, they were better for the cold New England climate. But the farmer scoffed. He grew his plants from his own seed, and he did not need any storekeeper or boy to tell him how to do it.

So Selim went his own way, and the second year he bought for two cents a package of new radish seeds. Behold, they sprouted earlier and grew faster than his master's, and Selim and the storekeeper were justified. But then, a few days later, Selim came to his garden to see that his radishes had all disappeared. He went to the farmer's garden, and there they were, neatly added to the rows.

That was Selim's last year on the farm.

When he was fifteen he went home to visit his mother, and she agreed that such happenings were too much for a boy to bear, so he was released from the bondage. Yet she could not keep him and there was no money for the boy's education, so he must be sent off again.

This time Selim's fate was kinder, and he went as an apprentice to a master builder. Luckily the builder was a reading man, and here Selim was introduced to the works of Robert Burns and other literary figures whose writings would never have found their way inside the library of his father.

For two years Selim worked at the carpenter's trade, but then he developed bad feet, and could no longer stand for many hours to work at building. He was sent home, where a doctor diagnosed his case as tuberculosis of the bone, promising a short time to live. But while there *was* life something must be done with it, and he had to earn his own way. He taught school in the village where his mother now lived, Randolph, Massachusetts, and he took a job binding shoes at nine cents a dozen pair, because he could do the work sitting down. He soon discovered, however, that housewives in the village could make more than he did each day by simply knitting socks and stockings, and he took up knitting as a trade. When some of the other boys chaffed him for doing women's work, he silenced them by pointing to his feet and saying he saw nothing amiss in earning his living in the best way he could.

Three years passed, and apparently whatever ailed Selim's feet became less of a problem, for he found at nineteen that he could get around again. He decided that since he could not farm, and had no money for a business, he must educate himself and become a professional man. He would not be a minister, that much was clear. He would be a teacher.

There was not enough money to send him to Harvard or Yale, but through the Hobarts of Vermont he was encouraged to come up to Burlington and matriculate at the much less expensive University of Vermont.

At this small school, Selim joined the Sigma Phi fraternity, which meant he had a little money, obtained by working for others at odd jobs, and by teaching school on the side. Selim's grades were not very good at first. His average was 82, which by the standards of the day would be called no better than fair. But he spent much time scouting for ways to make money. As a result of his poverty his quarters in Room 11 in the north hall were so bare that he never invited anyone to visit him.

There were many demands on the young scholar. He paid three dollars a week for his room, and one dollar a week for his board— but that low board bill meant he ate very few meals, only dinners, at the table. As for the rest, he subsisted by buying a great barrel of Vermont crackers. On weekends he would forage in the country-side, finding a farmer who would sell him cheaply a bushel of apples, or beechnuts or chestnuts. A friendly professor who owned a cow sold him a quart of milk every day and left it in a tin container on a fence post where Selim could find it every morning. And yet, in spite of such poverty, Selim spent six dollars on a subscription to the *Living Age*, a prominent magazine of the time. At about the time he wanted that subscription worse than anything else in his life he got a new job: he earned his daily dinner by carving the roast, whatever it might be, at the head of the dining room table where the more affluent students ate.

So the years proceeded. He read Ruskin, a favorite of this period, and he joined the debating club called the Owls—because they pretended wisdom, certainly not because they stayed up all night. One requirement of the Owls was to be able to talk extemporaneously for five minutes on any suggested subject, without even a moment of preparation. The club members had a good deal of fun from this requirement, and created speeches which would have brought amazement if not instruction to their teachers, because there was nothing in the rule that said the discussion must be pertinent or even truthful, but simply that it must take place. The Owls had another interesting custom in their prepared debates: while the debater was talking and consulting his notes his opponent held the candle for him, and it was common practice to drop as much candle wax on the notes as possible, and even to snuff the candle out entirely without seeming to do so intentionally. So there was much cheap amusement and some edification in their meetings, as there was also in another society to which Selim soon belonged, the campus glee club.

On May 16, 1850, Selim Hobart Peabody donned his broadcloth coat, his heavy black trousers and high button shoes, his white shirt with detached collar, black satin stock and and white kid gloves, put on his beaver hat and went to the college to deliver his entry in the Sophomore Exhibition. His speech was entitled "The

Unity of Purpose Necessary to the Success of a Student"—surely a subject serious enough to bring him the acclaim of his professors if no special award. Next year he was not nearly so concerned about his impact on his teachers, and he chose for the Junior Exhibition, the title "Influence of Climate on Society," perhaps prompted by the cold Burlington winters.

Selim was a good college man, well respected by his tutors. Because he was poor, when other youths were going home for vacation he took the eight-week winter term to earn money for his further schooling. The university let out on December 1 and did not reconvene for the spring term until January 31. Selim in his second year secured a job teaching at the Burlington High School during the winter term and managed to earn enough money to support himself during the ensuing spring, summer, and autumn terms. Then, in the fall of the next year he was allowed a singular dispensation: he was granted permission to teach at Burlington High and still attend college. It meant that he taught for six hours a day, sandwiched in his classes, and studied late into the night. But in this way he saved enough money so that in his senior year at Vermont he did not have to teach at all. He was elected to Phi Beta Kappa, the scholastic honor society, and graduated third in his class. Dr. Worthington Smith, President of the University, wrote of his high standing as a scholar, in mathematics and science particularly .

"He is of a mild and gentlemanly manner," said the President's letter of recommendation, "a man of honorable sentiment and Christian character."

Mild, gentlemanly, honorable, Christian—and also romantic, headstrong, and brave. That was Selim Hobart Peabody at the age of twenty-three. He was married that summer of graduation to Mary Elizabeth, daughter of David Knight Pangborn, and more important, cousin of his best friend, Zebinah Pangborn, a close companion all through his college years. He settled down right there in Burlington, as principal of the town high school.

Peabody served Burlington faithfully for a year, but then resigned to take a job as professor of mathematics and physics at New Hampton Seminary in Fairfax, Vermont. A year later he left New England for the first time in his life. He went to Philadelphia to accept a better job, as professor of mathematics and civil engineering at Polytechnic College of the State of Pennsylvania.

The journey south opened Selim Hobart's eyes to a new world— the non-Puritan world. For the first time, that year the Peabodys kept Christmas as a holiday and did not celebrate Thanksgiving. That was the Quaker way, as distinct from the old church. Seeking a new adherence Selim joined the Tabernacle Baptist Church, and was soon made head of the Sunday school because of his educational background, and his boyhood as a minister's son. During this stay in Philadelphia two babies were born to the family, so Sunday school began to have a real meaning to Selim Hobart Peabody.

He might have stayed on in Philadelphia indefinitely, had not the Panic of 1857 showed him how insecure his life had become. The college had no money to pay its bills or its professors. Some professors accepted payments in scrip, but Selim Hobart felt he should have the money and waited on the president until he secured at least part of his salary in cash. The college was forced to retrench until it suspended operations altogether, and Selim Hobart was left without any job at all. In this moment of indecision, the elders of his Baptist church came forward and pressed Selim Hobart to go west, where their church was expanding. Through a connection in Philadelphia and with the loan of two hundred dollars given him by one of the church elders, Selim Hobart went to Eau Claire, Wisconsin, where he secured a post as clerk in the federal government land office. Elizabeth remained in Philadelphia and awaited the word to sell their possessions and bring the babies to join her husband.

It was several months, springtime, before Selim Hobart was settled, and then the summer passed so quickly that it was autumn before Elizabeth made the long train journey. It was a hard trip through rough new country. The male passengers wore homespun and put their boots up on the plush seats while they played cards and drank whiskey from a bottle. There was another lady in Elizabeth's car, and they clung together for mutual protection. There was no dining car on the train, so they ate from wicker baskets, supplemented by what they could buy from station houses and peddlers along the road. There were no proper bunks or beds—their seats slid down and the backs flattened out to make rude beds, protected by curtains from the crowd. The end of the road for the western voyage of the Eastern Line was Chicago. There Elizabeth boarded a train of the new Chicago, Milwaukee, St. Paul, and Pacific Railroad for the trip to Milwaukee and then out another forty miles to the end of the line at Sparta. There she and the children were met by a beaming Selim Hobart, a "westerner" now, who had come another forty miles from Eau Claire in a sleigh drawn by two horses. While waiting he had loaded the sleigh with staples for the winter ahead, kitchen utensils, and a big barrel of lime which would be used to make plaster for the interior walls of the house he had built with his own hands that summer.

The train was late, and it was near noon before they got away from the Sparta tavern—really not much more than a saloon, but the only civilized spot in the village. There were another forty miles to be covered before night, and the horses might just make it by dark, as the days were growing short.

In his hurry, Selim was almost rude to the wife he had not seen for so many months. She did not know what to make of it, yet such was the strangeness and the excitement that she could forgive anything.

Selim piled Elizabeth and the babies into the sleigh, bundled them up in buffalo robes, and jumped up beside them. In a few moments they were off, Selim clucking to the horses as they glided along the track, out of the community. In a few minutes they were in the vast wilderness, with the clopping of the horses' hooves, the snorting of their nostrils and the gentle swoosh of the sleigh runners breaking the stillness of the afternoon.

About an hour's distance from the tavern, the worn tracings of the rig gave away, and Selim had to halt the horses so he could make repairs. The stillness then became almost overpowering. No bird called, no tree rustled in the cold quiet. Then Elizabeth did hear a sound, a baying that seemed to be behind them. She spoke to Selim. Was there a farm nearby? she asked. And if so, why didn't they stop there overnight and start again in the morning?

No, there was no farm, said Selim, smiling grimly. There was no human habitation between Sparta and Eau Claire.

Suddenly, Elizabeth realized the truth.

Wolves!

And she knew why Selim had been so hurried and why he had been almost brusque with her as she wanted to dawdle a little, taking in the full flavor of her new world.

The repairs took an hour, and Elizabeth grew cold. But they had no firewood, and the few evergreens promised scant assistance. They must press on, and hopefully make Eau Claire before darkness when the wolves would grow bolder.

Finally, Selim had the sleigh rehitched, and climbed back in. He brought out his rifle and a lantern. It was growing late. So they sped on through the afternoon, as the approaching darkness descended upon them, with the accompanying terror that they might be forced to face the wolves.

Night fell, and the ominous cries increased as the pursuing animals trailed closer. Selim spurred on the tiring horses as best he could, and they responded despite their fatigue because their ears told them what lay behind.

It was well after moonrise when the baying ceased, and a dim light moved into view, grew brighter, and then separated to become many lights. Soon they were in the middle of the tiny village of Eau Claire, a settlement of a hundred people, augmented that evening by three new inhabitants. They stopped at another tavern, where Selim passed on the news, then at last they arrived home at the unpainted, rough house that he had built for them.

Next day Elizabeth had a moment to go outside and look around her. Eau Claire was an old settlement in a way; the French had settled here in 1836 on the mail route from Prairie du Chien. It had a sawmill and a general store, and there were promises that it would have the railroad soon, but not yet.

So Elizabeth settled down as the wife of the land clerk. Selim worked out of a shack that was heated by a potbellied stove. He measured the land that was to be sold by the government, by the simple device of tying a knotted cloth around one wheel spoke, and counting the revolutions of the wheels as he drove across the prairie. He was also, as a preacher's son, the acting Protestant minister of the community. That first year he fell into disagreement with the Catholic community, who objected to an unordained man leading others in prayer. But Selim never gave in; he always invoked the blessings of the Lord on all, including himself. When the Catholics were shown the careful wording of his prayers and services, even they had no objection.

In a year the Peabodys had become acclimated; in two years they had all become "westerners." Experience made them one with the land, the kind of experience that teaches and gives a man a feeling of having conquered. Selim had to contend with the mosquitoes—"gallinippers" they were called in those parts—which came out in the spring in huge swarms and endangered the lives of men and beasts. Because he had to travel in the open, Selim soon developed the protective device of a hood and mask like a beekeeper's gown. Elizabeth made it for him out of netting, and the neighbors laughed at first to see their strange, ghostly friend, but soon Elizabeth was called on to make a dozen other gallinipper suits.

This was Chippewa and Sioux country, and the women soon learned to stay away from the Indians, avoiding giving anything to one lest the whole tribe descend on them.

Selim had a narrow escape on a river near Eau Claire. He was unfamiliar with the waterway and was suddenly catapulted in his birch canoe over a rapids that fell sixteen feet. He came out by virtue of skill and good luck, adding one more lesson to his course as a frontiersman.

In October, 1858, their third child was born, which meant they were really pioneers. The Midwest was great and open, filled with opportunity as well as hardship. Philadelphia seemed a long way away, and was half forgotten after Selim was appointed principal of the high school in Fond du Lac, Wisconsin's fourth largest city. Soon he became a power in educational circles in all the state. Two years after taking the Fond du Lac job he was appointed principal of the even larger school in the big city of Racine, where he also had responsibility as superintendent of the lower schools.

Early in the 1860s Selim became an active and ardent member of the Wisconsin State Teachers' Association, and at the height of the Civil War, 1863, he was chosen President of that organization. He volunteered at the beginning of the war for service even though he was a family man with three children. But at thirty-two he was a little old for soldiering, and the matter was settled when a doctor had a good look at his feet. His war effort was largely concerned with raising money and support for the United States Sanitary Commission, which provided medical, surgical, and nursing services for the men in the field.

Selim's professional career was progressing very well. He was a man of ideas and he proposed these for the betterment of the people of Wisconsin. He lobbied long and hard for a state-supported normal school, where teachers would be trained to serve the public schools. He worked for establishment of teachers' institutes, where those who taught might learn refresh themselves. He also recommended a grades system of high schools, normal schools, and the state university, integrating all the programs. Eventually Wisconsin adopted this plan, and the Peabody influence was at work again in the country, this time with an educational system that was regarded as a model for the Middle West.

Selim's work in Wisconsin was quite enough to give him a place in the history of American education, but he was far from finished. He was known throughout the Middle West for his interest in science and scientific affairs, and he kept in touch with others of the same bent. While at Racine he was offered the post of director of the Dearborn Astronomical Observatory, which was finished in

1862, but he declined the proposal in order to continue his teaching and efforts to better the schools through the state association. Perhaps, too, as a hot-tempered man well aware of his own worth, he felt that he was more valuable than what Dearborn offered. By this time, the woods and prairies had made their mark: Selim Hobart Peabody was a tall, slender man with a soft brown beard and high forehead. He was balding slowly, which gave him an air of grave intellectuality. He dressed formally, sometimes wearing a shawl, as was the fashion in the 1860s, with his inevitable frock coat, high button shoes, and black stock.

The big city of Chicago, with its greater opportunities for professional recognition and monetary advancement, continued to call Selim. In 1865 he gave in, and moved there to be professor of physics at the Chicago Central High School. The family continued to live in Racine, because he believed the smaller town to be more healthful, and Peabody became one of the Middle West's first weekend commuters.

These were busy years for him. He wrote many books of popular science on the moon and other objects of astronomy. He wrote a textbook for arithmetic and another for teaching astronomy. The result of the intensive scholastic work he projected and carried out in these years was his appointment in 1871 as professor of physics at the Massachusetts Agricultural College in Amherst.

The appointment was too good to turn down, and yet none of the family wanted to leave the Midwest. They were, adopted and born, confirmed midwesterners. The professor, himself, left Chicago and Wisconsin with deep misgivings about the climate and personality of his native New England, but the money was too much to refuse, nor could he ignore the professional advancement. It might have been better had he yielded to his instincts.

The family went to Amherst and found a big old house. The professor settled in to teaching and experimentation. He soon became acquainted with and impressed by Louis Agassiz, whose lead he followed in the study of natural history. Selim became a power in the intellectual community, entertaining such dignitaries as Harriet Beecher Stowe, who came to Amherst in the summers to visit her daughter, the wife of the Episcopal minister there.

Then, in 1874, after Professor Peabody had made a long study of the process of the ascent of sap in trees, valuable to Vermonters and other New Englanders, he was encouraged by President William Smith Clark of the college to publish his work, and prepared a monograph which was brought out under the auspices of Massachusetts Agricultural College. When the work was published, however, the name that appeared as author was that of William Clark Smith, and Peabody was quite ignored as the source responsible for it.

A small group of administrators took the position that anything appearing under the imprint of their institution should be attributed to them, but the general intellectual world did not agree, nor did Professor Selim Hobart Peabody. Beard bristling in fury, the professor told the president what he thought of him as man and scholar and resigned his post. (Nine years later, on the departure of President Clark, Professor Peabody was asked to become president of the college, but he was still angry, and refused.)

Back to the beloved Middle West went this branch of the Peabody family, glad to be away from the effete and dishonest East, going home to a land where they did not see men using false pretenses to mask their larcenous souls.

There was the old job at Central High School, and this time the family came to Chicago to live, because the professor intended to remain. He also became secretary of the Chicago Academy of Sciences and for three years lived a busy, happy life, spending his mornings at the high school and his afternoons at the academy.

Life in Chicago was happy for all the family. The Peabodys lived on West Adam Street between Ashland Avenue and Paulina Street. In the next block lived Mayor Carter Harrison—that was the kind of district it was then. They lived, as did all their neighbors, in a row house with high stairs leading to the parlor floor that were admirable for sunning in the daytime and gossiping in the long summer evenings.

For amusement they went to McVickers Theater or Hooley's Stock Theater, and saw *Uncle Tom's Cabin, East Lynne,* and *Jim the Penman.* But the professor did not always accompany the family to the theater, because he spent many hours writing books and articles, and also taught public night courses in the sciences two evenings a week.

The Chicago period came to an end in 1878 when Professor Peabody was asked to go to the Illinois Industrial University at Champaign, to become professor of mechanical engineering. He went, tentatively, and the family remained in Chicago. Champaign had little to offer the growing girls, and Elizabeth was now a club-woman of some importance, very active in the Chicago Women's Club.

As it turned out it was as well that the family stayed behind, because two years later the professor was asked to be editor of the *International Cyclopedia* in New York, so he went there. But it was a job that did not appeal at all, and in 1880 when the Illinois state authorities were looking around for a new regent, or chief executive, for the university at Champaign, it was known that he was not happy in the East. So they offered Selim the job and he jumped at it, in August, 1880. At first it was a temporary appointment, but it was made permanent in 1881.

Thus, Selim Hobart Peabody, a Vermont boy, became chief of the state's land-grant university. There was much trouble in the beginning because the school was heavily in debt, but Professor Peabody displayed remarkable facility in securing backing from the state legislators, and soon the university was supported by the legislature and by the sale of state-owned lands. It was not as easy as it sounds, however. When the new regent first went to the state capital to lobby, he was thoroughly chagrined to see how easily his major opponent, a lobbyist for the real estate interests, managed to defeat his plans. So he went to call on his chief opponent, congratulated him on beating him, and asked the man to teach him how to win. The professional, never having been asked to teach before, gave this willing student such good lessons that soon Peabody was one of the most successful lobbyists in Illinois.

In this post, Selim came to the full flower of his capacities. He made the University of Illinois—even the name was changed under his regency and then presidency—strong and independent of political pressures. At the same time it acted as an extension of the legislature with the creation of the agricultural experiment station, which then gave information to the legislators, who could pass it on to their constituents (largely farmers) and please the folks at home. So busy was he, so successful, that President Peabody declined many honors. For his work with agriculture, he was offered the post of Assistant Secretary of Agriculture in the Harrison administration, but he refused. He was offered the presidency at Amherst, and refused. He was offered the presidency of the Rose Polytechnic Institute, and refused. He preferred to work for the people of Illinois through the state university, and he did, championing the establishment of clubs and study groups that offered broad bases of democracy to the students, and stoutly opposing fraternities and sororities as antidemocratic, a grave and controversial position to take before the turn of the twentieth century. Under his presidency the university established high standards of scholarship and scientific attainment with a growing name even in the East.

But in 1889 Selim Peabody's health deteriorated, and he decided he ought to quit. He was persuaded to take a trip to Europe instead, and did so between October and the following April. When he came home, however, the daily routine brought on his affliction again, and in 1891 he resigned from the university at the age of sixty-two.

The cause of his illness proved to be gallstones, rather than overwork. Once these were removed, Peabody was ready for a new career, which developed as a specialist in international expositions. He was chief of the department of liberal arts at the World's Columbian Exposition at St. Louis. Then he went to Paris in 1899 to become editor of the various publications issued by the American exhibitionists at the Paris World's Fair. He was connected in a similar capacity with the Pan American Exposition at Buffalo and was assistant director of the Louisiana Purchase Exposition in 1902.

So he was at St. Louis at the end of his life, still in the Midwest, which he loved. He had achieved many honors, competing with easterners of his generation: he was listed in *Who's Who;* he was given an honorary LL.D. by the University of Iowa in 1881; he was offered a dozen posts as college president or chief administrator. He never lost his interest in education; it was his life and right down to the day he died of a stroke in the spring of 1903 he was working at educating the public in one way or another—and having a good time doing it. During those Paris exposition days, he made four trips across the Atlantic in one season; and what with that and the wolves of Wisconsin, the struggle with the larcenous President Clark, and his embattlements with the Illinois legislature, one might say that Selim Hobart Peabody lived an exciting life as well as a useful one.

CHAPTER 20

THE POETESS

THERE WAS A traditional air about the three girls who grew up to be known as the Peabody Sisters of Salem, and one might say they enjoyed every virtue of the gentility with which their family name and father's calling could endow young women in the middle of the nineteenth century. The three of them, Elizabeth, Mary, and Sophia, made their own ways in the world with a huge, unseen, helping hand behind them, the hand of respect for that gentleness of birth. Close after the careers of these three sisters came another girl of the Peabody line who did not share their advantages, but who exercised a serious influence on the writing, especially the writing of women, in the period of her own life.

She was Josephine Preston Peabody, the second child of Charles Kilham Peabody and Susan Josephine Morrill, who were living in Brooklyn, New York, at the time of the birth of this daughter. Josephine's early days were spent in a happy and protected home, where her father and mother took especial pains with the children's cultural education. But when little Josephine was ten years old, many of these advantages were taken from her. Charles Peabody died, and the widow took the children to Dorchester, Massachusetts, where she could live much more cheaply than in New York. Living economically, unfortunately, did not include much money for the arts, and little Josephine was reduced to learning about the theater by reading plays, not seeing them.

After a few years she went to high school in the city at the Girls Latin Shcool, but became ill after a few months and returned home to study under tutors. She kept up Greek and Latin, and in 1894 was admitted to Radcliffe College as a special student since she could not fulfill all the entrance requirements to be a regular member of the freshman class.

Two years were spent at Radcliffe, taking courses in the Elizabethan drama and others that interested her, and then again frail health forced Josephine from college and she went home. Instead of courses of study supervised by others, Josephine plunged into reading supervised by herself. She read hundreds, thousands of books. She had a good start, for in the years just before Radcliffe she had recorded six hundred important books she had read. Now she renewed her efforts to educate herself, to learn all there was to learn about the world she wanted to know.

Her world was the world of poetry and music and the theater. She did not disdain the music halls, and often took "standup" tickets.

In 1894 her first poem was published in the *Atlantic Monthly*, lines entitled "The Shepherd-Girl," which, in true teen-age fashion, concerned itself with the mysteries of lost sheep in a cold world.

> Within the twilight on the hill,
>   A shepherd-girl I met;
> And she was weeping as she went,
>   Nor may I well forget
> The darksome eyes she lifted up,
>   That bitter tears had wet.
>
> "My sheep are all astray, astray;
>   And since the sun arose,
> I have been searching all the land
>   Beyond the meadow-close;
> And all my sheep are gone from me,
>   And none are left to lose.

"We wandered, all the summer days,
    Where any cowslip led.
The little brook came with us, too,
    But now the leaves are dead;
The winds blow chill from yonder hill,
    And it is dark," she said.

"Oh, all the summer days I piped
    An answer to the lark.
My lambs were growing white as stars,
    And fair for all to mark;
And they have left me, one by one,"
    She said, "and it is dark."
"Nay, come, thou, lonely shepherd-girl,
    And find thy sheep with me!

The yellow moon will rise full soon,
    And lend her light for thee.
But thou art weary, wandering;
    Thine eyes are strange to see."

"Lad, I have called them long and long;
    Only an echo hears.
The grass blows gray beneath the wind—
    As gray as far-off years;
And even if the moonlight shone
    I could not see, for tears."

"The Shepherd-Girl" would scarcely have been published in the *Atlantic Monthly* of the last half of the twentieth century, but styles and requirements change. For the period, which was, after all that of Thomas Beer's *Mauve Decade*, visions of weeping shepherdesses wandering among the lost stars of the firmament were quite acceptable, and Josephine Peabody's efforts caught the eye of editor Horace Scudder.

Since it was unseemly in 1894 for a young girl to be putting her clean thoughts to dirty print, Josephine had pretended to be a boy, for the purposes of her poetry. But by the time she was ready, under Scudder's tutelage, to publish her first volume of verse, she had conquered enough of the girlishness to become sexually neuter in her poetry.

Two years later Josephine published her second volume of verse, most of which had appeared in magazines. This book was called *Fortune and Men's Eyes,* and it, too, was highly regarded by the literary community. Because Josephine was an uncommonly pretty poet, her work received considerable attention in all quarters and suddenly she was famous.

Those who acclaimed the slender, wasp-waisted girl did not know the wretchedness at home that inspired her poetry. Nor did all her readers get the message: beneath the lilac exterior and the apparently poor health beat the heart of a Trojan warrior who was dedicated to the principle of female equality and was fighting for that aim in her own sweet way.

Never, not once, had there been the slightest fear in her heart that she would not succeed as a writer. At eighteen, before she had any success at all, she had written scores of poems and sent them off, bemoaning only the callousness of such critics as the editor of the *Century,* who sent them back, and when she was established in 1898, she began to think of ways to get out and about in the world. Her great cause of concern that year was the Spanish-American War—not because there was war, but because she was not in it.

After 1900 the poems came pouring out, and her success increased. But even though she was so well established a poet as to achieve a lectureship in poetry and English literature, she was scheming in the privacy of her boudoir to attack a new field: the theater.

"Oh," she wrote, "if I could only have a hand in the tug at the Drama in America! If I could only pull and haul and boost and kick and push—and hear one responsive onward squeak!"

But she was pulling and hauling and boosting and kicking and pushing even then, making games out of the stage directions for the drama, cutting out pieces of cardboard and labeling them Enter, Exit, Exeunt, Re-Enter Discovered, and all the other stage directions, so she might become totally familiar with these tools and use them well in her art.

The flame of Josephine Peabody's inspiration burned fiercely, fanned by her personal unhappiness. She was sick, poor and lonely, and she poured out her thoughts in her diary as in December, 1900:

> I have lived by the spirit so long and so fiercely that my flesh fails and my spirit is infinitely wearied and only pants for space. And it is true that I sometimes feel that I can hardly help dying "tomorrow" from the terrible sameness of effort, effort, effort, without help or rather against the whole atmosphere of these years that I have been growing up. . . .

She wanted to flower in the world of letters, she wanted to become a personage more than anything else in the world. And so she continued to work.

With the second volume of poems out of the way, she turned her full attention in 1900 to her first major drama, in the tradition of the theater she loved best—Shakespeare. "Oh!" she once cried. "This man Shakespeare—one cannot get away from him."

So her first play, *Fortune and Men's Eyes*, had an Elizabethan setting and Elizabethan characters. The play's action opened in the interior of the tavern The Bear and the Angel in South London. The characters were named Wat and Dickon, Prentice, Chiffin, and one was simply The Player, who was Shakespeare.

The success was not great, but by the next year Josephine Peabody was working hopefully on *Marlowe*, a continuation of the Shakespearean period and themes.

Her teaching, her writing, and her presence continued to bring Josephine Preston Peabody public acclaim in a rarefied circle. In the spring of 1905 *Marlowe* was produced at the opening of the theater at Agassiz House at Radcliffe College, and this brought new acclaim within the academic community. By this moment of her life, Josephine Preston Peabody was reaching out for more. She wanted marriage, but not the kind of marriage most of her gentle friends aspired to. She would not settle down to be a housewife; she sternly insisted that she was a person before she was a woman. "We are not to be bounded by our sex," she wrote. "My sex is not the sum of me. I can live all around it."

Indeed, when it came time for her to marry the man she fell in love with, Lionel Simeon Marks, of the Harvard engineering department, she asked the bishop if she might not omit the word "obey" from the ceremony. The answer came on April 9, 1906, as her diary indicated:

> Letter from the Bishop this morning, very courteous and sincere, but, it also seemed to me, extremely guarded. He couldn't do anything about it, he said, etc., etc. He did not really say much 'cause there wasn't anything really left to say. . . . My Dear and I read it respectfully in the afternoon, and latterly danced about the room and praised heaven that we did not have to be bishops. . . .

So they were married, and Miss Peabody promised out loud in the church that she would "obey" her husband and promised inwardly that she never would, and they were happy ever after.

On their honeymoon, for reasons of her husband's they went to Berlin, where Josephine Peabody Marks began the study of German. Gone were the anxious days about money, the squabbles and the loneliness, and in their place were days of brightness and joy and love. Mrs. Marks wrote home to friends about speaking German:

> . . . a ridiculous four-footed *sprache*, with the most plodding, material point of view evident in seven words out of eight. I like the beer(!) better than the speech. . . .

And she wrote about how she liked the French:

> . . . French people repel me acutely; and it will ever be so. Mentally and physically, I can't abide 'em.

And the Italians:

> . . . we were both drawn; always excepting the well-dressed "ladies" of the upper classes who are curiously homely, brazen, devoid of ideas.

It was ideas that counted most of all with her, and she admired the German sense of value for ideas, even if the Germans were to her singularly devoid of charm.

The love for ideas led her next to a new play, *The Pipers*, which she began in the early winter months of 1907. The play consumed her for several months, then she settled down—home again in Cambridge—to having a baby girl and to writing *The Book of the Little Past*, a slim volume that won considerable critical acclaim.

She was a delightful woman and wife. She was capable of writing friends about "her child" in a manner that indicated immaculate conception—there was the independent spirit of her. She was also capable of showing great love, as in January, 1909, in her diary:

> What does the Lion of the House do but inveigle me into his den and let me relate my shoppings and my nothings with a tale as long as Juliet's nurse . . . and then he gets me to ask him questions that bring to light at length and at last that he is appointed Full Professor. Then I skerried and screeled like our Baby when she tries to be a peacock.

In 1909, the baby Aileen was growing, and her husband was away a good deal, occupied with the mysterious workings of engineering projects, and Josephine Preston Peabody had plenty of time to consider the world about her. With the same concern she wrote poems; "The Singing Man" was an excursion away from the poetic drama of the Shakespearean mold. Meanwhile, *The Piper* had become a raging critical success, winning the Stratford play competition in 1910 against 315 competing plays, and being performed at the Memorial Theater, Stratford-on-Avon, in July.

The Singing Man was the name for her book of verse published in 1911, and its opening poem, the title piece, began with the same old lilts for which Josephine Preston Peabody was famous:

> He sang above the vineyards of the world.
>   And after him the vines with woven hands
> Clambered and clung, and everywhere unfurled
>   Triumphing green above the barren lands;
> Till high as gardens grow, he climbed, he stood,
>   Sun-crowned with life and strength, and singing toil,
> And looked upon his work; and it was good:
>   The corn, the wine, the oil.

There was more lilt, more praise for nature and man as a creature of God, laboring with his hands in the open fields to produce the corn, the oil, and the wine. Then, suddenly, part two of the poem brought forth a new poet, a poet of protest who no longer used words to carry on the romanticism of Wordsworth or the visions of a Keats:

> Seek him now, that singing Man.
> Look for him,
> Look for him,
> In the mills,
> In the mines;
> Where the very daylight pines,—
> He, who once did walk the hills!
> You shall find him, if you scan
> Shapes all unbefitting Man,
> Bodies warped, and faces dim.
> In the mines; in the mills
> Where the ceaseless thunder fills
> Spaces of the human brain
> Till all thought is turned to pain.
> Where the skirl of wheel on wheel,
> Grinding him who is their tool,
> Makes the shattered senses reel
> To the numbness of the fool.
> Perish thought, and halting tongue—
> (Once it spoke;—once it sung!)
> Live to hunger, dead to song.
> Only heart-beats loud with wrong
> Hammer on,—*How long?*
> . . . *How long?—How long?*

Coming from any pen it was a scorching condemnation of big business:

> They knew it well, who took away the air,
> —Who took away the sun;
> Who took, to serve their soul-devouring greed.

Coming from the pen of the poetic dramatist it aroused hundreds, thousands, as Ida Tarbell aroused with her prose works.

To Josephine Peabody Marks, the most important things, as she listed them when *The Piper* won its prize, were international reputation, women's rights and suffrage, Harvard, Radcliffe, and Wellesley, local reputation.

A second baby came to the happy household (a boy, Lionel or Leo), and Professor Marks prospered in his profession. The family traveled to Europe, and came back to a New York production of *The Piper*. All Josephine Peabody's dreams seem to have been realized: *The Piper* was printed in Braille and the family was definitely among the well-to-do of Cambridge; *The Piper* bought them a handsome house with a garden and a long driveway.

Another poetic play, *The Wings*, cemented her establishment as one of the leaders of the poetic drama in America, at a time when the form was passing fast from the scene. It was produced in 1912 at the Toy Theater in Boston. Then came the *Wolf of Gubbio*, a drama of St. Francis of Assisi.

In 1911, when Josephine Peabody was thirty-seven she fell ill and underwent a series of operations. She continued to write plays and poetry, although she was in a good deal of pain much of the time, and finally she was afflicted with hardening of the arteries and what was known in those days as "softening of the brain"— what would be recognized later as a hardening of the brain arteries that prevented the free flow of blood.

Less and less efficiently than before, she continued to write. She traveled. Her letters were sprightly and full of life, but she did not have the energy to produce the work she once had done. A book of poems, *Harvest Moon*, was published in 1917, and she, whose formal education had been so sketchy, was elected an honorary member of Phi Beta Kappa.

But all this came after Josephine Preston Peabody was declared by the outside world to be an invalid, and her fame was referred to almost in the past tense. The trouble was that she must save up her strength by long periods of quiet in order to give intensive moments of public service. In 1920, she wrote "Song of the Pilgrim Women," for the Plymouth Pageant. It took a great deal out of her, but she insisted on doing it. She alternated between living in their house in Cambridge (192 Brattle Street) and their summer house on the coast of Maine.

Sick or not, in 1920 she was engaged in trying to write two plays and for inspiration was studying William Blake at the Fogg Museum. A thrombosis had caused her to have a limp and she walked with a cane, but she walked, and she went where she wanted to go.

By 1921 the family, although not impecunious, was not as well-to-do as in the earlier days. The generous Josephine gave too much away. When one of her uncles died in debt, she paid off his debts because she could not bear the thought of the world thinking ill of him, and it took all her personal money to do so. But she managed, and she kept up her interests. A firm advocate of women's suffrage, she did all she could to advance that cause. She also took up painting, going to the basement of the Copley Society building to join the daubing class in the mornings, and became intrigued with pastels and a bas-relief. That year she finished her prose play *Portrait of Mrs. W.*, and on January 22, 1922, she put the finishing touches to it:

> This A.M. I plunged a bodkin through my every member, and pinned myself to a leather seat beside the fireplace; and having Applied myself to the year old task of a *Preface* for my play . . . I hauled and kicked and pushed at it, from 9:30 until 11:30—and then felt so terribly Good and Innocent and Head Achey, and broken-down, that I decided to *call* it done and type-write it tomorrow.

By that summer, Josephine Peabody Marks was very ill, and although she had written some dear friends almost once a week, months went by in which she was too sick to write. She suffered an attack of uremic poisoning, and was unconscious for nearly two weeks. There was much talk in the family of all going off to Maine in June for a marvelous summer—but the end was very, very near, and after a great deal of pain, on December 4, 1922, Josephine Preston Peabody died.

The critics had much to say in memoriam. They recalled that

her artistic development was constant and sure, from the lyrical to the dramatic poet. Horace Scudder, with whom she had many delightful sessions in her youth, encouraged her to sacrifice design and symbolism to clear expression, and for this she found the dramatic form simpler. She never gave up her interest in symbolism; indeed, her personal letter signature was a symbol:

an eyebrow, a nose, and a pair of eyes, and it all meant J.P.P. She signed thus her letters to her intimates from early girlhood.

How would she be known, this dramatist, lyricist, fighter for women's rights who could dance about the room and be pleased that she was not a bishop to deny a girl and her man the right to be wed as they wished? There was one poem, "The Garden," which indicated how she would be known, for it betrayed her own love of nature and her own many happy hours in the flower-bursting garden of Brattle Street:

> Between two hard breaths of a parching day,
> I am rapt away
> Into some unkenned garden-place,
> Where for a space
> Dust nor demand may reach, nor human speech,
> Nor any far-off chime
> From walls of Times.
> But I wake up to coolness and the peace
> Of cedarn fragrances;
> And the remembered hush of grass made new
> With morning, and with dew.
> And all the darling trees of paradise,
> Leaning anear, let fall
> Vague petals in my eyes,
> And hands, and over all,
> Soft as the snow that fills the broken ground;
> Till every wound
> Is solaced; and no less

The air is thronged and white with happiness.
And still with one accord
They rain the petals down, soft blinding me,
So that I may surmise—but never see—
The Lord.

The *Dictionary of American Biography* gives her a "permanent place among American poets." Katharine Lee Bates, who wrote the foreword to Josephine Preston Peabody's collected poems, called her much more, for, she said, "true poet, eager artist, enraptured lover of beauty as Josephine Preston Peabody was, not the ecstasy of son, nor the passion for perfection, nor the Beatific Vision itself could wall in her heart from the footsore procession of humanity." And George P. Baker, calling her an unfulfilled dramatic artist, suggested that her path was converging with that of the realists like Eugene O'Neill, and that in *Portrait of Mrs. W.* she showed what might have been.

So there they were, the postmortem assessments, proving once again, in the case of Josephine Preston Peabody, the existence of that ephemeral Peabody influence upon the people of this land.

PART V

Men of Affairs

———

Nothing exists from whose nature some effect does not follow.

Benedict Spinoza, *Ethics*,
Proposition XXXVI

Among the Peabodys over the course of the years there were a number of men who definitely set out to mold the course of American affairs in their own ways. This was not always a life-long task, it was not always begun or finished at the usual times of men's lives, but there was a pattern in the affairs of several of the Peabodys which showed an awareness of the family tradition and a noblesse oblige *that it be used for good. There is no segregation of these men by profession or inclination, two of them were ministers of the Gospel, one was an architect, two were men of*

*business affairs, and one was a professional who became an out-
right politician (one of the few in the family history). They were
Ephraim Peabody, a minister and strong-hearted Abolitionist in the
days before the Civil War; Robert Swain Peabody, an architect
who became one of the leading of all American practitioners of
this art; Endicott Peabody, a minister who became one of the foremost of American educators, and knew precisely that he was training men for high position in America; Henry Wayland Peabody,
the businessman with the mien of a priest; George Foster Peabody,
businessman and industrialist, who became a liberal force in American politics and business; and finally, Endicott Peabody, Jr., the
young lawyer who went into politics, adding immeasurably to the
Peabody influence.*

CHAPTER 21

THE WRONG-HEADED ONE

ON MARCH 22, 1807, in Wilton, New Hampshire, was born Ephraim Peabody, the son of Ephraim Peabody, who traced his genealogy back to William, third son of Lieutenant Francis. This
Ephraim grew up a farm boy, then went off to Bowdoin College in
Maine, graduated, studied for the ministry, settled in Cincinnati
in 1831, but moved back to New Bedford to become pastor of the
First Congregational Society in 1838. There he became an ardent
foe of slavery, and a very talkative one—so efficient in his talking
that in 1846 he was asked to come to Boston to be pastor of King's
Chapel, and he did so. There, with more gusto than ever, the Reverend Ephraim Peabody took up the cause of the slaves and the
solution to the dilemma in which Americans found themselves in
the 1850s. In Boston, Ephraim could see that slavery was bringing
about the dissolution of what might become a great nation.

In the 1840s Ephraim Peabody made a particular study of slavery, with the hope that he and other men of good will might find
some manner of not only staving off but avoiding altogether the
"irrepressible conflict" to which most thinking people saw the
United States was heading. The Reverend Ephraim thought he saw
a way, which he considered long and hard, and he went with it to
the editor of the *North American Review*. That editor was none

other than Andrew Preston Peabody—so here we have an instance of Peabody influence on Peabody, cousin to cousin, like mind to like mind, with the result cast forth for the edification of the American people.

Editor Peabody accepted author Peabody's article, and it appeared in the October, 1851, issue of the *Review*, under the title "Slavery in the United States, Its Evils, Alleviations, and Remedies."

In a way, one might say Ephraim Peabody's article was the intelligent, loyal, generous American's statement of the conundrum, and so viewed, it gives a picture of the thinking of the day.

First, author Peabody stated the problem: Slavery, he said, was important because it had become the major element in determining the policy of the general government. Further, the political parties gravitated around the issue of slavery "as if it were a fixed magnetic centre." It exerted a controlling influence on the development of industry in the United States. It exerted prime influence on the regional relationships of the nation. "What is of not less importance," he said, slavery "creates around itself a peculiar social state and classes of interest which have been, and are likely to be, the occasion of perpetual irritation between north and south."

The nation, said the Reverend Ephraim Peabody, was sitting in the eye of the hurricane, the first winds, after blowing severely, having been brought to a temporary lull—or what seemed to be a lull—by the Compromise of 1850, which had been finally engineered in the autumn before publication of this article. During this entire year from October, 1850, to October, 1851, the issue was almost quiescent, because the admissions of states were not at the moment under consideration. The status quo was livable.

The Reverend Peabody welcomed this temporary lull because he felt the nation was given one more chance to treat the issue in the calm, serious way it deserved to be treated, to recognize the problem for what it was, with no political excitement to becloud it.

Speaking from a purely legal standpoint, the Reverend Peabody said, it was apparent to most men of good will that the right to legislate on the question of slavery belonged exclusively to the states. Each state had the right to abolish slavery within its own borders. The general government at the most had the right to exclude slavery from the territories, which were under its management in the interest of all the American people.

As matters stood, said the Reverend Peabody, there could be no doubt that slavery was "an essential and controlling element in the whole social organization of the southern people." And here was the crux of the American problem:

"To reconstruct the whole fabric of society—which is what is implied in any wise method of abolishing slavery—can never be the work of a day."

To get slavery off the statute books everywhere was easy compared to the difficult time any general government would have "to legislate into the minds of whites and blacks" the ideas which belong to the practices of democracy.

What, then, was to be done, granting, as the Reverend Ephraim Peabody certainly did grant, that slavery must be abolished in the interests of Christianity and national progress?

Any change—and the change must come—would have to be very gradual, not the result of revolution, but the result of growth. Revolution would never work, no matter how it might seem to work.

The Reverend Ephraim paused, and took a new point of attack on the problem: Consider the condition of the slaves of the South, he said. They had been brought, in considerable numbers, into the United States over the previous century and a half. In that time they had made great advances in the matter of civilization, picking up much of the moral, social, and religious idea of the South. Compare them, said the Reverend Ephraim, to the native African, who was "still a brute."

But here again was a part of the problem: the curse of slavery was that its existence depended on preventing the slave from developing just those qualities which would make him a decent citizen of the United States. He was shut off from education, and this was essential to his development.

Yet, there were remedies to the slavery question which were worse than the disease, and the United States was drifting toward one of them: civil war.

How could slavery end? Who could abolish it?

Not the North, said the Reverend Ephraim. "Any northern method of agitating the question of slavery . . . must be fatally erroneous." Then what did he offer? The responsibility must be given those who would take it, "that large class of men of the South . . . who desire to see slavery give place to free institutions."

Among these were the spiritual descendants of Jefferson, Madison, and Monroe, all of whom, in their declining years, saw clearly that slavery would in the future be the rock on which the ship of the nation might well founder.

Let there be no mistake, said the Reverend Ephraim Peabody, the South must abolish slavery. Otherwise there would be civil war. But if the South was not allowed to abolish slavery, then too there would be civil war. "Slavery agitation in the North . . . has paralyzed and struck dumb the southern friends of freedom." This northern social interference had resulted in the vast increase in the influence of John C. Calhoun and the immoderates of the South, and in the vast increase in value of slaves, because of the threats.

What must come, then, was the growth of an Emancipation party in the South, of which the seeds existed. Only thus could violence be averted.

Now, what were the prospects as the Reverend Ephraim Peabody saw them?

First, slavery was moving out of the border states and massing in the South. This might not be bad if the Emancipation party would organize, and if the northern agitators would stop frightening the South.

Second, the slaves were improving as human beings. They were more intelligent and more aware of the world around them than ever before, even though the number of free blacks had not increased substantially since the end of the Revolutionary War. In the census of 1850 there were 418,173 free blacks, of whom 233,691 were still in the South. And the tendency of life in America was toward the abolition of slavery.

Let no one fool himself, said the Reverend Ephraim Peabody, seeing clearly ahead through the years: the problem was a problem of race, and it would increase. The blacks were increasing at the rate of 75,000 a year, and so the problem would persist. The Africans should be set free, but they should not be kept in the South. That way lay danger. Either they should be given some territory of their own, or they should be sent back to Africa.

What the Reverend Ephraim Peabody feared, in the genetic and anthropological ignorance of his time, was a mongrelization of the races, and nearly every man feared such amalgamation. He referred to the product of intermarriage between blacks and whites as "a third race, inferior to both white and Negro."

His answer, delivered in all seriousness, was colonization. The black must be sent away, set apart, because in the American scheme he could "never rise above the firm lines of caste, even if set free."

He proposed to remove 100,000 blacks a year for twenty years, at the end of which time the blacks would nearly all be gone and slavery would have ceased to exist. Thus the blacks would prosper, going home to Africa with new skills, and the whites would be relieved of the "class whose presence . . . causes the South to look with dread on emancipation."

What was wanted was establishment of some place, whether it be in Africa, or a Caribbean island, or even in Mexico, which might be annexed in toto.

So, there was the Reverend Ephraim Peabody's program, delivered as the solution to slavery by a man of good will, who recognized, nonetheless, that if his proposal was not accepted, if the United States continued on its road of dissolution, still "we must preserve the Union. If the Union is dissolved, the fate of the Negro would be hopeless. All thought of the abolition of slavery, except through insurrection, would be at an end."

Because the Reverend Ephraim Peabody was known to be a man of good common sense, combined with sensitivity and the utmost purity of character, his article was given wide credence in the North, except among the most extreme Abolitionists, whose attitude was always that this transportation of slaves to Africa or anywhere else would not work. Fortunately for the spirit of the Reverend Ephraim Peabody, if not for his earthly presence, he died in 1856, when the debate was still raging, and some were still talking about the possibility of transportation. Yet while nothing the Reverend Ephraim wanted came to pass, his influence was pervasive, in North and South, and it was an influence for good. To the South he represented hope that the northerners might be amenable to southern reason, and to the North he represented an enlightened although moderate view of the problem of slavery. For his own sake, Ephraim Peabody was a lucky man to die at forty-nine, for the ten years that followed would only have convinced him of the folly of humankind.

CHAPTER 22

THE ARCHITECT

WHEN EPHRAIM PEABODY died at so early an age, he left behind him a legacy of gentleness and thoughtfulness, and not so very much else. His wife, however, was fairly well-to-do in her own right, being a Derby of Salem, daughter of a prosperous merchant, so her children had no fear of want. One of those children, Robert Swain Peabody, showed definite promise as an artist, even as a child. He was sent to the fashionable school run by Mr. Dixwell in Boston, and mingled there with the children of his father's parishioners at King's Chapel. But his father was gone when the boy was eleven years old, and the influences on him thereafter were maternal and what he might gain from being a boy among boys at the school.

In 1863, Robert Swain Peabody crossed the Charles and moved into the Harvard yard, to begin his studies as a freshman at the college. It was the same old grind, Greek and Latin, mathematics and rhetoric, and the Bible as a standby. He came under the influence of Old Doc Peabody, the college chaplain, and studied Christian morals and ethics under him. By this time, of course, Peabody scarcely knew Peabody, and although the boy might have marveled at the similarities of names, there was no closer relationship than that.

At Harvard, Robert Swain Peabody developed a strong body and a good mind. He rowed on the eight that swept its field in the Eastern Rowing Championships, and he was popular enough and stood high enough in his class to be chosen Chief Marshal on Class Day. Having finished the liberal arts education which made of him a gentleman of the Boston school, Robert Swain Peabody headed for Paris, for here was the soul of what he hoped to secure: a love and feeling for the arts.

Napoleon III had begun the revitalization of the city with the help of Baron Georges Haussmann. The streets were widened and the squares were filled with statuary and such objects as the Luxor obelisk in the Place de la Concorde. The railroad stations had been built, scattered intentionally throughout the city to give access to the north, south, east, and west. The Halles Centrales had been built and placed so that the people of Paris could reach their markets. Paris was in a period of architectural brilliance and the arts were flourishing. A universal exposition was held the year that Robert Swain Peabody arrived, 1867.

France, Germany, and Austria were all vying for leadership in the fields of the arts, but France was winning easily although the other two nations were making contributions, particularly in the fields of sculpture and architecture. The revolution that would be Impressionism was brewing in the streets of Montmatre and the sunny southland. Meanwhile Eugene Delacroix had just died, leaving a heritage of fine color. Hippolyte Flandrin was recognized as the greatest religious painter of the age, and Vernet, Delaroche, Fleury, and Cogniet were the old masters of the day (most of them had died within the decade). Paul Baudry was painting frescoes for the new Opera. Landelle was painting Italian scenes. Fromentin chose the Orient as his subject. A half-dozen French artists were doing battle paintings. But Jules Breton and François Millet were to emerge, painting peasants and the farm country. And then, of course, there was Corot, whose work was recognized for its silvery haze. Rosa Bonheur and her animals, Courbet and his landscapes, and Theodore Rousseau, who had just died, were all powerful figures in the galleries and the museums.

Soon Robert Swain Peabody had passed the entrance examinations and was enrolled in the Ecoles des Beaux-Arts in Paris, and entered the Atelier Daumet. He studied hard, and when he was not sudying he was roaming the countryside sketching great buildings. It was an era of great buildings: in Vienna, J. G. Muller had built the Altlerchenfelder Church in the Romanesque; Calgrin built the Arc de l'Etoile, and Vignon, the Madeleine; Gau, the Church of Ste Clothilde; Hittorf, the Church of St. Vincent de Paul; and the Hotel de Ville had just been extended, as had the Louvre. Then there was Garnier's new Opera, Duc's Palais de Justice and Beuilly's Tribune de Commerce. Peabody went to Italy to see the new Victor Emmanuel Arcade in Milan and he traveled to England to draw famous buildings there.

Robert's friends in Paris were Charles Follen McKim and Frank W. Chandler, who would both be heard from. And as for Peabody, he studied and loafed through the Continent, then came home with a fine hand and a fine eye and a grand memory of what he had seen and drawn. Without business experience, without knowledge of the functioning aspects of architecture, the practical matters of dealing with builders and clients and the world at large, he formed a partnership with John G. Stearns, also of Harvard, and they set out to conquer the world. Fortunately, Stearns knew all that Peabody did not—how to get along with tough contractors, how to superintend a job so that the costs did not skyrocket, and how to choose materials.

With Peabody's brains and artistic ability, as well as his strong connections in Boston through the old King's Chapel friends, together with Stearn's intense practicality, they did conquer their world, and became one of the leading architectural firms in all America.

They designed the Matthews Hall and Hemenway Gymnasium at Harvard, the railroad station that graced Providence for many years, and such landmarks in Boston as the Telephone Building, the

Customs House Tower, and the Exchange Building. They built the Groton School for another Peabody, the granite State House at Concord, New Hampshire, the stern Union League Club in New York, as well as the lodge house atop Pikes Peak, and the old Antlers Hotel at the foot of the mountains, looking straight down Pikes Peak Avenue in Colorado Springs—in its day the finest resort hotel in all America. They were represented at the World's Columbian Exposition in Chicago; and at the Buffalo Exposition, Robert went to rub shoulders with old Selim Hobart Peabody.

What did Robert Peabody bring to American architecture? For one thing, he was one who brought the Italian Renaissance style, which he admired from his student days. For another, he brought good taste rather than any style, and he trained dozens of the nation's architects in clean line and functionalism.

In Peabody's later years, many honors came to him. He was an overseer of Harvard for eleven years after 1888. He was many times president of the Boston Society of Architects. He was a serious and apt student of the problem of Boston rejuvenation, without destroying the old landmarks. He was one of the firm figures of the American Institute of Architects, working for the betterment of art in American building. He was a strong supporter of the effort begun around the turn of the century to beautify Washington, D.C., and he wrote widely, illustrating his own works with his drawings, showing cities, ports, and handsome buildings, for the education of his friends and other architects. His influence? Certainly he was one of the principal influences for the beautification of American cities with light, airy buildings, at a time when American millionaires leaned toward castles and Victorian gewgaws. In the last five years of his life he was ill, a semi-invalid, and he cut his work load drastically; and yet he still sketched and still considered new ideas in building up to the last, leaving in his notebooks, sketches, and his buildings an enormous influence on the style of American living.

CHAPTER 23

THE MAN FROM TOMBSTONE

When, on February 23, 1884, Endicott Peabody engineered the first meeting of the board of trustees of his new academy for boys, and when they appointed the architectural firm of Peabody and Stearns of Boston to build a schoolhouse for $37,000, the one Peabody was not turning to his cousin because of any relationship, but because Peabody and Stearns was the finest architectural firm in New England.

But who was Endicott Peabody and what was this new school, Groton, all about?

That is a story that began, as with all Peabodys, in the days of Lieutenant Francis. Endicott, who would found the school, came down through the line of Isaac, and old Joseph the merchant was his great-grandfather. Joseph's son Francis, the grandfather of the educator, was the inventor Peabody, the chemist who dabbled in powers and cements, manufactured sacking, and built his own pianola.

From the wealth accumulated and inherited, Francis built an estate called Kernwood on the Beverly side of Salem, where he liked to go, but he kept a brick house on Essex Street, too.

Francis had son named Samuel Endicott Peabody, who learned about life in school at Salem, at Harvard for a year, and then aboard one of the Peabody ships that sailed the eastern seas. He married Marianne Cabot Lee, whose father founded Lee, Higginson and Company. Samuel Endicott Peabody had a brother named Francis, who married a Providence girl named Helen Bloodgood (of the Bloodgoods who owned Perry's Pain Killer). Endicott Peabody was born to Samuel Endicott and Marianne in 1857; his first cousin Fanny Peabody arrived in 1860.

Endicott Peabody grew up a well-to-do boy in Salem with four brothers and sisters. He went to the Hacker school, and stayed there until he was thirteen years old. Then, old George Peabody, the banker, died in London, and his body was brought back for the ceremonious funeral recounted earlier. With the coming of the body, Junius S. Morgan, the banker, returned to the United States as well, and to show his appreciation for what George Peabody had done for the Morgans, Junius Morgan offered to take Samuel Endicott Peabody into the London firm. Samuel Endicott decided to go to London, as did Jacob Rogers, his brother-in-law, and so the Peabodys moved to England. They went by ship, the *Allepo*, whose captain made an adventure of the crossing by smashing into a brig just outside Minot's Light. Once in England, Endicott was sent to boarding school at Cheltenham.

At the school he shot himself in the hand while playing with a pair of dueling pistols one of the boys had brought down in his trunk. Cotty (as he was known) ran a mile to a surgeon's house for treatment. The surgeon was kindly but not very competent, and although Cotty Peabody insisted that the slug from the dueling pistol was still in the hand, the doctor bound him up and sent him off to bed at the school, where he stayed for five weeks before the authorities gathered that something was wrong, and he was sent down to London to visit a competent surgeon. His hand was stiff and took a long time to loosen up, even after the slug was removed by the London surgeon.

But that did not keep Endicott Peabody from athletics. He played cricket on the first eleven, and fives and racquets. He also played court tennis and other particularly English games and won cups for doing them well. Later, when his hand allowed it, he rowed. He was a prefect in his sixth form year, and eventually he managed to convince his English school companions that Americans—or some of them—were human and could be allowed in the drawing room.

In 1876 when Peabody was nineteen years old, after five years at Cheltenham, he went home to Salem for a visit, and then to Trinity College, Cambridge, where he studied, rowed and played cricket, with the vague idea of going into business somewhere, sometime, when the school days ran out.

The Cambridge adventure lasted three and a half years, and during that period Endicott Peabody decided to study for a degree in law. He took a walking tour through Normandy, and a trip through Italy with his mother and father, paying no attention at all to the art and architecture which so fascinated Robert Swain Peabody in his tours of the same general areas. Endicott became thoroughly Anglicized in his approach to life and in his humor, which biographer Frank Ashton later characterized as similiar to that of the *Punch* humor of the day.

Also, during this period, Peabody changed his religious affiliation. He had grown up, like many Peabodys, in the Unitarian church of New England. In England, he discovered the trappings and the friendliness of the Church of England, which contrasted so with the intellectuality of the Unitarian—after all an offshoot of the old Puritan faith, which rejected the trappings that so appealed to young Peabody. One might say, in a sense, that this Peabody was the first to make the trip "home" to England since Lieutenant Francis Peabody had looked back to say his private good-byes from the deck of the *Planter* in 1635. In any event, he was the first to come so completely full circle. It had taken nearly two and a half centuries for the circle to be completed, and for the ancient wounds to be wiped out.

The wounds were wiped out, although like most Americans who visited England he came up against the usual nineteenth-century superiority of the British.

"A man named Thompson was Master of Trinity when I got there," he said. "He was a dreadful fellow, so aloof. He used to have what were called 'stand-ups' where you went and stood around and wondered when you could get off."

But other aspects of life at Cambridge were better:

> I used to get up early in the morning to work and the bed-maker would come in and cook me some porridge. I would work for an hour, then breakfast would be sent up. I'd work through the morning, have lectures, then lunch either by myself or with a friend. The bed-maker would look after your lunch. Then you would go down to the boats if you were a rowing man; perhaps stop at the Pitt Club. You could post a letter there without putting a stamp on it. In rowing, you would always have a coach with you who would ride along the tow path. In the Bumping Races, the undergraduates would run along the bank with fog horns, bells, everything imaginable, and when they got near a bump it was the most complete presentation of a row.

Pleasant times in pleasant years. But they came to an end in 1878. That year events proved how well Junius Morgan had served the Peabodys in exchange for the great service George Peabody had done for him. Samuel Endicott Peabody had lived in London for less than a decade, yet he had made a large fortune in banking, and was ready to go home and retire. He might have retired in England, but he preferred Salem. So the family that spring was making ready to return to the United States. What would Endicott do?

The study of law in England was not the best manner to equip oneself for a career in the United States. But Endicott had learned in three and a half years that he did not want to be a lawyer, anyhow.

He was twenty-one years old when he came back to the United States, and having nothing else on his mind he took a job with the brokerage house of Lee, Higginson and Company, his maternal grandfather's firm. His future was obviously bright there, but the present could not be termed so. He was put to work learning to compute interest and run errands, and he found that the financial world bored him. He was a big young man, handsome in a way, with broad shoulders, blue eyes, and a face that wrinkled often in laughter. He was fair-haired and agile, and quite the young man of Boston society in that first year.

In the second year at Lee, Higginson things were not much better from Peabody's point of view. He was being groomed for a high management post, but he did not care for the attention, and he was constantly stirred about what he ought to do with himself His elder brother Jack had wanted to go into the ministry, but Samuel Endicott Peabody had the red-blooded businessman's distaste for the cloth, and had dissuaded the older Peabody boy. Then Jack drifted from art to architecture, without being interested or showing promise, and Samuel, who was a good father, decided he ought not to have interfered.

When Endicott evidenced the same inclination toward the ministry, his father did not interfere. The boy called on Phillips Brooks, the rector of Trinity Church, who persuaded him to an ecclesiastical career and supplied introductions to the Episcopal Theological Seminary at Cambridge.

Young Peabody studied theology under Dr. Henry Nash, and he started a mission, along with other students, in Boston's South End.

Endicott had found his calling. He was admirably suited for the ministry because he possessed a believing mind. Take the matter of immortality:

One day, Peabody was asked why he could believe in immortality.

"Why," he said in surprise, "the Bible states clearly that Christ assured us of life immortal."

"Where?" asked his questioner.

"When he turned to the penitent thief on the other cross and said 'Today thou shalt be with me in Paradise.' "

Peabody was a born believer, and nothing he ever saw on earth changed his mind about God. Perhaps that is what makes the remainder of this remarkable man's career credible.

The career began with a foray into the unlikely wilds (for a

Bostonian educated in England) of Tombstone, Arizona. Endicott Peabody and Tombstone were drawn together by Grafton Abbott, who knew the Peabodys. He had gone out to Tombstone to run a mine, and when the local church vestry quarreled with its rector and the minster left, Abbott asked if Endicott would come out and take over the church.

Endicott had not been at the seminary more than a few months, boning Greek, Latin, and Hebrew as well as his sacred studies, but he was fascinated by the offer. Still, he was also in love, with cousin Fanny Peabody. But on balance, the opportunity seemed to be to great to pass up, so in January, 1882, he packed up his bags and went west.

Endicott Peabody, a tenderfoot if there ever was one, arrived from the effete East, fittingly enough, on the midnight train, and he would never forget his first impression:

> Reaching Tombstone shortly after midnight, I was shown to a room in the hotel which was over-ventilated for mid-winter owing to both the windows and the transom being broken. As I began to unpack my suitcase, there came a loud knock at the door, and in marched three men. Standing in line, the chairman bade me welcome to Tombstone, apologizing for the late arrival of his committee owing to the fact that they had become interested in a game of cards. . . .

Next day, Endicott Peabody went out to look around the pastures of his new flock. Shortly before his arrival the brothers Earp and their friends had engaged in the famous gun duel that made the town's name in motion picture history. But that was the end of the bad old Tombstone, and by the time Endicott Peabody arrived, there was not even a murder a week any more. One of Peabody's friends, an assay man, was killed in the dead of night when he came to answer a knock on his door, and his friend the bank manager was in constant danger, as were all law enforcement officers, but affairs were relatively quiet.

Peabody busied himself tending his flock, burying the dead miners (often having succumbed to alcohol as deadly as any lead bullet) and putting to rest the prominent citizens. All were buried in Boot Hill, the town cemetery, the difference being that the miners were taken quietly in a box in a wagon, while the leading citizens were mourned by a procession led by a band and a black-draped hearse.

The churchgoers met in the courthouse at first, but Endicott Peabody raised funds and built a small church. He organized a baseball nine, amazed the miners by insisting on draping his window with a blanket when he took a bath, and received the following notice in the local *Epitaph:* "Well, we've got a parson who doesn't flirt with the girls, who doesn't drink beer behind the door, and when it comes to baseball, he's a daisy." High words of praise in the West in 1882.

Endicott, in fact, was a howling success as a frontier preacher because he was fatalistic enough to take life as it came. The Earps were still having trouble, after the "shootout" on the main street, and their enemies (including the town sheriff) were attempting to assassinate them from time to time. So there was some danger on the three streets of Tombstone every day and particularly at night. Endicott was not worried:

> The ordinary citizen is unmolested and the only danger is from a stray shot . . . but in my circumstances one is safe enough, so there is little cause for anxiety and I feel, perhaps more because of my errand, that it is best to leave it all with Him for whom I am trying to work. . . .

So he did work, building his church and his congregation. The man before him had let the Catholics, the Methodists, and the Presbyterians get a head start, but Endicott soon had some twenty-five parishioners and a church by May. Then came the great Tombstone fire of May 25, 1882.

It started at the back of a saloon next to the Grand Hotel, the largest building in the center of town. The wind was blowing hard, as it usually did in the spring in Tombstone, and soon the false fronts and awnings of the buildings nearby caught, and began burning like dry kindling. The hand engine was wheeled up from the fire station, but it had seen far better days and could not cope with the flames. The miners consulted and came up with a solution. They blew up the two houses at the ends of the block with gunpowder to keep the fire from spreading—there was no chance of dousing it and the skies were blue as the sea, so no help from God could be expected that day, either.

Endicott Peabody rushed to one of the general stores where there was a call for help and began unpacking cartridges and powder, lest the store catch fire. In the saloons the men rolled out fifty gallon barrels of whiskey and then the bartenders stood guard over them with cocked pistols, but still a quarter of the fire-fighters were nearly dead drunk in an hour.

The fire started at three o'clock in the afternoon. By five o'clock most of the business district was burned to the ground, and the drunks were prowling about, seeing what they could steal. Some shots were fired, and it was discovered that one fellow was burned to death in a saloon, whether shot first or not, he was in no condition to ascertain. From Endicott's point of view God was good because neither his church, nor his little parsonage, nor any other churches were harmed that day, although the fire was heading their way when it was stopped by gunpowder. That night the town was wild, and saloonkeepers rolled their barrels back into the ashes and set up planks, and business was declared open again. Cowboys and miners roamed the streets drunk and carrying guns. On one errand Endicott Peabody passed a drunken cowboy who was shooting up the street, but the minister was not noticed in the shadows. "I can assure you," he wrote, "I was pleased when I had got by him."

By late spring, after five months of writing sermons and dealing with new problems, Endicott Peabody felt the need for at least two more years of study, and referred to his "present condition of ignorance." In July he was showing extreme homesickness and decided to go back to the East in the autumn. His congregation protested. They did not want him to leave them, for they liked his attitude, and were able to forgive him his English ways. He was, they said, just the kind of minister they needed. Why? Well, an incident in July gave some indication: A drunken Mexican cowboy murdered a young deputy sheriff, and in the excitement that followed, a lynch mob was organized, but then it collapsed because nobody was brave enough to take the rope and actually hang the man. Mr. Peabody observed and commented:

"I really think that an example of frontier justice with the next white murderer would be a good thing—for the place is full of desperadoes who hold the lives of others and themselves very cheap."

Small wonder, was it, that the people of Tombstone liked their minister? He was just their kind of fellow, and they wanted him to stay.

But the need for education, the longing for Boston, and the loneliness for his first cousin drove Endicott Peabody home that fall. When he was twenty-five, then, he returned to theological school. He consulted with his father about marrying his first cousin (he had not asked her), and Samuel Endicott said it would be most unwise. Endicott gave her up, but then found a doctor somewhere who said the marriage was a fine idea, so he renewed his suit.

In the spring of 1883, his wooing continued, and Endicott Peabody began to have a glimpse of the life he would like to lead. It came during Holy Week that year. He accepted an invitation to go down to St. Marks School an Episcopal boys' boarding school, and make a talk each morning of Holy Week. He found that working with boys was just what he wanted to do. He came back, and was approached by the St. Marks trustees with the thought of coming down as headmaster, but the charter of the school called for an ordained minister and Peabody was not ordained. Nor did the Bishop approve of Peabody as the headmaster of St. Marks, which meant that he would never get the job.

Dr. Leighton Parks, the rector of Emmanuel Church, put the idea of starting a school into Peabody's head. Parks liked the student, and said he would try to help him. With his marvelous financial and social connections, why didn't he start a school of his own?

The idea was just what Peabody wanted. He could get money from family and friends. He could get boys from family and friends. Why not?

Peabody went to the Reverend Phillips Brooks with this problem, and Brooks gave him excellent advice. There was an opening at St. Paul's boys' school in Concord, New Hampshire. Why didn't Peabody take that for a year or so, and see how it went? Then he could make up his mind.

But Endicott Peabody was a forceful young man who had already made up his mind, and the fact that he had never taught in a boys' school made not a jot of difference to him. He would start a school.

Peabody friends, the James Lawrences, donated a farm of ninety acres at Groton, Massachusetts, a small rural community of rolling farmland and woods centered on a village with a few stores and an inn. Other Peabody acquaintances, friends of acquaintances, and people Peabody knew only by reputation agreed to give money for the foundation of this school. The Dean of the Episcopal Theological School (a Lawrence) agreed to be president of the board of trustees. Peabody's father was treasurer. J. Pierpont Morgan, son of Samuel Endicott Peabody's old partner, was a member of the board. So the school was launched. In October, 1884, it opened its first fall term with twenty-seven boys.

The announced purpose of the school was "to cultivate manly, Christian character, having regard to moral and physical as well as intellectual development." More than that, the idea of Endicott Peabody was to exert an influence on the world through these boys, by instilling in them a capacity for leadership and service. It was quite an ambition to be undertaken by a young man of twenty-seven years.

There were classes in Latin, Greek, grammar, mathematics, and French. There were no organized athletics because there were not enough boys to go around, but they played a kind of football, masters and boys, in which the whole school was divided into two sides and ran after the ball. The first house was called Brooks

House, which together with a red barn that was also the gymnasium, and a white frame farmhouse, constituted the school. The boys went to class in the mornings, studied in the evenings, and raised hob in the afternoons, playing practical jokes on one another and sometimes on some of the weaker masters.

Peabody was married in the summer of 1886, and the school acquired a lady, who brought a certain gentility.

Peabody, himself, held that a headmaster had to be a bit of a bully, and so he set about making the boys fearful of him, very respectful, thoroughly awed, and perhaps even liking him a little for his accomplishments. He dressed immaculately, in blue or gray suits with low collars and white or black bow ties with the ends tucked in, or in country fashion, in knickerbockers, wool stockings, and a tweed jacket. He rode a horse, a bicycle, and a motorcar when it became popular. He got up at six o'clock in the morning and began his work before the rest of the family awoke, held family prayers (eventually there were six children), had family breakfast, then went to the infirmary to see the sick boys, and then to chapel to see the well ones. Chapel began at 8:15, and then it was off to the schoolhouse where he worked until lunch, either at his desk or teaching, with a break for calisthenics at recess. Afterward he spoke with the senior prefect, chief of the student government, and then went to lunch, where if there was a roast he carved. Mrs. Peabody joined the school for lunch, and never managed to finish on time in fifty-six years, which annoyed the rector no end, but he could do absolutely nothing about it. It was her way of showing her independence. Then, after lunch, there was faculty coffee at which the ladies and gentlemen separated, a brief rest, exercise for an hour, then work for the rest of the afternoon, tea, supper at six, evening prayers, work until 8:45, perhaps a faculty supper, and then to bed by 9:30. The schedule changed, of course, but it was his program, more or less, for the next half century.

Almost immediately Peabody began raising money to enlarge his school. He built a gymnasium, and then the famous "fives" courts,

to introduce to his boys the unique English game he had learned
at his old boarding school. Then came Hundred House, named
because it was to house 100 boys, plus the headmaster, dining room,
and study halls. There followed the library, laundry, and chapel.
The Schoolhouse was built in 1900, and every few years it seemed
something new was added, to keep Groton strong and growing.

Starting with 27 boys, the school grew until in 1910 there were
160 boys. Since that time it has increased very little, as it was Endicott Peabody's belief that a small school was better than a large one.
The boys lived in alcoves in the school, washing with cold water
for a long time, in washpans and sleeping on hard cots. They
learned to be tough and polite, strong-minded, punctual, and independent.

Over the years Groton secured large endowments, from friends
of the school, friends of Peabody, alumni, and their families, and
became a thoroughly independent, self-supporting institution.

As his boys went out into the world, to college and beyond,
Endicott Peabody continued to take a personal interest in their
welfare and their conduct. He was never far from them, no farther
than the public prints and the post office.

One of the Rector's outstanding quarrels, which lasted for years,
was with the management of Harvard College. That university
had changed a very great deal from the days of Oliver William
Bourne Peabody and William Bourne Oliver Peabody. By the time
the Groton graduates began filing into the ivied halls of the "yard"
it was a free-swinging institution, where the undergraduates were
rather left to their own devices about such matters as morals and
social customs. Consequently, coming from the strait-laced and
highly protective atmosphere of Groton, some boys went wild.
Peabody thought something ought to be done, and he tried his
best to do it, but never succeeded in changing Harvard's ways.
After one scrape he resigned his honorary membership in the Por-
cellian Society.

When an old Groton boy was warned in a college football game

for trying to strike a member of the opposite team, Peabody sat
down and write a discourse on "dirty playing."

When a child was born to a graduate, he might write thus:

> My heartiest congratulations upon the birth of your little son!
> I am delighted to hear of the happiness of you and your wife and
> of the lad himself, for it is surely a good thing to be born into this
> world. After a long life, may the earth be better for his having
> been here. I am enclosing herewith a blank form of application,
> or rather, asking Mr. Andress to do so. . . .

The last, the application, was no joke. Boys had to be registered
at birth in order to be sure of getting places in the school. Groton
achieved a reputation for snobbery, which Peabody resented in a
way, but at least it was a reputation, and no one ever claimed it
was not a good school.

The graduates never went without the Rector's eye upon them,
and it could look sternly:

> You are one of four Groton boys whom the college reports to
> be on probation. Your record . . . will be as much of a disappoint-
> ment to your father and your aunt as it has been to me and the
> other Masters who tried to prepare you for College. . . .

He could also be downright shocking:

> I feel obliged to tell you that the contents of your letter from
> Bermuda have brought me great distress. I have been informed that
> Mrs. . . . obtained a decree of divorce from her husband for some
> reason other than that of unfaithfulness on his part. This being the
> case, she was not in my judgment free to contract another mar-
> riage. . . .

He could be outrageous as when he wrote one graduate object-
ing to a marriage which had been approved by the boy's parents,
and the boy told him so. "It seems very strange that you . . .
should step in and so candidly express your disapproval, especially when, as your letter clearly denotes, you knew nothing of
the circumstances. . . ."

But always he was interested in all of them. When Franklin
Roosevelt became engaged to Eleanor, Franklin wrote Endicott

Peabody and asked him to be sure to come to the wedding. For many, many years, both retired or departed members of the faculty and the boys kept up with their old mentor, despite his occasional churlishness.

One of the important aspects of the impact of Groton School on the United States was the quality of its faculty, which for a small, private school was very high. One teacher became a bishop. Another, Ellery Sedgwick, became editor of the *Atlantic Monthly*. One became president of Hartford's Trinity College, and many remained at Groton, teaching for twenty, thirty, or forty years. As for the boys, they included hundreds of famous Americans in many fields: Kermit Roosevelt, Frederick L. Allen, Lincoln Mac-Veigh, Oliver La Farge, Cass Canfield, Colonel Robert McCormick, in publishing and the literary fields. In diplomacy there were such men as Joseph C. Grew, Sumner Welles, and Dean Acheson. There were, of course, rich and social men, men in business and men too wealthy to be bothered with business. As noted by his biographer, Frank D. Ashburn, the Rector was a man of strong ideas.

Peabody and Groton were Hamiltonian and not Jeffersonian. He was a patrician and believed in patricians. If it is not the popular kind of democracy today, it is a very genuine kind from which the modern fashion originated. It would have been understood by Sir Harry Vane or Washington or the Adamses or Gladstone or Winston Churchill. It was a theory of democracy which holds that all men are entitled to justice before the law, with equal opportunity for equal talents as an unrealized goal rather than a realized fact. It made no pretense of considering all men equal, since, it held, experience and common sense proved they were not. It believed that democracy was the hope of the world, with free speech and the rights of conscience, but it also believed that the only hope of democracy was its ability to produce an ever devoted and intelligent and honest aristocracy. It objected to the theory that the average or mediocre is as good as the best.

He became stronger in his political and social opinions as time went on, and he gloried when some Grotonian achieved a place where he affected the course of human events, but he did not try to use his influence—whatever it might have been—to achieve ends in political or social change. He voted for Herbert Hoover in 1932, for example, although old Grotonian Franklin Roosevlet was running, but then when Roosevelt was elected, Peabody was pleased and convinced that Roosevelt would do his best for the country. And as time went on and many old Grotonians turned against Roosevelt, Peabody stuck by his guns.

For more than fifty years Endicott Peabody ran his school. Then in 1939, he felt his health deserting him. He was in his eighties, and he did not feel strong enough to continue running so vigorous a mechanism as a boys' school, so he retired, effective the following year. He could not keep away from Groton, of course, and he lived near the school grounds in a house built for him by the school. He lived on for a few years more, carrying on his correspondence with "old boys," watching them take the influence of Groton across the world. Francis Biddle became Attorney General. Sumner Welles became Undersecretary of State, Averell Harriman was American minister in London just at the outbreak of war, and then went to Russia. Grotonians were generals and admirals, too, and they were in the House and Senate and in the judiciary. Where they were, so was a little piece of the soul of Endicott Peabody, for no boy spent six or even four years under his tutelage without being influenced by his deep Christian beliefs, and his special brand of democracy.

Before Peabody retired there was an assessment of the school properties and values, and it was discovered that the little institution was worth more than five million dollars in plant, possessions, and endowment, which meant that Groton would long continue to have its impact on the American society, and that Peabody had accomplished something else in which he strongly believed. It was not enough to be right; one must also be successful to be effective, he said. In the 1940s, just before he died, Endicott Peabody could look out over his rimmed spectacles, beneath his broad-brimmed hat and smile broadly. Because he had done what he set out to do. Everything was just the way he wanted it.

CHAPTER 24

THE GENTLE MERCHANTS

IMAGINE, IF YOU WILL, a merchant who looks like a judge or a learned professor of medicine in neat black dress with a shining white wing collar and spotless gray silk cravat, white hair, white short beard, and full mustache—and you will have a picture of Henry Wayland Peabody, one of the merchant Peabodys, in his prime.

Henry Wayland Peabody never achieved great fame, and yet the story of him and his father is very much a part of the pattern of America.

This Peabody was descended from the line that included George Peabody. Henry's father, Alfred, was a gay blade with thick black hair, a widow's peak, long bristly sideburns, and a high color that gave him a look of perpetual excitement. His was an exciting life. He went to Buenos Aires in 1827 and liked it so well that he opened his own business there. He came home and married a local beauty, Miss Jerusha Tay, who had studied at Miss Perkins' Academy for young ladies, a slender, black-haired girl who never forgave her family for naming her Jerusha and always signed her name J.

Back they went to Buenos Aires to make a fortune in trade, and stayed for three years. Then Alfred Peabody saw opportunity in Buffalo, New York, with the surge of the Erie Canal, and took his bride there for a few months, but the Panic of 1837 wiped out his business. He raised enough money to return to Buenos Aires, where he became agent for the successful Salem firm of Robert Upton and remained six years, replenishing his fortune, after which he came home.

Again, he was wiped out when hides (his principal trade) fell to a new low on the market and remained there. As Jerusha did not want to go abroad again with the growing family, he entered the shoe business in Salem, forming a firm with John J. Ashby. But Alfred Peabody should have known better. He was not built to sell shoes to Salem ladies or to "tend store," and the moment that the discovery of gold in California offered a new chance to conquer the unknown, he was putting his affairs to rights. He found backers and sailed on the bark *Eliza* on December 23, 1848: his destination Sacramento.

On the morning of sailing from Derby wharf, a grand crowd assembled. Here, two days before Christmas, the young merchant was setting out without apparent regard for wife or children. But the fact was that Alfred Peabody knew precisely what he was doing, and why he must go. Gold had been discovered on Sutter Creek in January and had created a rush to the Sacramento area. But the news was not that quick to come east, nor was the impact that strong in Boston and New York in the very beginning. On December 5, however, President Polk mentioned the discovery in his annual message to Congress on the State of the Union—which meant that there must be a great deal of gold in California, that fortunes were to be made there, and that timing was all-important. Alfred Peabody knew that the first merchants to get in on the scene would have the inside track.

Of course, one did not assemble so serious an enterprise in a few days or weeks, and the California plan had been in motion for months. But the decision to leave just as soon as possible was made when the President acknowledged the discovery. Alfred Peabody knew only too well what would happen next, and he was determined to be on the scene before other Boston, Salem, and New

York merchants could steal the cream of the profits. So the cargo was rushed and loaded. The plans had been thorough. There were hams and barrels of salt pork, flour, sugar, coffee, butter in barrels, cheese, rice, figs, raisins, dried apples, bread, meal, pickles, boots, shoes, chairs, nails, cook stoves, pans and pots, axes, shovels, picks, and hundreds of other items of everyday living. Besides this Alfred Peaobdy brought along half a shipload of lumber for building, and plans for a store, materials for building a boat, which could go up the shallow rivers, a dredge, a steam engine, a lathe, and repair kits for every mechanical device. He took along boat builders, carpenters and machinists.

So they all assembled on the dock on the day before Christmas Eve and paid tearful farewells to their families, all the while casting nervous looks across the first wharf to a second where lay the brig *Mary and Ellen*, which was also getting ready for sea.

Soon everything was shipshape. The tide was right, the wind was fresh, and Captain Perkins ordered the lines cast off. One of the passengers, who had a banjo, had stayed up late, writing new words to the song "Oh! Susanna," and he now struck up a chord and began to sing.

> I came from Salem City,
> 　With my washboard on my knee,
> I'm going to California,
> 　The gold dust for to see.
> It rained all night the day I left,
> 　The weather it was dry,
> The sun so hot I froze to death,
> 　Oh! Brothers, don't you cry.
>
> Oh! California,
> That's the land for me!
> I'm going to Sacramento
> With my washboard on my knee.

Then began the second verse:

> I jumped aboard the 'Liza ship,
> 　And traveled on the sea . . .

By this time the passengers, the crew and the tearful friends and families standing on the dock were all joining in the chorus. The voices rose, smiles exchanged, and handkerchiefs were fluttering in the air. The passengers and all free men rushed aft as the ship headed out toward the mouth of the harbor, singing lustily, as the first verse was repeated. Then the distance grew so great that there were two songs, the song of the travelers and the song of the stay-at-homes. The people on the dock suddenly heard their own voices in the trailing notes of the banjo now far off, and they stopped singing and looked at each other self-consciously as the music died away.

Aboard the *Eliza* all was motion. These gold seekers were eager and ready, and the ship had scarcely cleared the Massachusetts coast than the shipwright and the carpenters were at work building the river craft. They were already first in one thing: the first ship bound for California with trade from Massachusetts. A handful of vessels had gone out from New York, but so far the rush was small, and the passenger trade was easily handled by the single pair of steamers that worked the Panama isthmus once a month.

Eliza and her passengers were lucky. The voyage around the Horn was made in uniformly good weather, and on June 1, 1849, the ship was in San Francisco Bay by 9:00 P.M., having made the passage in a hundred and sixty days.

As the first boat came alongside, the men rushed to the rail with a single question on their lips: "Has the gold held out?"

That was the important matter, for all they had chanced depended on the gold lasting.

But the gold had held out, and the reports of new finds were even better than expected. "We were very much pleased," said Alfred Peabody, "to learn that before we left home the half had not been told."

San Francisco was nothing to look at, one mangy wharf forty feet long, rough dirt streets without sidewalks, a ramshackle hotel and a customs house of adobe that dated from the Spanish times. There were, however, already a dozen shops of rude boards, selling mining tools and cooking untensils. Peabody went ashore and began to talk business with the merchants. It was Saturday, and the first merchant he came to was too busy to look at his wares or come to the ship. Peabody suggested returning the next week.

"Come Sunday," said the man.

Peabody never did business on Sunday, for he was a Salem Peabody.

"Oh, well," said the merchant. "You have just arrived; after you have been here a month you will do as we do."

"If nobody else in California keeps the Sabbath, I will," said Alfred Peabody.

"You are right," said the man. "I have gone with the crowd. . . ."

But Peabody did not go with the crowd, then or ever. Many who came out with the clear eyes of merchants were struck by the get-rich fever and abandoned trade for gold digging. They usually came home open-handed, while the traders, the middlemen, made their fortunes and multiplied them. Up in Sacremento, Leland Stanford would start a general store, and from that would come the capital that would help build the Central Pacific Railroad.

This was the crowd Peabody followed, the merchant crowd that knew precisely what they wanted and how to go about getting it.

The money lay upstream with the gold seekers, and Alfred Peabody could see that if the *Eliza* could be taken the 120 miles upstream to Sacramento he would save much time in the making of his fortune. No ship the size of the *Eliza* had ever gone upriver so far before, but Alfred Peabody found a pilot who said it could be done, and he persuaded Captain Perkins to try to do it. The *Eliza* was lightened by selling off some cargo in San Francisco. A schooner was engaged to go upriver with her; in case they did not make it, little time would be lost because the goods could be transshipped to the schooner which was in the river trade. It would be awkward but it could be done. Here is Alfred Peabody's report:

> We worked our way up the river, grounding several times, but by heeling the bark, by changing her cargo, chains and anchors, we got her off without discharging any cargo, and in six days

after we left San Francisco we moored her to two sturdy oak trees, at the foot of one of the principal streets, where she remained for years, having quite a history, as she was used as a store, a store house, a boarding house, and later, for years as a landing for steamers. . . .

If San Francisco was little, Sacramento was smaller. Seven buildings and a handful of tents constituted the town. It was a discouraging prospect, until Alfred Peabody made a tour and saw the heavily traveled dusty roads leading off in several directions. He took heart. Sacramento might not be much, but men came there by the hundreds, he could see.

He went to Sutter's Fort, a few miles away, where there was a printing press, and struck off fifty lists of his cargo. It cost him fifty dollars, or a dollar a list. Then he sent the lists into the mining camps and sat down to wait.

There was not long to wait: as soon as his own passengers went upriver to begin their mining careers, they told others of what the ship carried, and in two or three days the rush began. Soon the cargo was sold out, and Alfred Peabody and Captain Perkins were scouting the river for cargoes to buy from others and resell. It was not very long before some twenty-five ships were lying alongside the Sacramento River bank.

The profits were great, but the life was not. The mosquitoes were so thick that Peabody could not eat his evening meal, and one night he went up to the maintop just to get away from the insects below.

On the first Sunday, Alfred Peabody ran afoul of California custom. He was sleeping late, or hoped he was, having made arrangements to be undisturbed. But he was awakened by the cabin boy at daybreak. Three men and their mules were on the river bank, he saw, when he splashed his face and went on deck, and they wanted to trade.

"I don't sell goods on the Sabbath," said Alfred Peabody.

"Well, God damn," said one of the bearded miners to the others. "He don't sell goods on the Sabbath. What does that mean?"

"If I were you," Peabody shouted across the water, "I would keep the Sabbath myself. You and your mules will both live longer."

Then he told them if they would come at daybreak the next morning, he would sell them whatever they wanted to buy.

The three spat and shouted back that they wanted nothing more to do with a puritanical hypocrite and that they would not be back. But they were back the very next morning, and they liked what they saw and how they were treated, because they returned again and again, and finally made Alfred Peabody their banker.

Peabody had expected the miners to be an extremely rough crew, so he was surprised to find that a man he engaged to haul some lumber with his oxen was a Professor Shepard of New Haven. The professor was an educated man, a geologist, and soon became an ally of Peabody's in encouraging the keeping of the Sabbath free from business.

They succeeded, too, and found a Mr. Ball, a religious man from Salem, who had a cabinet organ and could preach. So service was held that first religious Sunday in California in a blacksmith's shop —and when the rough miners heard about it, they came from miles around until the shop overflowed. Next Sunday the service was held under a giant oak, whose trunk measured twenty-seven feet around. The only man who did not attend was a fellow who had set up shop under another oak tree near the *Eliza*, where he made rude coffins. On that first Sunday, he reported with satisfaction, while Peabody and the others had been wasting their time praising God, the coffin maker had earned sixteen dollars selling coffins.

"One of his coffins was taken for him before the close of the summer," reported Alfred Peabody with the satisfaction of one of his early Puritan ancestors.

After several weeks the immigrants began to arrive overland, as well as by sea, and the overland travelers brought oxen and horses with them. Sacramento grew to be a town of several long blocks, with new settlers arriving every day. One man wanted to build a restaurant and Alfred Peabody backed him. They put up a building made of Peabody's lumber, eighteen by thirty feet, covered it with sails from the *Eliza*, and charged the restaurateur $200 a month rent. A doctor came up and wanted a building; Peabody provided one the same size, and charged $250 a month rent. A storekeeper wanted a store; up went another eighteen-by-thirty-foot building with a sailcloth roof, and the rent was $300 a month. Mr. Peabody's lumber and Captain Perkins's sails were paying their way.

From the materials he had brought around through two oceans, merchant Peabody built two scows. One was used as a ferry boat across the Sacramento. The second was used as a market boat.

An old German immigrant had set up a market garden some four miles below the city. Captain Perkins took the second boat downriver and bought a load of vegetables and fruit. He paid sixty dollars a bushel for potatoes, for example. But then he brought the stuff upriver and sold it for much more. They bought squash at two dollars per squash, eggs at two dollars a dozen, milk at two dollars a gallon, used their own sugar, and made squash pies in the *Eliza*'s galley, which they sold for twenty-five dollars a pie. They sold a bag of onions they happened to have on board, two bushels, for eighty-five dollars and could have gotten twice as much.

The *Eliza* was their salvation in every way—particularly when the flood came. Nobody had expected flooding, although one old sourdough had reported seeing the Sacramento overflow its banks where the city was growing up; but it did flood and wiped out much of the tent city. Of course, merchant Peabody was safe enough, because the *Eliza* simply rode it out at her mooring, rising with the water, although along the Sacramento when the flood subsided, chairs were plucked out of the trees fifteen feet above the water.

Alfred Peabody grew homesick, but Sacramento was too good to leave. On December 1, 1850, however, he went down to San Francisco to meet J. P. Flint, of Boston, who had come out to join him in the merchandising business, and they decided that San Francisco would be a better bet than Sacramento as a headquarters for the future. So they built a store right next to the old wharf where the *Eliza* had first pulled in.

Times changed. Captain Perkins went home jangling his riches. And then one day in 1851 two little clipper tea ships arrived in San Francisco Bay with the amazing news that they had sailed around the Horn from New York harbor in just over 100 days. Alfred Peabody was quick to see a new opening—the firm of Flint, Peabody and Company (his partner was the wealthy one when the firm was founded) would go into the shipping business. He, Alfred Peabody, would go back to New England and build ships, and send them out loaded with cargo.

So Alfred Peabody took the July steamer to Panama—the first July steamer, for there were several by this time, and Commodore Vanderbilt was entering the California trade by way of Nicaragua. Peabody crossed the Isthmus on a mule, came down the Chagres River in a dugout canoe, and arrived back in Salem thirty-six days after he had left San Francisco.

The steamboats took the passenger trade, of course, but they did not even whittle at the freight trade because goods simply could not be shipped from New York to the eastern shore of Central America, offloaded, carried overland, onloaded, and then shipped to San Francisco. Speed just did not make that much difference in terms of goods.

Now Peabody set out to establish a shipping concern in combination with the firm of Glidden and Williams of Boston. A huge clipper ship was built, 1100 tons, in an East Boston harbor, and she sailed for San Francisco, bearing the cargo of Flint, Peabody and Company, on January 10, 1852. This ship was christened the *John Bertram*, after the man who had set Peabody up in the California trade. On her first trip she carried, among other things, 10,000 tins of eggs, a dozen to the tin, which sold at a dollar a dozen.

A year later, Peabody, John Bertram, and other Salem businessmen established the San Francisco ice trade, using five ships, which aggregated 3300 tons, and kept it up until it was discovered that ice could be shipped more cheaply from Alaska.

In five years between 1852 and 1857, Flint, Peabody and Company filled 207 ships with their merchandise, shipping 345,000 tons to California and earning a profit of perhaps ten million dollars on the trade.

Having been to California, Peabody knew what was needed, so he sent out peach, apple, pear, plum, and other fruit trees, raspberry bushes and currants—but so did everybody else, and although Flint, Peabody started their own farm, the fruit venture was a failure because of the competition. The California trade was no longer a certain money-maker. One had to be careful and the profits were no longer immense on each item. Flint, Peabody had some few other important tasks, however; one was to purchase and deliver the rails for the Central Pacific Railroad, and another was to market the first bonds of that road sold in the Boston area. They built a rope factory and a barrel factory, and the firm continued to be profitable. But the excitement was soon gone, and at the end of 1869 Alfred Peabody withdrew from the firm and settled down to a life of luxurious relaxation.

With this family background, Alfred's son Henry Wayland Peabody naturally felt a strong pull to become a merchant. In the 1840s and 1850s it was an exciting trade.

Henry's father was so busy trying to make a fortune in the early days that he was in Buenos Aires when the boy was born and did not cast eyes on him until little Henry was more than a year old. The family lived abroad during this boy's early years and at one point he could speak Spanish as well as English.

But by 1848 the family was settled in Salem, and Henry went to the Phillips School there, then to the Hacker School, where other Peabodys had gone before. Then he went to Jonathan Worcester's private school and finally to the Latin School.

During all these years J. Peabody did her best to inculcate Henry with a semblance of culture. He took French from a Frenchman and music from an Italian. The French went fairly well, but the music was another story.

One day, after several months, Henry came home with a note

from the music teacher, his mother having inquired as to his progress on the piano.

"He ver promising boy," said the note. "He no practice. He
ver promising boy."

So, hoping for a pianist in the family, or perhaps even a con-
ductor, J. Peabody continued to foot the bill for the lessons, ad-
monishing young Henry to practice.

Weeks went by, and eventually J. Peabody asked for another
report on the budding virtuoso. It came.

"He ver promising boy," it said. "He promise and promise he
will practice. He never do."

So Henry's musical career ended in a crescendo of understanding.

Henry was an active and enterprising youth. He managed to
have his head felt and a phrenological chart made of it: his brain
was the average size and he would probably be successful, it said.
Once, he turned his brother Ned into an Indian by staining him
brown from head to toe with "poppy juice," and the family discovered to J. Peabody's horror that whatever the juice was it did
not readily come off.

There was seldom any question in his mind about what he would
do for a living (the phrenologist said he had a strongly developed
acquisitive streak). He took a trip to Iowa when he was twenty,
and was satisfied that he had seen America. He took trips to Aus-
tralia and England and Cuba, as the scion of the Boston and Salem
house of Peabody. There was his calling, to be a rich young merchant prince. As a wealthy young man Henry Wayland Peabody
became a sporting yachtsman and owned a number of yachts; the
Curlew, the *Petrel*, and the *Halcyon* were a few of them. He developed business interests for the family (he built a hemp trade
with the Philippines to serve New England ships and a family
rope plant). In 1878 he served the United States as Commissioner
to the International Exposition in Sydney, and later he served the
Australians as Commissioner for the New South Wales Exhibit at
the Columbian Exposition in Chicago.

He became a member of the First Baptist Church of Salem, and a very good member indeed. On one trip to the Far East he devoted much of his time and a good deal of money to the inspection and support of Far East Missions.

Henry Wayland Peabody was a rich man's son, and as such he had no opportunity to show the spunk that his father had exhibited. Yet he was a brave man, as well as a good one, and his yachting experiences are enough to attest to that fact: for no man not brave keeps a yacht in New England waters and sails it in good weather and bad.

He did not go to college (not unusual among young merchants of his day) but learned "business" as a clerk in the house of Williams and Hall, East India merchants who were friends of his father's. His pay was only seventy-five dollars a year, but he had the privilege of using the company agents abroad for his own trading, in his own name, at his own expense, and soon he had laid up several thousand dollars. In 1866 he went broke in a panic, but his father endorsed notes to get him back into business on his own, and from then on it was clear sailing. It was not many years before he had branches of his foreign trading company in London, Liverpool, Sydney, Capetown, Manila, and Merida, Yucatan.

He married young, received assistance from his parents, and never had serious financial troubles. He lived a quiet Massachusetts Bay life of the kind lived by many a well-to-do descendant of the old Puritans. From his father's house on Sumner Street, Henry moved to Chestnut Street when he married Lila Mansfield, and here he raised his family in the three-story flat-topped columned house with its two big chimneys, shuttered windows, and walled garden. For a time he kept a cottage at Juniper Point in Salem, then at Beverly Cove, which was more fashionable, and finally he bought an estate, Paramatta, which he turned into a showplace of gardens —sixty-five acres in all, added piece by piece in what was a growing suburban district of the sprawling supermetropolis. He kept Pekin ducks and guinea fowl, and a large assortment of mallards. He even raised peacocks until they grew too noisy, and he sent them off to

Winston Churchill, the American author, who had a large farm in New Hampshire.

Alfred Peabody, the father, and Henry Wayland Peabody, the son, were both influential New England merchants, but the manner in which their various influences were used is indicative of the change in American society between the nineteenth and twentieth centuries. Alfred's influence was in taming California for one thing —who else did more to bring Christian principle to the roaring camps of the Sacramento? He was also a developer of the clipper ship, no small mark of achievement. In other words, he conquered physical frontiers, or some small parts of them, in Latin America and in the West. But what of Henry Wayland, the son who came to prominence a half century after his father? His influence was felt in the halls of Washington and in the business associations of America. Yes, the old day of laissez-faire was coming to an end at the turn of the twentieth century, and we see Henry Wayland Peabody speaking at meetings of business associations which had been organized for mutual comfort and protection against government control. Any associations organized fifty years earlier were dedicated to the principle of making more profits or even of fleecing the public, not for protection against anybody.

Henry Wayland was particularly interested in the matters that would affect a merchant in foreign trade: currency, the tariff, and subsidy of the merchant marine. He was, of course, a "sound money," or gold standard, man, who hated the easy credit idea of the Silver Age. He was a friend of President McKinley's and probably influenced McKinley on the tariff early in the game; McKinley was famous or infamous, depending on how one looked at it, for the protective tariff of 1890. Henry Wayland was long connected with the New York and Boston Chambers of Commerce and was a representative after 1908 on the National Council of Commerce, which was formed by Secretary of Commerce Strauss, and a member of the advisory board of fifteen until illness forced him to resign. And when Mr. Peabody traveled, the newspapers wrote about him. When he went to Havana, the *Post* called him "thoroughly posted on Cuba, past, present and future." When he went to Manila he made speeches, and when the newspapers criticized what he had to say (opposing United States annexation, favoring independence), he wrote letters to the editors. It is even said that Henry Wayland Peabody was responsible for adoption of the gold standard for the Philippines after the war of 1898, rather than the silver standard they were used to.

And here, from the *St. Louis Globe-Democrat* is an indication of a typical Peabody performance. He had been called as a witness before insular and Philippines committees of House and Senate, which were meeting to take testimony about the monetary standards. The Senate hearings began:

> There was a thin, modest-appearing old gentleman with sharp features and stoop shoulders and keen gray eyes, who quietly walked into the committee room and took a seat in one corner far back against the wall. One of the committee clerks looked him over and informed him that the meeting was not to be open to the public. Then the mild-mannered stranger said that he had been asked to come to the committee room by the Secretary of War, and was to be one of the witnesses. The young $1200-a-year clerk insisted that he "push back further to let these other gentleman have room nearer the table" and he did so. The other witnesses were disposed of one by one. Finally Senator Lodge called for "Mr. Henry Peabody, Merchant." The mild-mannered man came forward. He had ideas. It needed but a few questions to start his elucidation of them. He looked poor and unprepossessing, but in five minutes he had the undivided attention of every senator on the committee. He talked of "his branch house in Australia," of another in Calcutta, India, and another in Egypt, and explained as much as was necessary to show what a handicap his firm found in handling merchandise where there was no stable currency system. Then he took up the business of his firm in Manila, and in a plain businesslike way he pointed out definitely the need of a new currency system there and just why the standard should be based on a 12.8 fineness of gold and how it would have less of a tendency to disturb business conditions there. The shrewd Yankee merchant was not to be tangled up. Senator after senator, who had studied economics and the theoretical side of currency systems, fired at

him volley after volley of suppositive cases. These he shattered in a moment by the application of his hard business sense and backed them up with statements of actual transactions in his own business. Then when the Senate committee had finished with him, he journeyed over to the House end of the Capitol and told the insular committee the same thing. That is the way the present provision got into the Philippine bill.

Well, there are holes in the story. Senator Lodge was unlikely not to know one of his important constituents and undoubtedly a contributor to his political causes and campaign funds. Henry Wayland Peabody never looked "poor" in his whole life, although he dressed very conservatively. But as for the rest of it—it is how he would have acted, and how he probably did act in the hearings.

Peabody's influence was not confined to congressional testimony in this case. He was Chairman of the Advisory Board of the International Commercial Congress, and as such he pushed for the Panama Canal's building. Of course, many other people were pushing, too, but Peabody's shoulder was closer to the wheel than some of those others. Perhaps Teddy Roosevelt did not need persuading, but there were some in the Congress who did.

Peabody's last influence was exerted in 1908, when he spent a good deal of time and money working to elect William Howard Taft to the Presidency and to defeat William Jennings Bryan.

Surprisingly, for a businessman, he had some liberal quirks. At a time when the Republican party, by and large, opposed Oriental immigration, he wanted to open the doors, and he favored a friendly, even comradely relationship with China.

This Peabody died in 1908, just a few months after his son Alfred, who had contracted typhoid fever, and perhaps the death of this beloved son had something to do with his own passing.

When he died, the *Boston Transcript* had this to say:

> About as perfect a specimen as could be conceived of the Puritan of Massachusetts Bay and Cromwell's and Milton's Commonwealth transplanted this side of the Atlantic and translated into the New Englanders of today was Henry W. Peabody of Salem and Boston and Beverly.... Of not every man of successful busi-

ness can it be said, as it is said most earnestly of him, that he actually carried the Golden Rule into business. It was a matter both of principle and of method in business with him that the benefits and advantages of a bargain should be mutual. . . .

But in nothing of his action was ever withheld the religious element . . . inherited directly from Milton's Salem contemporaries and coworkers for democratic self-rule, as they believed, under the guidance of the most high. This kept him ever conscious of walking in God's sight, as he believed, in his daily work and conversation, and that without the least Pharisaism or pretension.

So went Henry Wayland Peabody in 1908, carrying out of this world the Peabody Puritan conscience.

CHAPTER 25

MR. WILSON'S FRIEND

In 1807 in the rustic woodland near Woodbury, Connecticut, George Henry Peabody was born. He was the son of William Henry Peabody, who was the son of Asa Peabody of Boxford, who moved to Pomfret, Connecticut; Asa was the first son of Richard Peabody of Boxford, who was the fourth son of William, who was the third son of old Lieutenant Francis Peabody, who came over from the old country in 1635.

George Henry Peabody is important to this tale largely because he moved to Columbus, Georgia, and thereby created a good deal of confusion as to which Peabody started that Southern Educational Fund. George Henry's name was similar enough to that of George the banker, and they were contemporaries, so the confusion was understandable enough. This George Henry Peabody had nothing to do with the southern educational effort of his banker cousin so many times removed; he was a moderately prosperous merchant in Columbus on the muddy Chattahoochee River.

Among the progeny of George Henry and his wife, nee Elvira Canfield, was a boy named George Foster Peabody, who was born on July 27, 1852, thus was nine years old at the outbreak of the Civil War. Perhaps the most important fact about his boyhood was that he went to school for a time with Nathan and Oscar Straus, who would later become important figures in the New York Jewish community and in American business affairs.

As far as the war was concerned, the Peabodys were physically untouched by it until April 17, 1865, when the horde of General Sherman was pressing through Georgia. A part of that army descended on Columbus on a Sunday afternoon and broke into the George Henry Peabody house, took the family dinner off the table, roughed up the family in the search of loot, and then went away, after burning the Columbus business district. A northern-born man himself, with a northern-born wife, George Henry Peabody had little use for the Union troops after that incident, and it was a long time before Peabodys of the southern branch could forgive.

George Henry Peabody's store was burned to the ground that Sunday, but he decided to stay in business. So he went North, concealed his distaste, and bought more goods. Further, in the destruction of the South, he sent young George and his brother to Deer Hill Institute, an Episcopal boys' school at Danbury, Connecticut. The parents followed their sons North in a few months, because in the black Reconstruction of the South it was impossible for George Henry Peabody to rebuild his business; and rather than lose his capital to the rapacious scalawags and carpetbaggers, he came North to Brooklyn. George Henry Peabody was fifty-nine years old and he was starting all over again.

Soon, the Peabody boys were forced to leave school and go to work to support themselves; George Foster Peabody found a job as an errand boy for a merchant in Brooklyn, earning eight dollars a month. Two years later he had risen to bookkeeper of another firm, and in 1870 went to Boston to work for White, Payson, and Company, an import house. Although he was there as a contemporary of Alfred and Henry Wayland Peabody, once again cousins passed as ships in the night. George Foster Peabody's evenings were not spent in the salons of the Peabody brahmins of Boston and Salem, but in lounge and library of the Young Men's Christian Association, where he read all the books he could find, by flickering gas lamps, and absorbed the education he could by himself.

Like his celebrated namesake cousin, George Foster Peabody became interested in the plight of the Negroes once Reconstruction had been overturned, and one Sunday while in Brooklyn he attended the Reformed Church in Brooklyn Heights when General Samuel C. Armstrong was preaching in behalf of his Hampton Agricultural and Mechanical Institute for Negroes. George Foster Peabody was impressed and made it a point to meet the speaker.

Churchgoing can be educational and can bring physical uplift as well as spiritual, as George Foster Peabody learned when in the Reformed Church Sunday school he met a wealthy young banker named Spencer Trask. The poor young Peabody fell in love with Trask's girl, Kate Nichols. She was a beauty, with a pink-white complexion, brown hair and blue eyes, and her family was well-to-do, but George Peabody wisely masked his feelings for her. How wisely becomes apparent: in 1879 Peabody, who had kept a civil tongue in his head, was offered a partnership in the firm of Trask and Stone, bankers (and later became a partner in Spencer Trask and Company, which succeeded the Stone alliance). But George Foster, although an Episcopalian by this time, had enough of the old Peabody conscience to make a confession as he went into business with Trask.

"Spencer," he said. "I am in love with your wife."

Trask looked him in the eye, calmly, and lit a cigar. "I don't blame you, Foster," he said. "I am in love with her myself."

So George Foster Peabody became a banker in true Horatio Alger style: he had studied hard beneath the gas lamps of the YMCA, run erands and done menial work for his meager pay, watched as his mother became careworn from taking in paying guests or renters, and his father died of heartbreak over the loss of the family fortunes to the damyankees among whom they were forced now to live; he had fallen for the right girl and had given her up to his superior (in wealth) friend. He had honestly spoken his mind; and here he was a rich banker.

But life at the rolltop desk was not easy, as he soon found out. There was still the problem of pleasing Spencer Trask, a rich

Princeton graduate. Peabody, twenty-nine years old, six feet tall, stalwart and rugged, did his best and satisfied the senior partner by being neither too obsequious nor too independent, and soon his brother Charles Jones Peabody was offered a job in the establishment—which meant that George Foster's seat was secure. Then, on May 27, 1886, George Foster Peabody went into his secret savings and brought forth $24,000 to purchase a seat on the New York Stock Exchange. From that point on there was no looking back.

George Foster Peabody emerged in Wall Street just at the end of what has been sometimes called the Era of Frenzied Finance. Jay Gould's great empire was crumbling; William Henry Vanderbilt had traded his railroad stock control in for government bonds, and the bully bulls of the street and the ragged bears were giving way in importance to lions like J. Pierpont Morgan.

Spencer Trask and Company started out in the Street dealing in stocks, but soon moved into the bond field, which was equally lucrative if one knew the right people and was not nearly so volatile. Peabody became the railroad man of the house, and traveled across the continent to learn the ramifications of the lines, from Ottawa to Manzanillo, and from Seattle to Pensacola.

Out west, Peabody ran into that old ramrod General William Jackson Palmer, who had built the Kansas and Pacific, the Denver and Rio Grande, the town of Colorado Springs, and was putting up a steel mill in Pueblo so he could run that town. Peabody, on a trip to Mexico, promoted a concession from President Porfirio Díaz for Palmer and James Sullivan to build a railroad from Mexico City to Juarez and another from Mexico City to Nuevo Laredo. It sounded marvelous, because there were great stirrings in Mexico, including those of the Guggenheims, who were coming down to build smelters and mine silver.

Palmer was a tough old fellow, and he impressed Peabody.

"You are building a railroad for the use of the Mexican people," Palmer told the hands as they laid the ties. "They have their own ways which it is not for you to criticize. Try to adapt yourselves to these ways in a spirit of sympathy."

This spirit of making a private Peace Corps of his road gangs was not unusual for the old General. When he built Colorado Springs on the edge of the Rockies, the General carefully drew the deeds to the land so that liquor was forever prohibited. Nobody could open a saloon or serve drinks in the General's town. He made one mistake: he forgot to put such a prohition into the deed of the local Episcopal church, which fell into disuse and became a saloon. But the General's mood continued if he was not always successful in enforcing it on the rough and ready West. He was a moralist to gladden the heart of any Peabody.

For sixteen years, George Foster Peabody associated with the crusty old General, and if he narrowly escaped a case of ulcers between 1885 and 1901, at least he earned his fortune in the old man's prescience about the western movement and the West in general. They organized and sold the Denver and Rio Grande Western to the American people and did the same with the Mexican National Railway. Peabody also went afield, he became involved in the St. Louis, Alton and Terre Haute road, and was at one time a director, at least long enough to handle the sale which put the little road into the hands of the Illinois Central.

Trask and Peabody made a fortune in the Edison Electric Company, and therein became closely associated with J. Pierpont Morgan, who was financing Edison. Trask was president of Edison Electric Illuminating, and when he was out of town Peabody ran the show. Then, in 1892, when Morgan merged all into the great General Electric Company promotion, Peabody became a member of the board of directors of that firm. And with so much experience in public utilities he helped with other stocks such as Cleveland Electric Illuminating and Detroit Electric Illuminating.

So the Peabody influence was considerable in the world of finance: this Peabody was even in attendance during the series of meetings in the Morgan house at 219 Madison Avenue in December, 1888, and January, 1889, when the gentleman's agreement was made to stop hurtful competition among the railroads in the matter of railroad freight rates. This was a historic period, and these were historic meetings: they marked the change in business attitude of fighting the government tooth and nail in regulation of utilities, and although there were skirmishes and rear-guard actions later, the principle of the public weal was here strengthened.

As Peabody's wealth grew, so did his influence. He became a member of the board of trustees of the Hampton Institute in 1884, and treasurer of this Negro educational institution a few years later. And, of course, as a man of affairs, he began showing off a little. He moved into a mansion on Monroe Place in Brooklyn Heights, and hired interior decorators and art dealers with a lavish hand. They bought art monstrosities for him in the best manner of the period, and he decorated his house with rococo statuary and bisque oil paintings, along with photographs of horses and the tombs of the Medici, a stained glass window, and a frieze of children. There were Oriental rugs on the floors and brass beds in the bedrooms along with cane chairs and clothes presses. His mother took up oil painting, and her works of art were also hung here and there in the house, since the musuems and art galleries did not seem to appreciate them.

George's branch of the Peabodys was a lively crowd and imaginative in the matter of giving names. One of Peabody's brothers was named Royal Canfield Peabody, and one of his little cousins was Pocahontas Peabody of Columbus, Georgia, who surmounted all and married a thoroughly respectable professor at the University of Wisconsin and used to come to 28 Monroe Place to admire the frieze and Mother Peabody's paintings.

In 1891 George Foster Peabody bought a chunk of land on Lake George near Trask's famous Yaddo estate, and created his own more modest palace, which he called Abenia (Algonquian for Home of Rest—the millionaires of the nineties were highly partial to mystical Indian names). A house with mansard roof stood, but he did not like it and spent as much rebuilding it as if he had started from scratch, with a crowning touch of a geranium bed around the edges of the flattened roof, piazzas built without any consideration for the frigid winter climate, and many effects of an Italian lake palazzo. This place ran to fur rugs instead of Orientals, oil paintings of madonnas and cherubs (and Mother Peabody's, of course).

In business, one matter led to another until Peabody was officer in half a dozen Mexican mining companies. Then he went into the sugar beet business, joining with Kuhn, Loeb to form a combine known as the American Beet Sugar Company, which was a twenty-million-dollar firm operating in Nebraska, California, and Colorado.

Early in the 1890s he became involved in politics, and since he lived in Brooklyn, it is not strange that this Peabody was a Democrat even though he was a businessman. But, of course, he was a Cleveland or sound money Democrat, which meant he, like Henry Wayland Peabody, had an instinct for the gold dollar. In 1892 George Foster Peabody took part in the Brooklyn Democratic move to upset Tammany, which was trying to maneuver former President Cleveland out of the nomination that year by calling a quick or "snap" convention in Albany a month after the call for the national convention had been made. George Foster was a leader of the revolution, and he and some twenty prominent Brooklyn Democrats met at the Clarendon Hotel, and he became a member of a committee of twenty-five which was to arrange a mass protest meeting at the Criterion Theater. They did so and managed to frighten Tammany so that the state Democratic convention was actually held at Syracuse on May 31, and there Peabody was chosen a delegate to the national convention in Chicago.

So the Peabody influence was at work again, to get Cleveland the nomination in 1892; Peabody was one of the New Yorkers instrumental in saving the day for the burly former President. And in 1896, when William Jennings Bryan captured the Democratic nomination with his cheap silver policy, Peabody was instrumental in the formation of the Gold Democrat movement, which was responsible in turn for defeating Bryan.

After 1896 George Foster Peabody took up the cause of Henry

George and the single tax, and, of all things, he became an ardent advocate of government ownership of the railroads. In this he might have supported Bryan, who held the same sentiments, but Bryan and silver were anathema to a gold man. All the while he was becoming more and more involved in educational affairs, and in 1898 became a member of the board of trustees of little Colorado College in Colorado Springs. Colleges liked to have multimillion-aires on their boards—it gave them a feeling of security.

Mrs. Peabody died in 1901, which left George Foster an orphan at he age of forty-nine. He was still in love with Kate, or Katrina Trask, and no other seemed to do for him. He spent his money on his table and on furs, rare gems, cut glass, and silver, which he lavished on his friends. There were many mink stoles, brooches, and white bearskin rugs, which might indicate that a number of those friends might have been out of the chorus line at White's, but Peabody was most discreet and no scandal touched him.

In memory of the old days with the gas lamps, Peabody was always an easy touch for the YMCA (the YMCA of Columbus got $35,000 for a new building in 1901), but his real charity was the Southern Educational Fund.

The other George Peabody, as noted, had given three and a half million dollars to this fund to promote education of whites and blacks in the South. A few years later John F. Slater gave a million dollars to the fund, and Daniel Hand gave one and a half million in 1888, and so forth, until a rich nest egg was established. But as for spending it, there was no unanimity that the best job was being done. So in 1898 a Southern Education Conference was called, and the millionaires began heading for Capon Springs, West Virginia, in their private railroad cars. Most millionaires brought other millionaires to such meetings, or needy relatives, but George Foster Peabody thoughtfully loaded up his private car with the Reverend S. D. McConnell of Brooklyn, along with Dr. Edwin Knox Mitchell of Hartford; Dr. Albert Shaw of the *Review of Reviews;* St. Clair McKelway of the *Brooklyn Eagle;* Clark B. Firestone of the *New York Evening Mail;* and Stanhope Sams of *The*

New York Times. Mr. Peabody was acquiring, very quietly, a reputation as a publicist.

In 1899 there was a second conference, and J. L. M. Curry, agent of the Peabody and Slater funds, gave the conferees a talk on education in the Southern States, which brought them enough to think about for the next ten years. Out of it all came the formation of the Southern Education Board, which established a relationship among Peabody and John D. Rockefeller Jr., as well as Robert C. Ogden, Walter H. Page, and Charles W. Dabney.

Peabody became a member of the Southern Education Board, which went back to New York to meet and plan the future of southern education. Meetings were held every day for five days in November, 1901. Eventually officers were elected (Peabody being treasurer) and a money-raising campaign was begun. The board began giving money to southern institutions for educational purposes.

In 1902 Peabody joined Rockefeller, Morris K. Jesup, and a number of others in meetings, and old John D., Sr., came through with a million dollars for the fund, which was entitled the General Education Board (Peabody was again treasurer). The General Board had as its credo the promotion of education without regard for race, creed, or color, and it was concerned with the whole United States rather than just the South. Eventually the fund amounted to forty-three million dollars, which Peabody invested and supervised for many years.

Out of this association, particularly the southern association, came many other connections. Peabody became a member of the board of trustees of the University of Georgia. But his real interest, shortly after the turn of the century, was Democratic party politics.

In 1901 Peabody supported Edward Shepard in his unsuccessful mayoralty race in New York against the reformer Seth Low, because Shepard was a friend of his and a regular Democratic party man, although Peabody believed in reform. He became involved with Tammany boss Richard Croker—and he was forever hooked by Democratic party politics. In 1904 Peabody boosted Shepard as a possible Presidential aspirant, but nobody thought much of that idea, at least in party circles, and he dropped it. This was the year that Alton B. Parker, a sound money man, was nominated by the Democrats, in between Bryan campaigns, and while Peabody could not get up much more enthusiasm for Parker than anybody else, he was persuaded to become treasurer of the Democratic party, and managed to raise about a million dollars for the war chest.

The Democrats lost to Teddy Roosevelt, as everybody expected, but the important cause of sound money had been supported and Bryan had been suppressed. That much was satisfactory.

Peabody retired from business in 1906, after a fall in a train. He decided to devote his life to education and philanthropy, and he had the connections to do so without taking on any more responsibilities. As for philanthropy, he gave away several million dollars: $250,000 to the University of Georgia; about $50,000 to Colorado College; about $25,000 to Skidmore College for women at Saratoga Springs; many thousands for YMCA buildings from Schenectady to Portland, Oregon. He gave $50,000 to Holy Trinity Church in Brooklyn, and $50,000 to Long Island College Hospital. And he gave away hundreds of thousands of books, subscriptions, magazines, and reprints of articles that interested him, including 100,000 copies of Mrs. Trask's poem "Christ of the Andes," and many thousands of copies of her other works, which were uniformly dedicated to peace on earth.

He was trustee of Tuskegee Institute and a trustee of a special Negro education fund called the Jeanes Fund.

In the beginning of 1910 came an accident which changed George Foster Peabody's life. Spencer Trask was killed aboard a New York Central train near Croton, and Peabody then became a lone wolf.

Actually, his turn was largely to politics, and he was one of the early movers in securing the nomination of Woodrow Wilson for the Presidency, starting his work to that end in 1911. Peabody, Henry Morgenthau, Oswald Garrison Villard, and William Gibbs

McAdoo were all involved. When Wilson was nominated, Peabody supported him. He was offered the post of Secretary of the Treasury in the Wilson Cabinet, but declined. He was appointed to the board of the New York Federal Reserve Bank and served from 1914 until 1922, and thus the Peabody influence was involved in the formation of the American fiscal system of the twentieth century.

During the war, Peabody sold war bonds and made speeches against the Germans. He wrote innumerable letters on every conceivable subject of public interest to the President, congressmen, and members of the administration—not forgetting the newspapers. He sent cables to Wilson at Versailles, and he carried on a long correspondence with Colonel House, offering advice and commenting on affairs.

During these latter years, much of Peabody's time was spent in and around Saratoga and his house at 19 Circular Street there. He gave up the estate Abenia as too expensive and too complicated to manage, for he was a bachelor and he wanted less trouble as the years rolled on. From time to time he called on his old love, Katrina Trask, at Yaddo, the Trask estate. She had closed the big house, but lived on the estate in Mansell Alsaada (Arabic for House of Happiness, they said). The visits were more frequent in 1920, and in 1921 on February 5, they were married—a marriage of late autumn for both of them, for Peabody was sixty-nine and Katrina was only a year younger.

They lived at Yaddo, for Katrina would not leave the place, and reopened the big house, but it was not a very happy opening, because Katrina was sick, suffering from heart trouble, and had to be carried from one house to the other by stretcher. She lived less than a year; then George Foster Peabody was a bachelor again.

Peabody now went back to his charitable activities and began taking an interest in the infantile paralysis center at Warm Springs, Georgia. Peabody had known Franklin Delano Roosevelt for many years, when Roosevelt was just beginning in New York's upstate politics, and when Roosevelt was Assistant Secretary of the Navy under Wilson. Now, Roosevelt was suffering from infantile paralysis or poliomyelitis, as it was beginning to be called, and Peabody suggested to Roosevelt that he go to Warm Springs and try the cure. In October, 1924, Roosevelt followed his older friend's advice and spent three weeks there. He wrote Peabody that he spent two hours every morning in the pool and that the muscles of his legs had strengthened noticeably in those three weeks.

Later, Peabody and Roosevelt met and planned the improvement of the springs for a better therapeutic center; Roosevelt became president of the foundation, and Peabody a trustee.

In 1924 Peabody was again a delegate to the Democratic National Convention, and he was one of the leaders of the fight against William Gibbs McAdoo; he supported John W. Davis, who was nominated after a struggle that nearly decimated the party. One reason Peabody did not like McAdoo was that McAdoo opposed government ownership of railroads. Norman Thomas wrote Peabody that he and the Socialists supported government ownership, and suggested that Peabody become a Socialist. Attractive as Thomas might be, Peabody could not accept the general Marxist principle of public ownership of *all* the means of production and the death of the machine by which Peabody had made his millions, the market of Wall Street. He did have hopes for the Fabian system of England, however, Peabody told Thomas.

Here is Peabody influence at work again: in 1924 Al Smith was governor of New York, and after the wounds he received at the national convention he was considering a total withdrawal from political life. But Peabody wrote to him and persuaded him that his services were needed by the people—and Smith (whether through more or less Peabody influence) decided to run again for the governorship.

So the charities and the good works continued. He helped lead a campaign in 1924 to raise $8,000,000 for Hampton and Tuskegee Institutes. He helped raise $20,000,000 for the American Church Institute and for its schools, including St. Paul's and St. Augustine's.

In 1922 he had given his house on Circular Street in Saratoga to the Katrina Trask Alliance, and hired Mrs. Marjorie Knappen Waite to be director of the center. She had earlier been associated with the Hollywood School for Girls in Los Angeles. In 1926 Peabody adopted Mrs. Waite, who then became Marjorie Peabody Waite (acquiring a maiden name by adoption) and began affectionately referring to the old man as Mon Père. Soon she came to Yaddo and brought with her a jolly atmosphere, as reported by Miss Pardee, a secretary, to Louise Ware, Peabody's biographer.

> Miss Pardee tells of the cheerful breakfasts at West House. The mail, brought from Saratoga by car, was heaped at Mr. Peabody's plate. Neglecting his food, he would open letter after letter, stopping now and then to read some bit that particularly appealed to him. Much hearty laughter accompanied these breakfasts.
>
> The memory of Kate was everywhere about the house; they spoke of her now as if she were in the next room. But he was now a man at ease from strain. He enjoyed a measure of lightheartedness in the complete acceptance by his womenfolk—Miss Pardee, like a sister; Marjorie, his daughter.

It was not long before Yaddo was converted into an artists' retreat. This idea had been Spencer Trask's; now it was carried out with gusto. The old mansion was restored to opulence, with new drapes, new paintings, and new coats of paint. Small buildings on the grounds were converted to studios for the artists, and ten or twelve were invited at a time. For a young practicing artist, an invitation to Yaddo was highly desirable, as can be seen in Miss Ware's description:

> On their arrival, guests were welcomed to the mansion by Mrs. Ames, the director. She showed them to their individual suites and made them feel at home. At eight o'clock the artists enjoyed a leisurely breakfast, served in buffet style in the spacious dining room. After breakfast they sauntered away to their various studios to work. Printed signs about the grounds requested silence, and only the whistling of the birds or the whir of an occasional car in the driveway interrupted the quiet of the scene. At noontime the guests returned to the mansion, or ate picnic luncheons on the

grounds. As the sun sank low, one figure after another reappeared along the pine-needled driveway. Dinner was a pleasant affair.

It certainly must have been. It was served by the hired help on Mrs. Trask's finest gold-embossed china at the huge tables in the dining room, and the dinner was followed by demitasses and perhaps other things to drink, and then people talked painting or music or writing.

"Many a young artist found stimulation in this pleasant company," said biographer Ware—and many a young artist had a succession of good meals, too, which might have been more important.

But there was a price. From time to time Mr. Peabody and Mrs. Waite would join the artists, and sometimes Mrs. Waite could be persuaded to sing for them in her rich, if untutored, contralto voice. At the end of the summer a concert was given, and the musicians who had been enjoying the summer as guests put on their work for the audience assembled in the library and the great hall.

Peabody loved the concerts, including Mrs. Waite's, although he was the first to admit he was not a musician. As a matter of fact (and this may have been a blessing), he was tone-deaf, but he always remembered how back in the 1860s when he was small he had heard *Tannhäuser* and was thrilled by it. And he said he liked Bach and Beethoven (he was a founder of the Bach Festival) and also Wagner and a handful of Russians.

But these were only his amusements between the political wars. The wars came again in 1928, when Al Smith ran for the Presidency on the Democratic ticket. Peabody unsheathed his sword and went to work, having 10,000 copies of this newspaper story printed and 10,000 copies of that one, assailing Walter Lippmann and other newspapermen with the arguments for his candidate, and otherwise unleashing the publicity machinery that only a rich man's fortune or a wealthy campaign chest can afford. But Smith lost, and it was quite a blow. However, there was still Mrs. Waite and the charities. For years Peabody had thought about old General Palmer, and now he caused to be placed on the wall of the Denver railroad station a memorial tablet designed by Evelyn Longmans Batchelder, with copies going to the Mexico City railroad station and Hampton Institute. And ever one to use the printing press, he had a volume of addresses and a sketch of Palmer compiled for selective distribution. Then it was back to the comforts of Mrs. Waite.

Peabody fell ill while on a tour of the South and was taken to Johns Hopkins Hospital in Baltimore. Just before Christmas he was being wheeled down the corridor toward the operating room, and a little girl saw him, the old white-haired gentleman on the stretcher.

"Oh," she said, "are they going to operate on Santa Claus, too?"

In a way, he was Santa Claus, at least to those who pricked his fancy and could muster his personal attention. He was a very good Santa Claus indeed to artists, friends, and adopted relatives. But he was more than a foolish old man: That spring he returned from his illness in the South and was appointed chairman of a commission to first survey and then promote Saratoga Springs. He served very ably, making a strong report to Governor Franklin Roosevelt which brought state assistance in its development as a spa.

In 1932, when George Foster Peabody was eighty years old, he considered long and hard, and then he supported Franklin Delano Roosevelt for the Presidency, which was considerably more than most of his Wall Street confreres would have done. Most of them were dead, of course, and Peabody was an agile old man, if he did suffer from angina pectoris. Biographer Ware suggests that he was a Brain Truster—with which Raymond Moley would not agree, since he was head of the Brain Trust—but Peabody did have counsel with Franklin Roosevelt, and the President listened, then did what he pleased. Peabody was still an advocate of federal railroad owner-ship, and he pressed for stronger controls. As time went on, to 1935, and many old Rooseveltian followers were falling off the bandwagon, George Foster Peabody became more enthusiastic for FDR, and went around the country speaking to Kiwanians and other service club groups about the administration and its great works. He liked the Agricultural Adjustment Act of 1933, and other measures. When they were in Warm Springs, Peabody had a certain access to Roosevelt, which gained at least one visitor a hearing on farm tenancy problems.

In one sense Peabody was particularly valuable to Roosevelt— and that was in his tireless plumping, through the machinery of publicity, for the projects that he liked. He liked the Tennessee Valley Authority, and spent thousands of dollars in publicity releases, advertisements, and telephone calls to friends to favor this controversial program. He also was a figure in the establishment of the Good Neighbor League, which presaged an important policy of the Roosevelt administration toward Latin America.

In the spring of 1934 Peabody moved his household to Warm Springs because of the salubrious climate—not that he did not like Saratoga Springs, but it did snow there. In the summer he was back in Saratoga, being referred to by Governor Herbert H. Lehman as "that splendid pioneer," which, of course, did not please him as much as Lehman thought—a man grows testy at eighty-two. Especially he can grow testy if he is sick, and George Foster Peabody was sick, most of 1936 and early in 1937. But he was determined to celebrate his eighty-fifth birthday, and he came to Saratoga Springs for the party. He survived until March 4, 1938, when he died quietly at Warm Springs, surrounded by Mrs. Waite, Miss Pardee, and other ladies.

All the formalities were observed; there were services at Warm Springs and at Brooklyn, too, and the body was cremated and the ashes were buried at Yaddo.

But George Foster Peabody lived on, in his good works and his various foundations. The George Foster Peabody Memorial Highway in Georgia was named for him, and besides that—how many philanthropists were ever honored by having radio and television awards named for them, as was old George Foster?

CHAPTER 26

THE POLITICIAN

THE INFLUENCE of old Endicott Peabody, the educator of Groton, can be measured in many ways, not the least of which is the choosing of this salty old character by Louis Auchincloss the novelist with a thin disguise to be hero of his novel *The Rector of Justin*.

But there is another measure of his immortality, and that was to be seen in the career of his grandson, Endicott Peabody. In 1962 when the second Endicott Peabody ran for governor of Massachusetts, for some reason or other everybody knew who he was although he had not been that prominent before. Perhaps Louis Harris or some other poll-taker could feel the public pulse and discover the manner in which the surnames of certain figures embed themselves in the public consciousness as standing for certain types of activity. When anyone in Massachusetts thinks of Peabody, if they do not think Endicott, then they are even more genteel and think George or Frank Wayland or Ephraim or Nathaniel, or any one of the figures mentioned in this book—and perhaps even of some of the lesser Peabodys who have shared the family characteristic of iron-bound conscience and will to do public good.

Endicott Peabody, the younger, was fortunate when he chose politics as his métier, in that he had two distinguished families on which to lean for background. First was the Peabody family. He was son of Malcolm Peabody, who grew up at Groton, went off to teach at a school in the Philippines for a time, and ended up as Episcopal Bishop of Cenral New York. This Endicott's sister, Mrs. Marietta Tree, is herself an indefatigable public servant on the international level and has served in several positions in the United Nations, and was a very close friend of Adlai Stevenson's. And then there was also the Endicott family. Old John Endicott was governor of Massachusetts Bay Colony in 1629—which the politicians liked to use as a harking point when Endicott was running for public office.

By the time that young Endicott was born in 1920, the Reverend Malcolm Peabody was long gone from Groton, back from the adventurous days, and had a church of his own, Grace Church. For a time the boy attended Penn Charter School near Philadelphia, and then, of course, he went to Groton to study under his grandfather, where he acquired the nickname Chub. He was elected to the presidency of the first form, or seventh grade, achieved honor and responsibilty as a junior prefect, and showed himself to be something of a dramatist in the school productions. During the summers he honored an old church school practice of giving time to the underprivileged, working at a New Hampshire camp.

At Groton, where boys have sports every afternoon except perhaps in the slush season between the hockey season and the spring games, Peabody opted for football and played ardently if not very skillfully.

Still six years of organized athletics gives any boy a certain skill and poise, and by the time he got to Harvard in 1938 young Peabody showed enough promise to interest the football coach, Dick Harlow. He played football for four years.

"Peabody was practically indestructible," said Harlow, "and played fifty minutes of the Yale game with a charley-horse severe enough to keep most football players in bed." How little Coach Harlow knew of the rough school in which young Peabody had been trained—boys at those church prep schools just played the game from start to finish without worry about minor injuries. A broken bone would take them out of the game, but little else would, unless the coach yanked them, usually for discourtesy to other players or some ineptness. The squads at these schools were small, and the play was intense, particularly at Groton, which was often matched with schools two or three times its own size.

By 1941 young Peabody had achieved the distinction of being chosen All-American guard on five of the teams so named by various sportswriters, including the most authoritative, which was then Grantland Rice's choices made for *Collier's* magazine.

But football was not his only sport. A Groton boy was well rounded, and Chub Peabody also played varsity hockey and varsity tennis. Again, six years of intensive training counted. And to cement the old Rector's case that his kind of education made leaders, his grandson was chosen a member of the student council at Harvard, and in his graduating class was chosen second marshal. He was a member of the Varsity and Hasty Pudding Clubs, and ranked about the middle of his class academically. All of which added up to a good solid record.

Early in the game he joined the naval ROTC program, and since he graduated in June, 1942, a few minutes after the ceremony he was commissioned an officer in the Navy Submarine Corps and prepared to go to war. In the Navy, the qualities of determination and responsibility that his grandfather stressed at the school turned out, also, to be the qualities of heroism. He served ably aboard the submarine *R-6*, one of the old class, in the Atlantic and the Caribbean. Then in 1944 he was assigned to the new fleet-class submarine *Tirante*, and went on a cruise that Commander Edward L. Beach, the executive officer, has described in detail in a book. The *Tirante* was sent off into the Pacific to harry Japanese shipping, with special emphasis on the new Japanese practice of trying to disguise motor ships as innocent junks in the Pacific trade. In March they went out toward the China Sea and ended up off Quelpart Island in Korean waters. Lieutenant Peabody found himself engaging a Japanese surface force in the harbor there, for which he was decorated with the Silver Star, and the *Tirante* received a Presidential Unit Citation for general bravery under fire.

During the war, Endicott Peabody decided to go into politics, went home to Massachusetts where he studied law at Harvard, and graduated in 1948. That year he dedicated himself to the campaign of Harry S Truman for the Presidency, and when Truman won, this young campaigner was rewarded in a small way with appointments as assistant regional counsel for the Office of Price Administration and then as regional counsel for the Small Business Administration. In 1952 he went into private law practice as senior member of the firm of Peabody, Koufman, and Brewer in Boston.

Peabody kept working at his political career in the approved fashion. He campaigned for Adlai Stevenson in 1952. Two years later he was elected to the Massachusetts executive council, which controls gubernatorial appointments and expenditures. In 1956 he decided to strike out for election to high state office on his own and ran for the Democratic nomination as Attorney General of Massachusetts, but lost, both that year and in 1958. In 1956 Peabody supported Adlai Stevenson.

Back in the days of the war, Peabody had wagered with Commander Beach one day that he would get himself elected governor of Massachusetts, and in 1966 he made a bid for the Democratic nomination, but lost. The Democrats, long in high office, had succumbed to the usual political temptations, and the people turned out the Democrats from the state administration and elected a reformer, John A. Volpe. But Volpe was hampered severely by being the only Republican elected to statewide office that year, and so many of his reforms went begging.

Thus in 1962, Volpe's record was not what he would like to have written, and when Peabody did secure the Democratic nomination, he had a chance to win. He had good support, from such diverse interests as the Kennedys and James MacGregor Burns, the political scientist. Basically, Peabody himself was independent in politics, and while there were certain disadvantages in his failure to lean on the old Democratic machine, still he won election by

3000 votes over his Republican opponent. The Kennedy support may have done the trick for him.

And then came a two-year term as governor. It started off badly enough, with a head-on collision between the new governor and the combined old guard of Republicans and Democrats. Yet the governor managed to salvage much from the fighting and to have an influence on the affairs of his state for some time to come. He was able to reform taxation programs, reorganize public works programs, and increase the expenditures for highway safety. But many of his other programs were either scuttled right away or simply stalled until 1964. That year Peabody lost the election, as was more or less expected for someone who had won so closely but had failed to win over the old guard. He went back to private law practice, and then disappeared into the maw of bureaucratic Washington, whence men sometimes reappear and sometimes not.

His influence, this Peabody's, on the state and the nation had not been very prominent by 1968, but the potential was that he might turn out to be the most influential of all Peabodys in terms of the American scene. Much remained to be seen, but it was certain that he was a young man of strong character (his mother was arrested when she insisted on marching in the civil rights demonstrations in St. Augustine, Florida, in 1964, and that shows where at least part of the character derives), and he was an impressive man. James MacGregor Burns characterized him in 1962 as more like a scoutmaster than the survivor of three political campaigns, and also said that Peabody continued to be an idealist although immersed in practical politics. No mean feat that, and if he could retain some of the idealism after the bath in Washington, and was not either stalled or sidetracked along the way in the next few years, there was no telling how far this Peabody would go.

POSTSCRIPT

> The days of palmy prosperity are not those most favorable
> to the display of public virtue or the influence of wise and
> good men. In hard, doubtful, unprosperous and dangerous
> times, the disinterested and patriotic find their way, by a
> species of public instinct, unopposed, joyfully welcomed, to
> the control of affairs.
>
> Edward Everett
> Mount Vernon Papers, No. 14

I think the case for the Peabody influence is made, and that in
the overall it is the case for any and every American family. The
Peabodys can be proud of their heritage, as I have tried to show.
The heritage has told; there is something of the same stuff in
Nathaniel Peabody the revolutionary politician of 1776 and Endi-
cott Peabody, who bumped his head against the Massachusetts
Democratic machine in the 1950s and 1960s and who cannot be
counted out as of this writing.

The Peabodys have changed history. I do not mean to imply
that their influence has been overwhelming, or that the Puritan
influence they represent in its best fashion has been the controlling
factor in the growth of America, but it is there, in all its aspects
and ramifications.

Consider, to simply gloss over material stated in the body of the book, how Nathaniel Peabody changed the course of history. He went to Washington's headquarters at Morristown in those deep dark days when Washington and the American troops felt deserted, arriving just at the time of the rebellion of the Connecticut men of the line. He and his Congress Committee associates saw the picture as it was, described it in all its depression, and managed to carry enough weight to bring help to Washington when otherwise the Revolution might have collapsed. That is no mean achievement, no unimportant influence.

Consider the influence of Stephen, the pastor of a small congregation in a village in New Hampshire. He married into the family that produced John Quincy Adams, and somehow, somewhere he had influence on Adams, if no more than by his character. What that influence was or how it worked in the course of American affairs is an unravelable mystery, but its existence cannot be denied.

Consider Oliver, Oliver William Bourne, and William Bourne Oliver and their influence on American intellectual life through their writings and publishings, or even as workers at Phillips Exeter Academy. Consider George, the banker, and George Foster, the Wall Street man, and Joseph, the international merchant, and Alfred and Henry Wayland, and all the other Peabodys of business: one thing, they at least all shared records for moral integrity that are enviable in any business society, and their other activities have been described here.

Consider the literary Peabodys, the Oliver family as noted, the Peabody sisters of Salem, Josephine Preston and Andrew Preston. Consider Ephraim, the preacher, and his understanding of the slave problem—not his solution (to send the blacks back to Africa) but his sense of the future is what stands out in Ephraim's appraisal of slavery. It is as if he stood in his Boston pulpit a century and a quarter ago and told us Americans that if we did not solve the problem sensibly, honorably, without violence, we were simply storing up dozens, scores, perhaps even hundreds of years of trouble for future generations.

Consider Selim Hobart, and his bridling at the attempt of the college president to steal credit for his work. What the president at the Massachusetts college was doing was common enough in the period; does anyone doubt that the furor Selim Hobart Peabody made did not help bring an end to such shoddy practice?

Consider Endicott Peabody, who had so much influence on the molding of men, and on American education—or Elizabeth, for that matter, who helped establish the American kindergarten and struck blows for the emancipation of women through her own activities as bookseller and publisher at a time when ladies did not follow such careers.

Or consider George Foster Peabody, and the simple tale of one little bit of influence: had he not spoken to Franklin D. Roosevelt about the therapeutic values of Warm Springs, had Roosevelt not gone there, then the thirty-second President of the United States might never had recovered the aplomb, let alone the strength, to seek public office again.

That last is an indication of the type of influence of the Peabodys that is surprising, and yet common to the American experience; it is an indication of the complex, interdependent actions of a community on the making of history. I am not trying to say that Nathaniel Peabody stemmed the tide in the black days of Morristown, that like Horatius, he stood at the bridge and held back the enemy by himself; no, the Peabody influence, or the influence of any family or collection of individuals, does not work that way, and it never will. But by tracing the course of the more important members of the Peabody family, I do hope to have given a glimpse of the hidden threads of history, to have shown how the Peabodys are an inextricable part of the American story, and by exposing this one family, to point out how we all have our place in the scheme.

SPECIAL BIBLIOGRAPHY

Ashburn, Frank D., *Peabody of Groton*, Coward-McCann Co., New York, 1944.

Baker, Christina Hopkinson, *Diary and Letters of Josephine Preston Peabody*, Houghton Mifflin, Boston, 1925.

Biography and Other Articles, William C. Todd (Nathaniel), New Hampshire Historical Society, Concord.

Chapple, W. D., *George Peabody*, Peabody Museum of Salem, 1933.

Collections of the New Hampshire Historical Society, Vol. III, Concord, 1832.

Current Biography, 1964 (Endicott Peabody, Jr.).

Endicott, W. C., and Whitehill, W. M., *Captain Joseph Peabody*, Peabody Museum, Salem, 1962.

Gannett, E. A., *A Discourse at the Funeral of W. B. O. Peabody, June 1, 1847*, Springfield, 1847.

Girling, Katherine Peabody, *Selim Hobart Peabody*, University of Illinois Press, 1923.

Hanaford, Phebe, *The Life of George Peabody*, B. B. Russell, Boston, 1870.

Hoyt, Edwin P., *The House of Morgan*, Dodd, Mead & Co., New York, 1966.

Hunt's Merchant Magazines, April, 1857, "Biographical Sketch of George Peabody," Baker and Godwin, New York, 1857.

Leavis, M. H., *Henry Wayland Peabody, Merchant*, M. H. Leavis, West Medford, Mass., 1909.

Merriam, S. O., *Ancestry of Franklin Merriam Peabody*, privately printed, unplaced, 1929.

Morris, Richard B., *Encyclopedia of American History*, Harper & Row, New York, 1953.

Parker, Franklin, *George Peabody, Founder of Modern Philanthropy*, George Peabody College for Teachers, Nashville, Tenn., 1955.

Peabody, A. P., *Harvard Reminiscences,* Tichnor and Co., Boston, 1888.

——*Reminiscences of European Travel,* Hard and Houghton, New York, 1869.

Peabody, Ephraim, *Slavery in the United States,* a pamphlet, reprinted from the *North American Review* of October, 1851.

Peabody, Everett (ed.), *The Literary Remains of William B. O. Peabody,* Benjamin H. Greene, Boston, 1850.

Peabody, Josephine Preston, *Collected Plays,* Houghton Mifflin, Boston, 1927.

——*Collected Poems,* Houghton Mifflin, Boston, 1927.

Peabody, O. W. B., *Memoir and Sermons of W. B. O. Peabody,* B. H. Greene, Boston, 1849.

Peabody, Selim Hobart, *Peabody Genealogy,* Chicago, 1909.

Peabody, William S., *A Genealogy of the Peabody Family as Compiled by the late C. M. Endicott of Salem,* David Clapp and Son, Boston, 1867.

Proceedings of the New Hampshire Historical Society, Biographical and Other Articles, The Rev. Stephen Peabody and Wife, Concord, New Hampshire, undated.

Publications of the Colonial Society of Massachusetts, Vol. 22.

Schuchert, Charles, and LeVene, Clara Mae, *O. C. March, Pioneer in Paleontology,* Yale University Press, 1940.

Stearns, E. S., *Genealogy and Family Histories of the State of New Hampshire,* Vol. II, Lewis Publishing Co., New York, 1908.

Tharp, Louise Hall, *The Peabody Sisters of Salem,* Little, Brown and Co., Boston, 1950.

Ware, Louise, *George Foster Peabody, Banker, Philanthropist, Publicist,* The University of Georgia Press, Athens, 1951.

Winthrop, R. C., *Eulogy at Funeral of George Peabody,* Press of John Wilson and Son, Boston, 1780.

INDEX